National Politics and Sexuality in Transregional Perspective

National Politics and Sexuality in Transregional Perspective explores how modern identity politics around the world are gendered and sexualized in multiple ways. Constructions of the imagined collective "self" often contain references to a heteronormative order, whereas relevant internal or external "others" are often felt to deviate from this order through their gendered or sexual practices. By contrast, some Western countries have witnessed the evolution of LGBTQI-friendly discourses by certain political actors in recent years, often in the context of the post-9/11 culture wars.

This pathbreaking book focuses on perceptions of "self" and "other" in Europe, the Middle East and North Africa from a gendered perspective. It deals with anti-LGBTQI as well as LGBTQI-friendly aspects of modern culture and politics in countries within these regions, focusing on the functions such discursive markers play in nationalist and racist imageries, in discourses legitimizing class differences from the nineteenth century to the present day, including globalized discourses in the context of 9/11 and its aftermath. It shows that discourses on sexuality and gendered performances in everyday life often undermine the stability of such binary constructions, as they point to the multiplicity, ambivalence and the indeterminate character of individual and collective identities under conditions of modernity. Addressing contemporary identity politics both in a wider historical context and within a transregional comparative framework thus helps to discern differences and similarities between different world regions and serves to dislocate essentialized notions of cultural differences based on gender and sex. This book will appeal to those with an interest in Political Sociology, Gender Studies, and Globalisation.

Achim Rohde is a Middle East historian and scientific coordinator of the research network "Re-Configurations: History, Remembrance and Transformative Processes in the Middle East and North Africa" at the Center for Near and Middle East Studies, Philipps-Universität Marburg.

Christina von Braun is the co-director of The Center for Jewish Studies Berlin-Brandenburg, established in 2012. She was nominated full professor in 1994 at Humboldt University, Institute for Cultural History and Theory. Before, she worked as a freelance writer and film maker in New York, Paris, and Bonn, authoring 13 monographs, many edited books and more than fifty films.

Stefanie Schüler-Springorum studied Modern History, Ethnology and Political Science at the Universities of Göttingen, Germany, and Barcelona, Spain. She gained her PhD in 1993 from the University of Bochum, Germany. She has been head of the German branch of the Leo Baeck Institute since 2009, and Director of the Center for Research on Anti-Semitism, Berlin, since 2011.

Sexualities in Society

Series editor:
Helen Hester, The University of West London, UK
www.routledge.com/Sexualities-in-Society/book-series/ASHSER1428

Sexualities in Society offers a dedicated and much-needed space for the very best in interdisciplinary research on sex, sexualities, and twenty-first-century society. Its contemporary focus, methodological inclusivity, and international scope will provide a distinctive vantage point in terms of surveying the social organization of sexuality. It critically addresses numerous aspects of sex and sexuality, from media representations, to embodied sexual practices, to the sometimes controversial issues surrounding consent, sexual fantasy, and identity politics. It represents a critically rigorous, theoretically informed, and genuinely interdisciplinary attempt to interrogate a complex nexus of ideas regarding the ways in which sexualities inform, and are informed by, the broader sociopolitical contexts in which they emerge.

Titles in this series

Rethinking Misogyny
Men's Perceptions of Female Power in Dating Relationships
Anna Arrowsmith

Consumer Sexualities
Women and Sex Shopping
Rachel Wood

Radical Sex Between Men
Assembling Desiring-Machines
Edited by Dave Holmes, Stuart J. Murray and Thomas Foth

Sex in the Digital Age
Paul G. Nixon and Isabel K. Düsterhöft

National Politics and Sexuality in Transregional Perspective
The Homophobic Argument
Edited by Achim Rohde, Christina von Braun and Stefanie Schüler-Springorum

National Politics and Sexuality in Transregional Perspective
The Homophobic Argument

Edited by Achim Rohde, Christina von Braun and Stefanie Schüler-Springorum

LONDON AND NEW YORK

First published 2018 by Routledge

2 Park Square, Milton Park, Abingdon, Oxfordshire OX14 4RN
52 Vanderbilt Avenue, New York, NY 10017

Routledge is an imprint of the Taylor & Francis Group, an informa business

First issued in paperback 2019

Copyright © 2018 selection and editorial matter, Achim Rohde, Christina von Braun, Stefanie Schüler-Springorum; individual chapters, the contributors

The right of Achim Rohde, Christina von Braun, Stefanie Schüler-Springorum to be identified as the authors of the editorial material, and of the authors for their individual chapters, has been asserted in accordance with sections 77 and 78 of the Copyright, Designs and Patents Act 1988.

All rights reserved. No part of this book may be reprinted or reproduced or utilised in any form or by any electronic, mechanical, or other means, now known or hereafter invented, including photocopying and recording, or in any information storage or retrieval system, without permission in writing from the publishers.

Notice:
Product or corporate names may be trademarks or registered trademarks, and are used only for identification and explanation without intent to infringe.

British Library Cataloguing-in-Publication Data
A catalogue record for this book is available from the British Library

Library of Congress Cataloging-in-Publication Data
A catalog record for this book has been requested

ISBN: 978-1-4724-8264-8 (hbk)
ISBN: 978-0-367-33281-5 (pbk)

Typeset in Times New Roman
by Out of House Publishing

Contents

List of figures vii
Notes on contributors viii

Introduction. National politics and sexuality in
transregional perspective: The homophobic argument 1
ACHIM ROHDE, CHRISTINA VON BRAUN AND
STEFANIE SCHÜLER-SPRINGORUM

PART I
Europe 17

1 A post-progressive nation: Homophobia, Islam, and the
new social question in the Netherlands 19
PAUL MEPSCHEN

2 Becoming family: Orientalism, homonormativity, and
queer asylum in Norway 39
DENIZ AKIN AND STINE HELENA BANG SVENDSEN

3 Homophobia as identity politics and a tool for political
manipulation in the former Yugoslavia 55
HANA ĆOPIĆ

4 Contemporary art versus homophobia: Selected Eastern
European cases 69
PAWEL LESZKOWICZ

5 "How gay is Germany?": Homosexuality, politics, and
racism in historical perspective 88
CLAUDIA BRUNS

PART II
Middle East / North Africa 105

6 "An oriental vice": Representations of sodomy in early
  Zionist discourse 107
  OFRI ILANY

7 Arabic literary narratives on homosexuality 121
  JOLANDA GUARDI

8 Gay in North African literature? 138
  MAX KRAMER

9 The struggle of LGBT people for recognition in
  Turkey: An analysis of legal discourses 156
  PINAR ILKKARACAN

10 Gays, cross-dressers, and Emos: Non-normative
   masculinities in militarized Iraq 172
   ACHIM ROHDE

Index 189

List of figures

4.1 Igor Grubic, *East Side Story*, video installation (2006–2008)   75
4.2 Igor Grubic, *East Side Story*, video installation (2006–2008)   76
4.3 Minna Hint and Liisi Eelmaa, *Heard Story*, video installation (2011)   77
5.1 "Wie schwul ist Deutschland?", *Bild*, July 22, 2004, p. 1   89
5.2 *Titanic. Das endgültige Satiremagazin* No. 2, February 2009, p. 1   98
10.1 Baghdad Restaurant, *Babil*, January 13, 1994   175

Notes on contributors

Deniz Akin holds a BS in Sociology and M.Phil in Gender and Development. She is currently a PhD candidate at the Department of Interdisciplinary Studies of Culture, Norwegian University of Science and Technology. Her PhD project is entitled "Queer challenges to the Norwegian Policies and Practices of Immigration: Asylum-seeking in Norway on the grounds of sexual orientation." Her research interests include sexuality, migration, and queer studies.

Christina von Braun is the co-director of The Center for Jewish Studies Berlin-Brandenburg, established in 2012. She was nominated full professor in 1994 at Humboldt University, Institute for Cultural History and Theory. Before, she worked as a freelance writer and film maker in New York, Paris, and Bonn, authoring more than fifty films. From 1996–2005 she was head of the Department of Gender Studies at Humboldt University, from 2005 to 2012 she directed a state-funded PhD program on "Gender as a Category of Knowledge." Her research fields comprise media theory, religious history, history of antisemitism and gender. Among her recent monographs: *Der Preis des Geldes: Eine Kulturgeschichte* (2012); *Nicht ich: Logik – Lüge – Libido* (1985/2009); *Glauben, Wissen und Geschlecht in den drei Religionen des Buches* (2008); *Versuch über den Schwindel: Religion, Schrift, Bild, Geschlecht* (2001/2016), together with Bettina Mathes, *Verschleierte Wirklichkeit. Die Frau, der Islam und der Westen* (2007/2017).

Claudia Bruns is Professor for Historical Anthropology and Gender Studies at Humboldt University Berlin, where she is director of the Institute for Cultural History and Theory. Her research focuses on the cultural history of modern Europe, racism and antisemitism, memory of the Holocaust, history of (homo-)sexuality, and of European borders. Publications (in English): *Fundamentalism and Gender. Scripture, Body, and Community* (2013) (ed. together with Ulrike Auga et. al.); "Politics of Eros: The German 'Männerbund'-Discourse between Antifeminism and Anti-Semitism at the beginning of the twentieth century," in: *Masculinity, Senses, and Spirit in German, French and British Culture*, ed. by Katherine Faull (2011), 153–190.

Notes on contributors ix

Hanna Ćopić was born in Belgrade, Yugoslavia. She studied German language and literature, was the recipient of the 1999/2000 DAAD scholarship in Heidelberg and a scholarship of the German Bundestag (2006). She completed her post-graduate studies (Women's Studies) at the Faculty of Political Sciences, University of Belgrade. She has been a translator from German to Serbian since 2003, with focus on politics and philosophy, and project coordinator at the Belgrade office of the Heinrich Boell Foundation since 2008. She's a PhD candidate at the Centre for Research on Antisemitism (ZfA), Technical University Berlin – her thesis dealing with antisemitism and emergence of the Kingdom of Serbs, Croats and Slovenes.

Jolanda Guardi is currently scientific director of the ILA-Arabic Certificate Program and Editor of Barzakh's Series (Translation from Arabic) at Jouvence Publishing House. Guardi holds an International PhD in Anthropology from the Universitat Rovira i Virgili of Tarragona. She completed an MA in German Language and Literature (University of Milan) and an MA in Arabic Language and Literature (University of Turin) and holds a Master's degree in Islamic Feminism (University of Madrid). Her research focuses on dynamics of intellectuals and power especially as deployed in Arabic literature and gender issues and is based on feminist research methodology. Guardi acted as guest editor for a special issue of DEP Deportate Esuli Profughe on *Queerness in the Middle East and South Africa* (2014); she is the author of "The 'Urmann' is a Woman. A Re-reading of Yūsuf Idrīs' Abū ar-riǧāl." *Kervan. International Journal of Afro-Asiatic Studies*, 18 (2014).

Ofry Ilany is a Polonsky postdoctoral research fellow at the Van Leer Jerusalem Institute. His book, *In Search of the Hebrew People: Bible and Enlightenment in Germany*, has been published at the Leo Beck Institute and Zalman Shazar (2016). The book describes the use of the ancient Hebrew cultural and political ideal as a model for German nation-building. Ilany's research interests include the history of sexuality, Orientalism and Bible research. His column, "Under the Sun," is published in the Haaretz newspaper's weekly supplement.

Pinar Ilkkaracan is a researcher, activist and trainer on gender equality and sexual and reproductive health and rights at national, regional, and international levels. She is trained in both psychotherapy and international relations. She is the editor of *Women and Sexuality in Muslim Societies, Deconstructing Sexuality in the Middle East*, and *The Myth of the Warm Home: Domestic Violence and Sexual Abuse*. She has received the International Women's Human Rights Award of the Gruber Foundation in 2007, and has authored many articles on gender equality and sexual and reproductive health and rights. Currently an adjunct professor at the Bosporus University in Istanbul, she serves on the supervisory board of CSBR, the editorial board of the International Journal of Sexual Health,

x *Notes on contributors*

on the International Steering Group of BRIDGE, University of Sussex and the advisory board of the Sexuality and Development Program at the Institute of Development Studies, UK, among others.

Max Kramer is Assistant Professor of Francophone and Comparative Literature at the City University of New York. His theoretical background lies in gender and sexuality, metaphor, translation, and in literary criticism in combination with cultural studies and anthropology. He is a specialist of the contemporary Maghrib and of the modern and postmodern literatures of Europe and the Americas. In his current research project, he contrasts the depictions of sexuality in European Orientalism with the way sexual issues have been treated in North Africa and the Middle East in a postcolonial context.

Pawel Leszkowicz is a Reader in the Department of Art History, Adam Mickiewicz University, Poznan, Poland. He is an academic lecturer and a freelance curator specializing in international contemporary art/visual culture and LGBTQ studies. He is the author of the *Ars Homo Erotica* (2010) exhibition at Warsaw's National Museum. He has written four books: *Helen Chadwick: The Iconography of Subjectivity* (2001), *Love and Democracy. Reflections on the Homosexual Question in Poland* (2005), *Art Pride: Gay Art from Poland* (2010), and *The Naked Man: The Male Nude in post-1945 Polish Art* (2012). He was a Marie Curie Research Fellow at the University of Sussex in Brighton (2011–2014) and a Senior Fulbright Research Fellow at One Gay and Lesbian Archives at the USC Libraries in Los Angeles (2015–2016). Currently he is a EURIAS Fellow at the Helsinki Collegium for Advanced Studies (2016–2017).

Paul Mepschen is a social anthropologist, working as a postdoc in the Political Sociology program at the University of Amsterdam. He is working on questions relating to sexual practices and subjectivities, as well as on the politics and history of Pride. He received his PhD degree from the University of Amsterdam for his dissertation *Everyday Autochthony: Difference, Discontent, and the Politics of Home in Amsterdam* (2016). His work deals with the politics of belonging, citizenship, and urban politics in Western Europe. His interests include cultural and sexual politics, migration, race and racism, queer theory, and religion and secularism.

Achim Rohde is a Middle East historian and scientific coordinator of the research network "Re-Configurations: History, Remembrance and Transformative Processes in the Middle East and North Africa" at the Center for Near and Middle Eastern Studies, Philipps-Universität Marburg. Rohde has published widely on the recent history of Iraq, in the fields of gender and sexuality studies, education, arts and literature, and state–society relations. He has previously been an assistant professor at the Center for Research on Antisemitism, Technical University Berlin, a research fellow at the Georg-Eckert-Institute for International Textbook Research, Braunschweig, and a lecturer at Hamburg University's Asia-Africa Institute.

Stefanie Schüler-Springorum studied Modern History, Ethnology and Political Science at the Universities of Göttingen, Germany and Barcelona, Spain. She received her PhD from the University of Bochum/Germany 1993; in 1994/95 she was researcher at the Berlin Foundation "Topography of Terror"; from 1996–2001 she was involved in research projects on German-Jewish History and on the History of National Socialism; from 2001–2011 she was director of the Institute for German-Jewish History and professor at Hamburg University; since 2009 Schüler-Springorum has been head of the German branch of the Leo Baeck Institute, and since 2011, director of the Center for Research on Antisemitism, Technical University Berlin. She has authored *Geschlecht und Differenz* (2014); *Krieg und Fliegen. Die Legion Condor im Spanischen Bürgerkrieg 1936–1939* (2010; Span. version 2014); *Denkmalsfigur. Biographische Annäherung an Hans Litten* (2008); and *Die jüdische Minderheit in Königsberg/Preussen 1871–1945* (1996).

Stine Helena Bang Svendsen is Associate Professor of Pedagogy at the Programme for Teacher Education, Norwegian University of Science and Technology (NTNU), Trondheim, Norway. Svendsen's research focuses on how sexuality, gender, and race come to matter in current Nordic cultural politics and education. In 2014, she defended her doctoral thesis "Affecting Change? Cultural Politics of Sexuality and 'Race' in Norwegian Education." With Professor Åse Røthing, she has written the book *Seksualitet i skolen. Perspektiver på undervisning* (2009) about sex education. She also writes about sexuality in Norwegian immigration policy, and the role of LGBTQI issues in new northern European racist discourses, and gender equality more generally. Svendsen's educational background is in American Studies (MA) and Gender Studies (BA), both from the University of Oslo. Her PhD is in gender studies, from NTNU. Among her most recent publications are "Feeling at Loss: Affect, Whiteness and Masculinity in the Immediate Aftermath of Norway's Terror," in *Affectivity and Race*, Eds. R. Andreassen and K. Vitus (2015), and "Learning Racism in the Absence of Race," in *European Journal of Women's Studies*, 21(1), 2014.

Introduction: National politics and sexuality in transregional perspective
The homophobic argument

Achim Rohde, Christina von Braun and Stefanie Schüler-Springorum

This volume focuses on gendered perceptions of *Self* and *Other* in Europe and the MENA-region (Middle East and North Africa).[1] Because of their geographic proximity, these two regions are inextricably linked through a long history of cultural exchange, the legacy of colonialism, migratory movements, and economic ties. The idea of two distinct regions, as implied by meta-geographical concepts delineating both as separate and self-contained entities, therefore seems questionable (Derichs 2016; Braune & Rohde 2015). The influx of refugees to Europe from war-torn Middle Eastern countries, temporarily halted as a result of newly erected physical barriers and murky political deals with countries bordering the war zones, has heightened awareness of the multifaceted connectivity linking both regions (Ribas-Mateos 2016; Aksaz & Pérouse 2016). Yet, at the same time, for the last few decades, and increasingly so in the context of the ongoing movement of refugees, Europe and the Middle East are often represented by a range of actors on both sides of the perceived cultural divide as opposing and radically different civilizational blocks. Such political discourses and practices reflect the rise of right-wing populism, with its rigid identity politics, in various parts of the world. More generally, there seems to be a growing tendency to challenge the hegemony of a world system ever more integrated along neoliberal lines by reinstating spatial border regimes and cultural and national boundaries that, until recently, were widely considered outdated (Clifford 2012; Ivarsflaten 2008; Swank & Betz 2003).[2]

This book examines such identity politics through the lens of gender and sexuality. While recognizing important differences among the countries in both regions, it identifies structural and phenomenological similarities in the contexts of gender and sexuality between the European and Middle Eastern/ North African political discourses and practices that are designed to delineate Self and Other. The book focuses, specifically, on issues related to LGBTQIA communities in European and MENA countries.[3] How and to what degree are these subjectivities acknowledged and represented in public discourse? How and why are these non-normative gendered positionalities and bodily practices either integrated into the perceived national/cultural Self or declared corrupting elements endangering its coherence? To what extent and for what purpose are so-called "excluded identities" appropriated by political movements? By juxtaposing original and meticulously researched case studies from various (Eastern and Western) European and MENA countries, the book illustrates the structural connections and even mutual dependence that exist between antagonistic gendered identity discourses. It also shows how projections of Otherness are used to outline conceptions of the Self, thereby creating extreme polarizations that in turn reinforce mutual prejudices.

For pragmatic reasons, the book frames the discussion in terms of nation-states at specific times in the twentieth and twenty-first centuries, and it is divided into two parts along the lines of the established meta-geographical concepts of Europe and the Middle East/North Africa. At the same time, the case studies it presents are designed to deconstruct and transcend the seeming coherence and materiality of nations and civilizations. The book thus builds on an established body of scholarship that critically engages with modern constructions of national and cultural identities. The study of anti-Semitism has developed many productive tools in this pursuit (Benz & Königseder 2002; von Braun & Ziege 2004), and some of the essays contained in this volume hark back to such methods and analyses and point to the intersections between anti-Semitism and homophobia in European history.

Uffa Jensen and Stefanie Schüler-Springorum (2013) have argued that it is precisely the emotional dimension of identity discourses that helps to explain the effectiveness and, at times, deadliness of exclusionist ideologies based on fantasies of pure, homogeneous societies. Gender and sexuality seem to be pivotal for embedding aversive emotions deep in the body. Similarly, the gendered and sexualized dimensions of modern nationalism can be analyzed not only normatively but also in terms of their substance and practices (Brunotte, Ludewig, and Stähler 2015). In his classic work, George Mosse demonstrated that the link between nationalist identity politics and a heteronormative gender order, centered on conservative family values and a heroic kind of masculine agency (Mosse 1985), while Benedict Anderson stated that nations tend to be understood in terms of a deep horizontal "comradeship," that is, as "fraternities" (Anderson 1983). Despite nationalism's usual emphasis on popular unity, rarely, if ever, in the history of nationalist movements have women's experiences been taken as a starting point for political organization (Blom, Hagemann, and Hall 2000). Rather, as Cynthia Enloe notes, "nationalism has typically sprung up from masculinized memory, masculinized humiliation and masculinized hope" (Enloe 2000). Nira Yuval-Davis and Floya Anthias identified five major ways in which women have been integrated into nationalist discourses and nation-building projects: as biological reproducers of the members of the national collective, as reproducers of the boundaries of national groups (i.e. through controlling women's sexual and marital relationships), as producers and transmitters of national culture, as symbolic signifiers of national difference, and as active participants in national struggles (Yuval-Davis & Anthias 1990; Yuval Davis 1997). Building on Homi Bhabha's poststructural and Lacanian concept of nationalism, Anne McClintock has explored the gendering of the national imageries of black and white South Africans. McClintock does not subscribe to Anderson's Marxist view that the development of print capitalism was at the root of the popularity and mass currency of nationalist narratives. Rather, the appeal of nationalism is, according to her, mainly an effect of the technique of performing the nation through ritualistic mass spectacles and various other forms of popular culture, and it is by looking at South African nationalisms from this angle that she renders visible their gendered character (McClintock 1995; McClintock, Mufti, and Shohat 2004).

This volume adds to this body of scholarship by focusing specifically on homophobic and LGBTQIA-friendly discourses and practices from a transregional comparative perspective. These discourses and practices are crucial elements for regulating boundaries in modern and contemporary identity politics, which is understood here to be a set of historical practices through which social and cultural difference are both invented and performed. The invention of imagined communities, such as nations, cultures, and civilizations, is a performative process that takes place on a daily basis as part of a permanent struggle between the social groups and actors in a society (Bhabha 1994). In this context, internal or external Others are often considered as deviating from a normative order through their gendered or sexual practices (Bob 2012, 36–71).

A majority of authors in this volume have chosen to focus on maleness and masculinity in this context, while female queerness and discourses on women are not explicitly discussed in most chapters. Of course, given the overlapping of national and sexual boundaries in identitarian discourses outlined above, "deviant" sexualities, whether male or female or queer, are perceived as a danger to the reproductive survival of the nation by nationalist or culturalist voices in Europe and the MENA region alike (Mosse 1985; Nagel 2003; Habib 2007, 2010; Cohler 2010). Indeed, many chapters address political reactions to LGBTQIA communities in a general sense, without specifically emphasizing male or female attributes. At the same time, the masculinized character of powerful modern identity discourses, certain laws, and other state sanctioned practices in various countries imply that male homosexuals and male to female transgender persons have been and are still being perceived as a more acute threat to the perceived national or cultural Self than other LGBTQIA communities. Hence, they are more widely debated in this particular context. The collection mirrors this empirical fact, but it does not constitute a male-centered politics of visibility on the part of the editors and authors.

A masculinized and heteronormative national identity is poignantly illustrated by the contributions of Claudia Bruns and Ofri Ilany about early twentieth-century Germany and the Zionist Yishuv (Hebrew for "settlement," a term used to refer to the Jewish colonies in mandatory Palestine before Israeli statehood). Bruns discusses the close relationship between the discourse on male homosexuality and the realm of political space in both the German Empire prior to World War I, when the discourse was evolving, and the unified Germany of the 2000s. In the early twentieth century, when the nascent movement for the emancipation of homosexuals was fighting for the repeal of Paragraph 175 (criminalizing homosexual acts), the figure of the homosexual was described in new medical and racialized terms that linked male homosexuality with the degeneration of the state and the race. This linkage became the basis of the ensuing debate about homosexuality in Germany.[4] Prior to the rise of the Nazis, the law itself was not applied to female homosexuality (Marhoefer 2016). As contemporary debates show, homophobia, *raison d'état*, and (anti-)racism remain complexly interlinked to this day. The similarities discovered by Bruns between these two different periods in German history point to the perseverance of a sexual dimension in modern and contemporary identity politics.[5]

Moving from Europe to a European enclave in the Middle East, Ilany discovers similar interrelations in his study of early Zionist society, which deals with representations of what was called "sodomy" in the Hebrew press of the British Mandate era. On the basis of this material, he argues that the Hebrew–Zionist discourse of the time construed sexual intercourse between men as an "oriental" vice, that is, a sanitation problem somehow endemic to the "Orient." This sort of discourse is typical of colonial situations. In this case, when Jews – especially Zionists of European descent – "contracted" sodomy, it was a symptom of ideological weakness and the "destructive influence" of the Arab environment. In this way, incidents of sodomy were used to caution Jews about the terrible effects of befriending Arabs. Thus, the battle against "sodomy" should be read as part of the Jewish-Zionist (Yishuv) community's leaders' intensive effort to construct a physical distinction between Jews and Arabs and eliminate the interactions with Arabs that were taking place on the margins of the Zionist camp. Similar to imperial Germany, public debate concerning "sodomy" in the Yishuv centered on male homosexuality.

In Europe and North America over the last few decades, a contradictory duality of practices and discourses regarding LGBTQIA communities has evolved. Some Western countries have witnessed a proliferation of gendered lifestyles and embodiments, and previously marginalized LGBTQIA groups have gained legitimacy, rights, and political clout. A certain diversification of hegemonic masculinity (Connell & Messerschmidt 2005) is occurring in those metropolitan centers where a growing proportion of the population is embracing metrosexuality as it comes to accept gay and queer masculinities, which coexist with homophobia and established notions of heroic heterosexual masculinity. As a variety of scholars and several authors in this volume have noted, a discourse of sexual democracy is often used to delineate the borders between "the West" and its enlightened liberalism and internal and external Others, most significantly, in the context of the culture wars ongoing since 9/11, the "Muslim world" and Muslim immigrants in Western countries (Haritaworn, Tawqir, and Erdem 2008; Fassin 2010). Thus, in his contribution, Paul Mepschen shows how sexuality is pivotal to the moralization and culturalization of politics in the Netherlands. Culturalists of various stripes characterize the presence of (post)immigrants, and especially Muslims, as disturbing the Dutch moral order. They insist on the need to educate (post) immigrants culturally and morally in order to mold them into well-integrated citizens in the Dutch, and European, moral community. Western ideals of sexual freedom are mobilized in this individualization offensive directed at Muslims, who are asked to show their loyalty to the dominant secular and liberal order by unequivocally embracing gay rights and sexual diversity. So, while "homonationalism" (Puar 2007) is a component of right-wing populist rhetoric, Mepschen shows that its salience is clearly wider than the neo-nationalist right. He examines "progressive" articulations of homonationalism in the Netherlands, focusing on the "moralist reinvention" of social-democratic and social-liberal discourses in the neoliberal Netherlands.

Queer life has also proliferated in post-Soviet Russia and Eastern Europe.[6] Compared to their more established counterparts in Western Europe, these communities face an uphill battle in gaining legitimacy and securing their rights. During the 1990s, local societies in post-communist Eastern Europe often saw LGBTQIA emancipation as part of the painful transition to the neoliberal global order (Ther 2014). In some countries, for example, Russia and Poland, this transition is also confronted with the return of religious allegiance, for many decades suppressed by the communists. This double tailwind – the rejection of neoliberalism and the embrace of the Church – pushes many of the region's anti-LGBTQIA movements. Rising neo-conservative populist forces in these countries use LGBTQIA issues as a weapon in their fight to preserve what they portray as an authentic national Self against corrupting Western influences (Graff 2010). Such portrayals symbolically resurrect the Iron Curtain in new (but really old) garments as a cultural divide separating the "old West" from Eastern European countries both in and outside of the European Union. Anti-LGBTQIA practices and discourses, as well as organized enmity toward other minorities, such as refugees, are also instruments for implementing authoritarian political agendas. Thus, the leaders of Russia and Serbia use the old discourse of Western decadence and its sexual deviance in their struggle for power and discursive hegemony, and the leaders of Poland and Hungary resist the EU's non-discrimination laws and practices to preserve their imagined national Selves. LGBTQIA rights are a familiar battleground in this context. In his contribution to this volume, Pawel Leszkowicz shows how queer rights and representations spark cultural tensions, political conflicts, acts of censorship, and violence in many parts of Central and Eastern Europe. But he also describes the evolution of LGBTQIA activism in the arts and shows how art is now one of the few fields where these conflicts can still be dealt with. The post-1989 transition has given rise to a new dissidence of love and sexuality against the legacy of totalitarianism, religious fundamentalism, social complacency, and the new far-right governments. Therefore, despite the EU's protection, queer culture and activism function in a volatile climate of culture war. In his chapter, Leszkowicz focuses on selected works by artists from Croatia, Estonia, Poland, and Romania that address homophobia. The artists interrogate homophobia within the space of their art works with far-reaching implications for sexual politics and society at large. Focusing on ex-Yugoslavia, Hana Ćopić discusses LGBTQIA issues in Croatia and Serbia from the perspective of state manipulation of human rights. She contends that while LGBTQIA people enjoyed a period of fairly far-reaching freedom during the time of Socialist Yugoslavia, today the political elites of the subsequent nation-states use homophobia as a strategic tool to advance a crude kind of gendered and ethnicized identity politics directed against both queer dissidence and allegedly corrupting Western European influences.

The supposed global imposition of a universal sexual epistemology by the neo-imperial West (Massad 2002, 2007), on the one hand, unites regions as diverse as Eastern Europe and the MENA countries, while, on the other, it forms the core of controversies about homonationalism (Puar 2007, 2013). LGBTQIA-friendly policies have become a potent symbol of the liberal values of the educated middle class. Thus, over the last decade, sexual orientation has been widely included in the scope of international asylum law and practice as reasonable grounds for offering protection.[7] While we do not downplay the legitimacy and value of such progress, Deniz Akin and Stine Helena Bang Svendsen, in their thoughtful contribution to this volume, remind us that even the most enlightened asylum practices can become caught up in the contradictions of identity politics and may end up reinforcing the difference between "us" and "them." Because of their malleability, the reification of gay and lesbian identities has been a contested subject in diverse academic disciplines and also in the field of immigration law. Akin and Svendson discuss the case of an Iranian refugee who sought asylum in Norway on the basis of persecution for his sexual orientation. His request was rejected in 2010, but he was granted asylum in 2013 after the Norwegian practice for assessing claims based on sexual orientation had been revised. Akin and Svendson use this case to explore how the change in asylum policy that occurred in 2012 can shed light on the different constructions of homosexuality that Norwegian immigration policy and practice have erected. They also explore how the lived experiences of the applicant were transformed to create a credible narrative of persecution that ensured his entitlement to protection in Norway. They argue that the case shows how Orientalism has been resurrected as a constitutive part of the new Nordic homonormativity that applicants have to negotiate to become legitimate queer asylum seekers under the new regulations.

Liberal values are increasingly being attacked by populist right-wing parties and movements in Eastern and Western Europe alike, as well as in the US. They have won national elections in Eastern countries like Hungary and Poland and have also had notable success in Western EU member states such as France, the Netherlands, and Germany. The notion of an LGBTQIA-friendly Western Europe serves as a trope for diagnosing a rising tide of homophobia in non-Western contexts, and it is grossly homogenizing. Furthermore, it obscures political and economic differences in incidents of anti-queer animus and pastes over the historical evolution of attitudes and practices toward non-normative sexualities in both regions (cf. Thoreson 2014). Several contributions to this volume offer historical cross-sections of the evolution of sexualized identity politics in Europe. They highlight the fragmentation of the discourses over European identity, which have framed the conversation between Western Europe and Eastern and Southeastern Europe.

An interesting hybrid case is Israel, with its strong sense of self-identification as belonging to the Western cultural space and its Middle Eastern location, its important minority of Palestinian citizens, and manifold display of Middle Eastern influences in its everyday culture. The country is home to a thriving gay and queer community that enjoys more rights than anywhere else in the Middle East and most Western countries. Israeli governments use this fact to project an image of Israel as an icon of liberal democracy in order to counteract its loss of stature in the West, resulting from its ongoing occupation and seizure of Palestinian territories, which is widely seen as undermining a solution to the Israeli–Palestinian conflict on the basis of territorial compromise (Puar 2011; Schulman 2012). Ofri Ilany takes a historical perspective on the debate over Israeli pinkwashing and reminds us of the heteronormative foundations of Zionism and the practice in the pre-state Yishuv of Othering non-normative sexual practices and embodiments as Oriental by associating them with Arabs. Ironically, this practice mirrored nineteenth-century European nationalist discourses and the anti-Semitism that came along with them. Modern European anti-Semitism included the trope of Jews as an Oriental people that could never be integrated into European modernity, and this rejection included a contradictory gendered dimension, namely, the image of the masculinist Jewish rapist polluting the non-Jewish female (von Braun 1996, 2006, 2015) *and* the image of Jewish male effeminacy that leaned toward perversion and homosexuality (Rohde 2005, 2014; Schüler-Springorum 2017). In trying to liberate Jews from the yoke of European anti-Semitism, modern Zionism re-invented the Jews as a manly European people transplanted to an Oriental setting from which they struggled to remain separate (Boyarin 2000). The Israeli case illustrates the historical mutability of gender regimes and gendered identity discourses. However, more research is needed to understand the degree to which the emancipation of the LGBTQIA community in contemporary Israel actually impacted Israeli society's hegemonic notions of heroic, military masculinity rooted in the heterosexual family (Cohen 2012; Yosef 2004). Alas, the early Zionist refusal to become or be seen as Oriental has consistently been a trope in Jewish-Israeli society until today. As Ilany demonstrates, the same behavior that in the Yishuv was depicted as a symptom of unhealthy fraternization with the natives is today used to justify a regime of deepening ethnic segregation in Israel/Palestine. He claims that the necessary condition for legitimizing homosexuality in Israel was its shedding of all of its prior association with Arabs.

The visibility of non-normative gendered identities and subjectivities is growing also in Muslim majority countries in the MENA region like Turkey,

Lebanon, Morocco, and Tunisia.[8] But this proliferation stands in marked contrast to the simultaneous rise of dichotomous discourses on gender difference centered on the heterosexual patriarchal family, which delegitimize gender non-conformity of any kind (Tolino 2014; Zengin 2016; Whitaker 2006). While these developments are reminiscent to some extent of the rise of neo-right populist homophobia in Eastern Europe, queer communities are particularly threatened in a number of Middle Eastern countries where LGBTQIA communities are often persecuted by state organs as well as victimized by non-state actors like militias in times of state failure and civil war. Achim Rohde in his contribution explores ruptures and continuities in organized violence against sex and gender nonconformity in recent Iraqi history. He shows that the Ba'thist regime's turn toward social conservatism and religious discourse during the 1990s included a notable homophobic dimension. Nevertheless, the regime tolerated the existence of a queer subculture in Baghdad and other cities until its fall in 2003. Organized violence against queers began in earnest only after 2003, when it was the work of Shi'ite militias during and after the civil war of the mid-2000s. He argues that violence against non-normative gender and sexual behaviors, enactments, and identities is attributable to the general erosion of the Iraqi state and the normalization of violence after decades of war, embargo, and societal conflict. The radical and traumatic changes that Iraqis have experienced since 2003 have increased organized gender and sexual violence and outbreaks of moral panic that scapegoat nonconformists.

These findings do not sit well with Joseph Massad's (2002, 2007) diffusionist argument, according to which exposure to global gay culture has heightened the cultural significance of homosexuality in Middle Eastern society in a way that helps to trigger negative reactions to anyone associated with it. Massad is probably correct in arguing that "western interactions are [...] reshaping the way men who have sex with men in Islamic countries self-identify, and how locals see that behaviour" (Luongo 2010, 103; Altmann 2002). In this context, some of the actions of American and British forces in Iraq, most notably in the infamous Abu Ghraib prison, certainly come to mind. Raping male Iraqi prisoners and stripping them naked and forcing them to simulate homosexual acts in front of a camera as a way to humiliate them must have had a heavy impact not only on the victims but also on the whole of Iraqi society once these practices became publicly known.[9] Indeed, as Ann Laura Stoler (1995, 1997, 2002) reminds us, the legacy of colonial encounters has been a constitutive element in the evolution of sexualities and gender norms on both sides of these encounters. But, at the same time, there is abundant evidence that non-normative gendered lifestyles have been practiced in Iraq and elsewhere in the MENA region for centuries prior to any colonial encounter. Through the centuries, there have been periods of pronounced hostility as well as leniency toward non-normative sexualities in non-Western countries, which were not triggered by encounters with the West.[10] In re-enacting a familiar anti-colonial habitus, Massad constructs a bipolar picture of the West and non-West that is strangely reminiscent of the narratives he criticizes (Hasso 2007; Dalacoura 2014). Still, it is indisputable that recent years have witnessed "an increasing culturalization of thinking about the West" in Islamist and in nationalist circles in the MENA region, and this trend reflects "the concern with authenticity that is itself stimulated by globalization" (Woltering 2011, 159). Gender issues are a familiar battleground in this context, as they have been in others over the centuries (Schüler-Springorum 2014).

This book includes several contributions that illustrate this point. In analyzing recent LGBTQIA legal struggles in Turkey, Pinar Ilkkaracan argues that recognizing LGBTQIA people and their rights is a significant part of the democratic process in Turkey. Although LGBTQIA people began to demand their rights at the beginning of the 1990s, their demands were regarded as marginal issues in Turkey until recently. The growing number of LGBTQIA organizations throughout the country and their increasingly powerful calls for recognition has slowly changed the situation. Yet, the conservative Turkish government continues to reject their demands. In light of recent developments in Turkey, including the government's anti-European rhetoric and violent attacks against LGBTQIA activists in 2015/16, Ilkkaracan expects the struggle for the recognition of LGBTQIA people and their rights to increasingly be a topic of public and political debate in the near future.

Interrogating female and male homosexuality in contemporary MENA societies from the perspective of literary studies, Jolanda Guardi considers the evidence that she finds in a number of Arab novels whose main hero or heroine is homosexual. Such novels became the subject of public debate in newspapers and on television, where they were often acclaimed as "the first Arabic novel on homosexuality" or "the unveiling of a taboo." In her chapter, Guardi inserts these novels into a socio-political frame, and she separates out three different discourses in her readings of them. One involves the West, where Arab culture is today used to redefine the role of women. Another relates to the Arab world, where "sexual deviance" is used to defend a conservative female role that is part of a repressive political strategy. The third concerns the Academy, where queer Arabic literary studies are still too often confined to the Middle Ages.

Also working from the perspective of literary studies, Max Kramer inquires into same-sex sexuality in Maghrebi literature. Aided by gay tourism, satellite television, and global media (online dating services, virtual social networks, instant messengers, Internet telephony, etc.), the dominant Western-style gay way of life, which makes being exclusively gay one's social identity, has over the last two decades disrupted prevailing notions of gender and sexuality in the Maghreb, where it is often the case that young male Maghrebis can conceive of themselves as gay only by renouncing their cultural heritage and becoming Westernized. At the same time, LGBTQIA-rights organizations outside of the West are increasingly agitating for the emancipation of sexual outcasts. The novels that Kramer analyzes show that the hybrid Berber-Arab-Muslim-French Mediterranean culture of the Maghreb has a much less fixed concept of the gendered Other than Westerners assume. Indeed, the frequently unstable Maghrebi subjectivities staged in many of these narratives deconstruct the post-independence homophobic official discourses of North African nation-states and the traditional segregation of the sexes, but they also deconstruct the polarized hetero- and homonormative identity discourses that come from the West and segregate not sexes but sexual orientations. Contrary to typical Western expectations, the sexual imaginations portrayed in the novels that Kramer examines and the deconstruction of the Muslim closet that they carry out reflect a reality that shares crucial elements with what queer theorists in the West have promoted.

One of the aims of this volume is to deconstruct the notion of a homogeneously anti-queer Middle East and North Africa by offering a view into the sexual and gender diversity of the region's societies and culture and the historical mutability of attitudes and practices toward non-normative sexualities in MENA countries. The volume thereby contributes to the emerging field of transregional comparative sexuality studies in a way that demonstrates the "interarticulation and coimplication of Eastern and Western bodies, desires, aesthetic paradigms and analytical paradigms," thus eventually "confounding the very terms by which our understandings of East and West are derived" (Traub 2008, 12).

By focusing on the intertwined identity politics of Europe and the MENA countries, this collection constitutes a comparative study of negative stereotypes and exclusionary political practices toward internal and external Others in both regions. The authors it has assembled deal with both anti-LGBTQIA and LGBTQIA-friendly aspects of the modern cultures and politics of countries in the two regions, and they focus on the functions of these discursive markers in nationalist and racist imageries and in discourses legitimizing class differences all through the twentieth century and until today, including globalized discourses in the aftermath of 9/11. Several contributions show that discourses on sexuality and gendered performances in everyday life often undermine the stability of such binary constructs, for they point to the multiplicity, ambivalence, and indeterminate character of individual and collective identities under the conditions of modernity. Addressing contemporary identity politics in a wider historical context and a transregional comparative framework helps to reveal differences and similarities between different world regions and serves to destabilize essentialized notions of cultural difference based on gender and sex. By examining notions of inclusion and exclusion within the framework of gender and sexuality, a queer approach can highlight the marginalization of alter/natives in scholarship and social movements regarding empire and diaspora (El-Tayeb 2011; Coloma 2006).

Notes

1 This book came about as part of collaborative work in the "Research Network Gender in Anti-Semitism, Orientalism, and Occidentalism" (RENGOO), a European network project funded by the Netherlands Organisation for Scientific Research (NOW). See https://researchnetworkaoo.wordpress.com/.

2 Yet, the multiculturalism embraced by liberals in Western countries displays some troubling similarities to the kind of racial thinking resurrected by right-wing populists because multicultural ideology fetishizes, like the racial theories of yore, ethnic diversity understood as a set of fixed and separate identities existing side by side. See Adamson (2015).
3 We use LGBTQIA as the most inclusive acronym currently in use to signify nonnormative gendered embodiments and sexual practices. Yet, given the different scholarly and regional contexts of the authors assembled in this volume, they also use different acronyms in their respective chapters.
4 See also, Brunotte (2010).
5 See also, Dietze (2010).
6 See, for instance, Kulpa and Mizielinska (2011), Renkin (2009), Stulhofer and Sandfort (2004), Roman and Judit (2007), Essig (1999), Fejes and Balogh (2013), Baer (2009).
7 See, for example, various court cases listed in EDAL. European Database for Asylum Law, www.asylumlawdatabase.eu/en [Accessed January 30, 2017].
8 See, for instance, Bereket (2006), Altinay (2008), Ozbay (2017), Lundqvist (2013), Kilbride (2014), Hayes (2000), Lachheb (2016).
9 The feminization of colonial men has long been known to be an imperial strategy of projecting power, and American and British investigators of Abu Ghraib prison in 2003/04 followed this well-trodden path (Razack 2005; Tétreault 2006; Butler 2009, 89–91).
10 Ze'evi (2006), Babayan and Najmabadi (2008), Habib (2007, 2010). Evidence ranging from the time of the Prophet to the nineteenth and early twentieth centuries points to the continued existence of institutionalized practices of gender crossing and same-sex relations in what was later to be Iraq as well as in neighboring countries (Rowson 1991; Murray 1997a, 1997b; Westphal-Hellbusch 1997).

References

Adamson, Goran. 2015. *The Trojan Horse: A Leftist's Critique of Multiculturalism in the West*. Malmo: Arx Forlag.

Aksaz, Elif and Jean-Francois Pérouse eds. 2016. *"Guests and Aliens": Re-Configuring New Mobilities in the Eastern Mediterranean After 2011 – with a Special Focus on Syrian Refugees*. Les Dossiers de l'IFEA, http://books.openedition.org/ifeagd/1829.

Altinay, Rustem Ertug. 2008. "Reconstructing the Transgendered Self as a Muslim, Nationalist, Upper-Class Woman: The Case of Bulent Ersoy." *Women Studies Quarterly* 36, 3–4: 210–229.

Altmann, Dennis. 2002. *Global Sex*. Chicago, IL: Chicago University Press.

Anderson, Benedict. 1983. *Imagined Communities. Reflections on the Origins and Spread of Nationalism*. London: Verso.

Babayan, Kathryn and Afsaneh Najmabadi eds. 2008. *Islamicate Sexualities. Translations across Temporal Geographies of Desire*. Cambridge, MA: Harvard University Press.

Baer, Brian James. 2009. *Other Russias: Homosexuality and the Crisis of Post-Soviet Identity*. London/New York: Palgrave Macmillan.

Benz, Wolfgang and Angelika Königseder eds. 2002. *Judenfeindschaft als Paradigma: Studien zur Vorurteilsforschung*. Berlin: Metropol.

Bereket, Tarik. 2006. "The Emergence of Gay Identities in Contemporary Turkey." *Sexualities* 9, 2: 131–151.

Bhabha, Homi K. 1994. "DissemiNation: Time, Narrative and the Margins of the Modern Nation." In *The Location of Culture*, 139–170. London: Routledge.

Blom, Ida, Karen Hagemann and Catherine Hall Blom eds. 2000. *Gendered Nations: Nationalisms and Gender Order in the Long Nineteenth Century*. Oxford and New York: Oxford International Publishers.
Boyarin, Daniel. 2000. *Unheroic Conduct. The Rise of Heterosexuality and the Invention of the Jewish Man*. Berkeley, CA: University of California Press.
Braune, Ines and Achim Rohde. 2015. "Critical Area Studies." *Middle East Topics & Arguments* 4: 5–11, http://meta-journal.net/issue/view/108.
Brunotte, Ulrike. 2010. "Masculinity as Battleground of German Identity Politics. Colonial Transfers, Homophobia, and Antisemitism." In *Grenzregime. Geschlechterkonstruktionen zwischen Kulturen und Räumen der Globalisierung*, ed. Waltraud Ernst. Münster: LIT, 165–184.
Brunotte, Ulrike, Anna-Dorothea Ludewig, Axel Stähler eds. 2015. *Orientalism, Gender, and the Jews. Literary and Artistic Transformations of European National Discourses*. Oldenbourg: De Gruyter.
Butler. Judith. 2009. *Frames of War: When is Life Grievable?* New York: Verso.
Clifford, Bob. 2012. *The Global Right Wing and the Clash of World Politics*. Cambridge, MA: Cambridge University Press.
Cohen, Nir. 2012. *Soldiers, Rebels, and Drifters: Gay Representation in Israeli Cinema*. Detroit, MI: Wayne State University Press.
Cohler, Deborah. 2010. *Citizen, Invert, Queer. Lesbianism and War in Early Twentieth-Century Britain*. Minneapolis, MN: University of Minnesota Press.
Coloma, R.S. 2006. "Putting Queer to Work: Examining Empire and Education." *International Journal of Qualitative Studies in Education* 19, 5: 639–657.
Connell, R. W. and James W. Messerschmidt. 2005. "Hegemonic Masculinity. Rethinking the Concept." *Gender & Society* 19, 6: 829–859.
Dalacoura, Katerina. 2014. "Homosexuality as Cultural Battleground in the Middle East: Culture and Postcolonial International Theory." *Third World Quarterly* 35, 7: 1290–1306.
Derichs, Claudia. 2016. *Knowledge Production, Area Studies and Global Cooperation*. London/New York: Routledge.
Dietze, Gabriele. 2010. "'Occidentalism', European Identity and Sexual Politics." In *The Study of Europe*, eds. Hauke Brunkhorst and Gerd Grözinger, 87–116. Baden Baden: Nomos.
El-Tayeb, Fatima. 2011. *European Others. Queering Ethnicity in Postnational Europe*. Minneapolis, MN: University of Minnesota Press.
Enloe, Cynthia. 2000. *Bananas, Beaches and Bases: Making Feminist Sense of International Politics*. Berkeley, CA: University of California Press.
Essig, Laurie. 1999. *Queer in Russia: A Story of Sex, Self, and the Other*. Durham, NC: Duke University Press.
Fassin, Eric. 2010. "National Identities and Transnational Intimacies: Sexual Democracy and the Politics of Immigration in Europe." *Public Culture* 22, 3: 507–529.
Fejes, Narcisz and Andrea P. Balogh. 2013. *Queer Visibility in Post-socialist Cultures*. Bristol/Chicago, IL: Intellect.
Graff, Agnieszka. 2010. "Looking at Pictures of Gay Men: Political Uses of Homophobia in Contemporary Poland." *Public Culture* 22, 3: 583–603.
Habib, Samar. 2007. *Female Homosexuality in the Middle East: Histories and Representations*. New York: Routledge.
———. 2010. *Islam and Homosexuality*, Vol 1 & 2. Santa Barbara, CA: Praeger.

Haritaworn, Jin with Tamsila Tawqir and Esra Erdem. 2008. "Gay Imperialism: Gender and Sexuality Discourse in the 'War on Terror.'" In *Out of Place: Interrogating Silences in Queerness/Raciality*, edited by Adi Kuntsman and Esperanza Miyake, 9–33. York: Raw Nerve Books.

Hasso, Frances. 2007. "'Culture Knowledge' and the Violence of Imperialism: Revisiting The Arab Mind." *MIT Electronic Journal of Middle East Studies* 7: 24–40.

Hayes, Jarrod. 2000. *Queer Nations: Marginal Sexualities in the Maghreb*. Chicago, IL: University of Chicago Press.

Ivarsflaten, Elisabeth. 2008. "What Unites Right-Wing Populists in Western Europe? Re-Examining Grievance Mobilization Models in Seven Successful Cases." *Comparative Political Studies* 41, 1: 3–23.

Jensen, Uffa and Stefanie Schüler-Springorum. 2013. "Gefühle gegen Juden. Die Emotionsgeschichte des modernen Antisemitismus." *Geschichte und Gesellschaft* 39, 4: 413–442.

Kilbride, Erin. 2014. "Lebanon Just Did a Whole Lot More Than Legalize Being Gay." *Muftah*, March 8. Available at: http://muftah.org/lebanon-just-whole-lot-legalize-gay/#.VomhD4luvfs/ [Accessed September 29, 2016].

Kuhar Roman and Judit Takacs eds. 2007. *Beyond the Pink Curtain. Everyday Life of LGBT People in Eastern Europe*. Ljubljana: Peace Institute.

Kulpa, Robert and Joanna Mizielinska eds. 2011. *De-Centring Western Sexualities: Central and Eastern European Perspectives*. London: Routledge

Lachheb, Monia ed. 2016. *Être Homosexuel au Maghreb*. Tunis: IRMC – Karthala.

Lundqvist, Erica Li. 2013. *Gayted Communities. Marginalized Sexualities in Lebanon*. Lund Studies in History of Religions 35.

Luongo, Michael T. 2010. "Gays under Occupation: Interviews with Gay Iraqis." In *Islam and Homosexuality*, vol. 1, edited by Samar Habib, 99–110. Santa Barbara, CA: Praeger.

Marhoefer, Laurie. 2016. "Lesbianism, Transvestitism, and the Nazi State: A Microhistory of a Gestapo Investigation, 1939–1943." *American Historical Review* 121, 4: 1167–1195.

Massad, Joseph. 2002. "Re-Orienting Desire: The Gay International and the Arab World." *Public Culture* 14, 2: 361–385.

———. 2007. *Desiring Arabs*. Chicago, IL: University of Chicago Press.

McClintock, Anne. 1995. *Imperial Leather: Race, Gender and Sexuality in the Colonial Contest*. London/New York: Routledge.

McClintock, Anne, Aamir Mufti and Ella Shohat eds. 2004. *Dangerous Liaisons. Gender, Nation, and Postcolonial Perspectives*. Minneapolis, MN: University of Minnesota Press.

Mosse, George M. 1985. *Nationalism and Sexuality: Middle Class Morality and Sexual Norms in Modern Europe*. Madison, WI: University of Wisconsin Press.

Murray, Stephen O. 1997a. "The Sohari Khanith." In *Islamic Homosexualities: Culture, History, and Literature*, edited by Stephen O. Murray and Will Roscoe, 244–255. New York: New York University Press.

———. 1997b. "Some Nineteenth-Century Reports of Islamic Homosexualities." In *Islamic Homosexualities: Culture, History, and Literature*, edited by Stephen O. Murray and Will Roscoe, 204–221. New York: New York University Press.

Nagel, Joane. 2003. *Race, Ethnicity and Sexuality: Intimate Intersections, Forbidden Frontiers*. Oxford: Oxford University Press.

Ozbay, Cenk. 2017. *Queering Sexualities in Turkey: Gay Men, Male Prostitutes and the City*. London: IB Tauris.
Puar, Jasbir. 2007. *Terrorist Assemblages: Homonationalism in Queer Times.* Durham, NC: Duke University Press
———. 2011. "Citation and Censorship: The Politics of Talking About the Sexual Politics of Israel." *Feminist Legal Studies* 19, 2: 133–142.
———. 2013. "Rethinking Homonationalism." *International Journal of Middle East Studies* 45, 2: 336–339.
Razack, Sherene H. 2005. "How Is White Supremacy Embodied? Sexualized Racial Violence at Abu Ghraib." *Canadian Journal of Women and the Law* 17, 2: 341–363.
Renkin, Hadley Z. 2009. "Homophobia and Queer Belonging in Hungary." *Focaal – European Journal of Anthropology* 53, 1: 20–37.
Ribas-Mateos, Natalia ed. 2016. *Migration, Mobilities and the Arab Spring. Spaces of Refugee Flight in the Eastern Mediterranean.* Cheltenham/Northampton: Edward Elgar.
Rohde, Achim. 2005. "Der Innere Orient. Orientalismus, Antisemitisimus und Geschlecht im Deutschland des 18. bis 20. Jahrhundert." *Die Welt des Islams* 45, 3: 370–411.
———. 2014. "Asians in Europe. Reading German-Jewish History through a Post-Colonial Lens." In *Orientalism, Gender, and the Jews. Literary and Artistic Transformations of European National Discourses*, eds. Ulrike Brunotte, Anna-Dorothea Ludewig and Axel Stähler, 17–32. Oldenburg: de Gruyter.
Rowson, Everett K. 1991. "The Effeminates of Early Medina." *Journal of the American Oriental Society* 111, 4: 671–693.
Schüler-Springorum, Stefanie. 2014. *Perspektiven deutsch-jüdischer Geschichte: Geschlecht und Differenz.* Paderborn: Schöningh.
———. 2017. "Gender and the Politics of Anti-Semitism." *American Historical Review* (forthcoming).
Schulman, Sarah. 2012. *Israel/Palestine and the Queer International.* Durham, NC: Duke University Press.
Stoler, Ann Laura. 1995. *Race and the Education of Desire: Foucault's History of Sexuality and the Colonial Order of Things.* Durham, NC: Duke University Press.
———. 1997. "Educating Desire in Colonial South-East Asia: Foucault, Freud, and Imperial Sexualities." In *Sites of Desire, Economies of Pleasure: Sexualities in Asia and the Pacific*, eds. L. Manderson and M. Jolly, 27–47. Chicago, IL: University of Chicago Press.
———. 2002. *Carnal Knowledge and Imperial Power. Race and the Intimate in Colonial Rule.* Berkeley, CA: University of California Press.
Stulhofer, Aleksandar and Theo Sandfort eds. 2004. *Sexuality and Gender in Postcommunist Eastern Europe and Russia.* London/New York: Routledge.
Swank, Duane and Hans-Georg Betz. 2003. "Globalization, the Welfare State and Right-Wing Populism in Western Europe." *Socio-Economic Review* 1, 2: 215–245.
Tétreault, Mary Ann. 2006. "The Sexual Politics of Abu Ghraib: Hegemony, Spectacle, and the Global War on Terror." *National Women's Studies Association Journal* 18, 3: 33–50.
Ther, Philipp. 2014. *Die neue Ordnung auf dem alten Kontinent. Eine Geschichte des neoliberalen Europa.* Berlin: Suhrkamp.
Thoreson, Ryan Richard. 2014. "Troubling the Waters of a 'Wave of Homophobia': Political Economies of anti-Queer Animus in Sub-Saharan Africa." *Sexualities* 17, 1–2: 23–42.

Tolino, Serena. 2014. "Homosexuality in the Middle East: An Analysis of Dominant and Competitive Discourses." *DEP (Deportate, Esule, Profughe)* 25: 72–91.
Traub, Valerie. 2008. "The Past is a Foreign Country? The Times and Spaces of Islamicate Sexuality Studies." In *Islamicate Sexualities. Translations across Temporal Geographies of Desire*, eds. Kathryn Babayan and Afsaneh Najmabadi, 1–40. Cambridge, MA: Harvard University Press.
von Braun, Christina. 1996. "'Le Juif' et 'la femme': deux stéréotypes de 'l'autre' dans l'antisémitisme allemand du XIXe siècle." *Révue Germanique Internationale* 5: 123–139.
von Braun, Christina. 2006. "Scripture and Community." In *Gender in Conflicts. Palestine, Israel, Germany*, edited by Ulrike Auga, Christina von Braun, 63–74. Berlin/Münster: Lit Verlag.
———. 2015. "The Symbol of the Cross: A Visual Symbol Become Flesh in Anti-Semitism." In *Ethics of In-Visibility*, edited by Claudia Welz, 119–130. Tübingen: Mohr Siebeck.
von Braun, Christina and Eva-Maria Ziege eds. 2004. *Das "Bewegliche Vorurteil". Aspekte des Internationalen Antisemitismus*. Würzburg: Königshausen und Neumann.
Westphal-Hellbusch, Sigrid. 1997. "Institutionalized Gender-Crossing in Southern Iraq." In *Islamic Homosexualities: Culture, History, and Literature*, edited by Stephen O. Murray and Will Roscoe, 233–243. New York: New York University Press
Whitaker, Brian. 2006. *Unspeakable Love: Gay and Lesbian Life in the Middle East*. London: Saqi.
Woltering, Robbert. 2011. *Occidentalisms in the Arab World: Ideology and Images of the West in the Egyptian Media*. London: I.B. Tauris.
Yosef, Raz. 2004. *Beyond Flesh. Queer Masculinities and Nationalism in Israeli Cinema*. New Brunswick, NJ: Rutgers University Press.
Yuval-Davis, Nira. 1997. *Gender & Nation*. London: Sage.
Yuval Davis, Nira and Floya Anthias eds. 1990. *Women – Nation – State*. London: Macmillan.
Ze'evi, Dror. 2006. *Producing Desire. Changing Sexual Discourse in the Ottoman Middle East, 1500–1900*. Berkeley, CA: University of California Press.
Zengin, Aslı. 2016. "Mortal Life of Trans/Feminism: Notes on 'Gender Killings' in Turkey." *Transgender Studies Quarterly* 3, 1–2: 266–271.

Part I
Europe

1 A post-progressive nation

Homophobia, Islam, and the new social question in the Netherlands[1]

Paul Mepschen

Sexual democracy in the Netherlands

In recent decades, the Netherlands has witnessed a shift in the social location of gay politics as it relates to the rise of anti-multiculturalism in Europe (Bracke 2012; Jivraj & De Jong 2011; Mepschen et al. 2010; Wekker 2009, 2016). LGBTQIA rights and discourses are employed to frame Western Europe as the "avatar of both freedom and modernity" (Butler 2008, 2) but to depict its Muslim citizens, especially, as backwards and homophobic. In the words of the queer theorist Jasbir Puar (2007), who coined the term "homonationalism," gay rights have been recast as an "optic, and an operative technology" in the production and disciplining of Muslim Others (see also Rahman 2014). Cases of homophobia among Muslim citizens are highlighted, treated as archetypal, and cast within Orientalist narratives that underwrite the superiority of European secular modernity. Homophobia is increasingly represented as peripheral in Dutch culture. Central to this process of representing Dutch culture is a political and social anxiety about the recent achievement of sexual democracy, that is, the extension of full civil rights to citizens who do not conform to heterosexual "normality." As Fassin and Salcedo (2015) argue:

> We live in societies that claim to define their own laws and norms immanently, from within, and no longer from above or beyond, through some transcendent principle (be it God, Nature, or Tradition). This self-definition extends to sex; indeed, sex has become a primary battleground in our societies as it raises the question of the limits of this democratic logic: Does it apply everywhere, to everything, or is sex an exception? This accounts for the political battles about sexual liberty and equality – from same-sex marriage to violence against women, sexual harassment, prostitution, and pornography. Sex becomes our ultimate democratic truth.
>
> (2015, 1118)

Sexual democracy thus raises important questions concerning political democracy and citizenship in pluralistic societies. Sexual liberty is incorporated into a cultural protectionist discourse that associates it with secularism and liberalism, and pits it against the allegedly backward cultures and religions of post-immigrant citizens, especially Muslims. In commenting on the intellectual and activist travels of the concept of homonationalism, Jasbir Puar (2013, 337) argues that it is not simply a synonym for gay racism. Similarly, "sexual nationalist" denotes not an identity that scholars and activists can attribute to those with whom they disagree but, rather, a political lens through which many people view political and sexual dynamics in Europe and the United States. In this chapter, I analyze the discourse of sexual nationalism in the case of the Netherlands beyond its articulation in far-right or right-wing populist neo-nationalism. Sexual nationalism is, in my view, an element of a culturalist discourse that expresses a way of thinking that carves Dutch society up into distinct, internally homogeneous, and delimited cultures and represents autochthonous Dutch culture as a threatened entity that must be protected from the cultures and moralities of minoritized and racialized outsiders (Mepschen 2016, 23). However, I shall argue that important elements of this culturalist perspective on sexuality are also found in progressive circles, and they even play a role in shaping liberal and progressive subjectivities.

In an attempt to understand the power and performativity of Dutch sexual nationalism, I shall look critically in this chapter at my conversations with the liberal Muslim Ahmed Marcouch, an MP for the social-democratic Labor Party (PvdA), about homophobia, sexual liberty, and religion. Part and parcel of a broader research project on the culturalization of citizenship and the politics of "autochthony" in the Netherlands (Mepschen 2010; 2016a; 2016b), these conversations highlight a number of pivotal conundrums in the analysis of sexual politics in the Netherlands today. I zoom in on Marcouch's political discourse because it represents broader developments in Dutch society. First of all, I understand it as an aspect of a broader post-progressive discourse in the Dutch Left; second, I see his discourse as representative of what the sociologist Justus Uitermark has called "civil Islam" (2012). While I focus, empirically, on a single case study, I place the case of Ahmed Marcouch in broader political and social developments in the Netherlands today: the culturalization of citizenship; the rise of a "new social question" surrounding immigration and migrant integration; and the transformation of the Left.

In recent years, scholars have pointed to the centrality of sexuality in constructing majoritarian Dutchness as secular, and the extent of secularization in Dutch society is indeed remarkable. In one generation, the Netherlands has transformed itself from one of the most religious societies in the world to one of its most secular (Van Rooden 2004; Verkaaik 2009). As secular ideologies and practices have grown increasingly important in Dutch cultural practices of belonging and identity, religious practices and ideologies have been framed as out of sync with liberal secular morality, as bastions of deviant cultural alterity. Muslims, or those with Muslim backgrounds, have been the most conspicuous targets in recent years of what Sarah Bracke refers to as "secular nostalgia," in which certain groups are represented as trespassing on a secular moral landscape and distorting the perception of a unified, secular, and morally progressive nation (Bracke 2012; Mepschen & Duyvendak 2012; Wekker 2016).

Oskar Verkaaik and Rachel Spronk (2011) have advocated an anthropological, ethnographic approach to secularism and secularity. Their argument builds on the work of the feminist historian Joan Scott, who developed the notion of "sexularism" to describe the ways in which secularism plays out in the intimate spheres of desire, sexuality, and the body. Sexularism includes the assumption that secularism "encourages the free expression of sexuality and that it thereby ends the oppression of women because it removes transcendence as the foundation for social norms and treats people as autonomous individuals, agents capable of crafting their own destiny" (Scott 2009, 1). According to this perspective, secularism has broken the hold of tradition and religious particularism and ushered in an era of individualism, rationalism, and sexual liberation. Thus, secularism is understood in public discourse to be neutral and modern and, at the same time, intimately connected with gender equality and sexual freedom.

However, as Scott argues, such simple dichotomies between the religious and the secular and the traditional and the modern must be brought into question. For, secularism is not a sufficiently historical explanation for the "admittedly more open, flexible kinds of sexual relations that have gained acceptance in some countries of the West in recent years" (Scott 2009, 6). I agree. The explanatory relationship between secularization and the increase in sexual freedom cannot be taken for granted because other factors are at play. In other words, religion and secularism – faith and secularity – are not separate spheres. Rather than taking secularization "as the standard intrinsic to modernity," the rise of secularity must be understood as redefining the place, role, and understanding of religion in society (Meyer 2012). For, the dominance of secularism and the secular nostalgia that construes religious people as cultural Others *transform* religious practices, emotions, and modes of binding (Meyer 2012; Beekers 2015). My analysis in this chapter of Dutch sexual politics demonstrates one way in which the relationship of religion and secularity has transformed in post-progressive times.

A post-progressive nation

The analysis of sexual nationalism brings into focus the "dynamics of power" at work in discussions in the Dutch civil sphere about the integration of immigrant communities and the nation's moral and sexual order (Uitermark 2012). The culturalist position is dominant there (Uitermark et al. 2014), and the pundits of culturalist politics see themselves as rebelling against the entrenchment in public administration and political debate of a leftist and relativist approach to cultural diversity and integration (Prins 2004; Uitermark et al. 2014). Policies pertaining to minorities have traditionally been the province of moderately left-leaning pragmatists who have tried to deal with integration issues as pragmatically as possible through a combination of paternalism and management (Uitermark 2012). By taking a managerial approach focused on regulation, dialog, and conflict resolution, they attempted throughout the 1990s to prevent the politicization of these issues. It is against this sort of pragmatism, and an alleged lack of political debate on immigration and integration, that culturalists, from Frits Bolkestein in the 1990s to Fortuyn, Hirsi Ali, and Wilders in the 2000s and 2010s, have rebelled.[2]

Culturalists have emphasized the so-called "Judeo-Christian" roots of Dutch and European, society and the need, in light of the growing presence of Muslims, to guard these roots with tough stances on immigration, Islam, and integration (Van den Hemel 2014; Geschiere 2009b). In the eyes of culturalists, the presence of Muslims in postcolonial Europe marks the end of the secular contract. They ground their post-secular appeal to Judeo-Christian roots precisely on the notion that particular religious values are needed to safeguard society from the practices and ideas of minoritized Others, especially Muslims (Van den Hemel 2014, 28). It is through this dynamic that Dutch culturalist nationalism, in its various articulations, has appropriated some of the central achievements of the progressive and radical politics of the recent past: for example, women's and lesbian and gay emancipation, secularism, and individualism.

This is not to say that culturalists have a purely instrumental view of these progressive values or, as Oudenampsen (2013) seems to suggest, that progressive principles play only a minor role in the neo-nationalist project. Oskar Verkaaik (2009, 91), for instance, reports that lesbian and gay emancipation was the subject *most* discussed in the naturalization ceremonies that he studied. Still, I agree with Oudenampsen that it is important to understand the essentialism underlying the nationalist construction of Dutch society. Cultural nationalists abstract liberal achievements in gender and sexual emancipation from the processes in which they were embedded and understand them not as products of an ongoing contingent, historical, progressive social struggle but as inherently Dutch. That is to say, they naturalize them. Therefore, Oudenampsen argues, Dutch neo-nationalism should be called "post-progressive":

> While progressive values are assimilated in post-progressive discourse, the ideal of progress itself is discarded. The idea of a fluctuating but persistent progression on the field of social equality and civil liberties has been replaced with cultural essentialism: progressive values are given a static quality, they are seen as ingrained in Dutch culture, something that must be conserved, and defended from threats from without.
> (Oudenampsen 2013)

This essentialism with respect to progressive politics plays an important role in the politics of citizenship. The growth in popularity of sexual nationalism relies on neoliberal constructions of subjectivity, and it seems to me that post-progressive sexual nationalism has become possible exactly because of the neoliberal emphases on individual autonomy and responsibility, choice, and personal advancement. Indeed, Willem Schinkel and Friso van Houdt (2010) have argued that the amalgamation of neoliberalism, nationalism, and cultural assimilationism is a new form of governmentality, which they call "neoliberal communitarianism," a mode of governing populations and a process of subject-formation that is simultaneously individualizing and homogenizing and that is grounded in the entanglement of a number of historically progressive values – for example, individual autonomy, secularism, free sexual object-choice – which are represented in communitarian, nationalist terms. In short, this sort of discourse focuses on the formation of an exclusionary community of individualized and individually responsible people who are made into "lean" consumer-citizens (Sears 2005).

Post-progressivism, therefore, is neither conservative nor progressive but must be seen as part of a neoliberal project of producing individually responsible subjects. Alan Sears (2005) has used the notion of "lean citizenship" in arguing that it is no coincidence that in a large number of Western countries lesbians and gays have won full citizenship in the current neoliberal period, which is marked by a transformation from a Fordist welfare state to a post-Fordist "lean state" that prioritizes market morality. While not denying the power of political mobilization or the importance of patient and resilient social struggle, Sears has pointed out that neoliberalism has made a certain amount of sexual freedom possible, as the state moved away from established practices for the ethical and cultural formation of the population while enabling a market rationality and morality that frames human relations and human needs in terms of individual agency. Market rationality, in other words, often undermines conservative moralizing (Drucker 2015, 228). Peter Drucker notes that middle-class lesbian and gay identities, anchored in consumption and embodying the liberal values of self-fashioning, autonomy, and individual freedom, are not at odds with market rationality and morality.

As such, the ascent of neoliberalism has been a factor in the success of social movements struggling for full citizenship for LGBTQ people. In fact, neoliberalism has, arguably, made possible a form of biopolitics that mobilizes sexual autonomy to produce a community of individualized, "autonomous" subjects. Whereas the Fordist state was invested, for a number of reasons, in protecting the heterosexual family and heteronormative morality, the lean state employs sexuality in its moral regulation of those citizens – mostly those with immigrant backgrounds – whom it considers to be not fully assimilated into a post-progressive society of individualized subjects (Puar 2013; Scott 2009; Verkaaik & Spronk 2011).

The post-progressive construction of Dutchness goes hand in hand with the construction of immigrant, and especially Muslim, culture as "pre-progressive" (Mepschen 2016). The implication that these minoritized groups are still in need of emancipation has become hegemonic because it has salience beyond the populist neo-nationalist Right. The reasons for this are, first, that liberal and progressive critics of the neo-nationalist Right can show their commitment to progressive values and gay rights only by distancing themselves from Muslims' alleged sexual and gender conservatism. In this way, liberal and leftist politicians and public figures participate in culturalist rhetoric (Uitermark et al. 2014). Second, the construction of immigrant and Muslim "cultures" as pre-progressive makes minoritized communities the ideal targets of progressive political passions, especially in contemporary social-democratic politics, in post-political times.

There is an important link here with the debate on postfeminism (McRobbie 2004). The feminist sociologist Sarah Bracke has argued that feminism, understood as a progressive social practice, in the Netherlands has become framed as intrinsically Dutch. In other words, Dutch society is understood to be postfeminist (Bracke 2012). She has also pointed out that the right-wing populist Pim Fortuyn's invocations of women's emancipation in the early 2000s located the necessity for feminism among white women in the past while simultaneously construing "allochthonous" women as in need of emancipation from pre-progressive cultural and religious constraints. In other words, what emerges in this discourse is a substantialist conception of gender equality as the property of white European liberal secularists and a similarly substantialist view that those "in but not of Europe are always already excluded from this state of being" (Lentin & Titley 2011, 90; Brown 2006, 8). These representations made it possible that a central figure in Dutch feminism, Ciska Dresselhuys, the long-time editor-in-chief of the feminist monthly *Opzij*, could argue that Fortuyn was an ally of feminists. Political differences between Fortuyn and Dresselhuys (who identifies as a leftist) notwithstanding, "they aligned in the absolute priority granted to the emancipation of Muslim women, which elsewhere Dresselhuys affirms as the "third wave" of Dutch feminism" (Bracke 2012, 239).

Bracke argues that the alliance between progressive feminists like Dresselhuys and right-wing populists like Fortuyn was less strange than it might seem at first sight. She points out that Western feminism has long relied on a civilizational script that construes certain women – working-class, black, and colonized women – as subjects needing to be rescued (Bracke 2012, 241). Important strands of feminism in the Dutch public sphere today build on this civilizational script, now according to which Muslim women are always already oppressed, an oppression symbolized by the *hijab* (see also Scott, 2009). This liberal-feminist script has become the handmaiden, to paraphrase Leila Ahmed (1992), of a culturalist, "muscular" liberalism that focuses on the regulation of cultural diversity and the disciplining of racialized Others in the name of women's liberation.

Social democracy and the "new social question"

The post-progressive and postfeminist construction of Dutch society as a modern, emancipated nation creates a conundrum for the social-democratic

Left by raising the following question: What targets of progressive political passion can be found in a society in which emancipation is seen as a more or less finished project? The analysis of this conundrum contributes, I think, to our understanding of the dominance of culturalist representations of contemporary social problems, including the pivotal role played by sexual nationalist figurations.

This is well illustrated by the contribution to the debate on integration of the prominent social-democratic intellectual Paul Scheffer (2000; 2006). Scheffer's contribution shows that the critique of pragmatic, managerial cultural appeasement in the field of immigrant integration has not been limited to the New Right, but its genealogy reaches back into Dutch social-democratic politics. In 2000, Scheffer published an influential article in which he argued that the Netherlands was then in the midst of a "multicultural drama" and pleaded for acknowledging and promoting Dutch national identity as a first step toward a stricter integration policy targeting immigrant communities (Scheffer 2000; Uitermark 2012, 66–67). As the anthropologist Peter Geschiere has argued, Scheffer took for granted a substantialist approach to culture, while building on the opposition between traditional and modern cultures "in which, as usual, the 'traditional' pole turned out to be in all respects the negation of the qualities of the 'modern' one" (Geschiere 2009a, 155).

The similarity between Scheffer's analysis and rightist culturalist views is important but seems to me not to be the most significant aspect of his contribution. What is most important is that Scheffer, unlike right-wing culturalists, positioned himself firmly in the tradition of the social-democratic Left. In 2004, in his inaugural speech upon becoming a professor of European Studies, he looked back at the early development of Amsterdam New West, in the construction of which his grandfather had played a cardinal role (Scheffer 2006) and where I conducted my fieldwork. Scheffer's speech was an exercise in social-democratic reasoning; his concerns were deeply rooted in social-democratic passions and politics. In discussing the history and present state of social engineering and the politics of state-led progress in Amsterdam New West, he referred to the social problems arising from the growing marginalization and segregation of the racialized urban poor in New West as a "new social question." Moreover, in line with the culturalist approach, Scheffer connected the cultural backgrounds of immigrants – for instance, their having come from non-modern, non-industrial countries – to their socio-economic marginalization and urban segregation. Fundamental for Scheffer was cultural integration. People, he argued, must not only dwell in the same physical spaces; they must also share the "mental space" of the Dutch majority (Scheffer 2006, 29). In a global era in which, in his view, the relationship between modernity and tradition – "cosmopolitanism" and what Scheffer referred to as "tribalism" – is the most important point on the agenda of large cities, cultural integration can result only from stricter state regulation. In line with his article from 2000, he argued in favor of a forceful integration policy and a more self-conscious Dutch nationalism as the answer to "the new social question."

In raising "the new social question" and thus referring to the nineteenth-century's *sociale kwestie*, Scheffer links contemporary social issues to the general historical project of social democracy and progressive liberalism. Scheffer's approach to integration taps into older civilizational tropes in social-democratic politics. Without an ideal of civilization, he argues, every political project lacks direction. Just as pre-war social-democratic and progressive liberal elites responded to the "old" social question with a moral-cultural agenda grounded in civilizational ideals and paternalism, contemporary urban elites should develop an interventionist moral agenda, a moral-cultural politics focused on the integration and social elevation of those who do not have full access to political, social, and cultural resources (Swierstra & Tonkens 2008).

In reflecting on this project, Scheffer (2006, 31) emphasizes the necessity of creating access to cultural resources, for example, collective narratives and reference points, grounded in European and Dutch cultural history. In accord with his reading of Manuel Castells (1993), Scheffer points out that the "new social question" has emerged from a dichotomous urban reality, a cosmopolitan urban elite, on the one hand, and "tribalist" local communities, on the other. The central question, according to Scheffer, is how we can bring modernity and tradition into balance. What is needed is the reinvention of a modernist civilizational project, a moral-cultural offensive of the sort that was historically central to the social-democratic project and that goes against the grain of what he understands to be postmodern relativism (Scheffer 2006, 33).

In response to the "new social question" and the dominance of the culturalist framework, a new social-democratic moral politics that appropriates aspects of the culturalist agenda while tapping into the older civilizational traditions of the Left has been born. This demonstrates that, first, the culturalization of citizenship is nothing new, and, second, it is not confined to the neo-nationalist or populist Right. Discourses of sexual nationalism fit well with progressive articulations of culturalism. First of all, in the context of a post-progressive society sexual nationalism offers clear targets for moderate leftist passions concerning minoritized lesbians and gays, who must be defended against conservative and homophobic *pre-progressives*, who themselves must be civilized and brought into the fold of post-progressive common sense.

Civil Islam: sexuality and liberal Muslims

After Paul Scheffer's influential article in 2000, social democrats with immigrant and Muslim backgrounds, like Ahmed Aboutaleb (the Labor Party mayor of Rotterdam) and Ahmed Marcouch (a Labor Party MP), have played a key role in extending culturalist topics. They have been particularly vocal about the need to defend tolerance, gay rights, and sexual progress, even if that means criticizing Muslim and immigrant communities. Marcouch and Aboutaleb occupy a particular position in the dynamics of power, operating in discussions of immigrant integration in the Dutch civil sphere (Uitermark 2012). Their position offers an alternative to New Right culturalism while at the same time incorporating some of the central elements of the post-progressivism of culturalists. Whereas culturalists have claimed that Islam is incompatible with civil engagement in Dutch society and have therefore advanced confrontational politics focused on either the assimilation or exclusion of Muslim communities, figures like Aboutaleb and Marcouch have developed a discursive position that challenges the culturalist construction of Islam as incompatible with Dutchness. Uitermark has coined the term "civil Islam" to describe this position in the civil sphere:

> Civil Islam is an integration discourse based on the idea that Islamic and civil commitment can and should go hand in hand. Cultural problems are readily identifiable and have considerable explanatory relevance for analyzing integration issues. Contrary to Culturalism, religion – properly understood – can and does provide solutions, as it demands civil behavior from Muslims. Muslims should be assertive in public debate and clearly state what they do or do not consider civil behavior. Public policy should manage the integration of migrant groups because this is necessary to help migrants emancipate as Muslim citizens.
> (Uitermark 2010, 263)

In debates on lesbian and gay emancipation, an increasing number of people with Muslim backgrounds take up a certain position, one that is important in the analysis of Dutch sexual nationalism because it blunts the secular imperative of sexual nationalism and undermines the notion that support for lesbian and gay emancipation relies entirely on so-called "Judeo-Christian tradition." Marcouch and others promoting LGBTQIA rights and visibility in Muslim and immigrant communities do so in large part because of their religious convictions and post-immigrant backgrounds. As Muslims, they call upon other Muslims to take seriously their civil responsibilities, which in the Netherlands include support for LGBTQIA rights and lifestyles. They do so on the basis of their interpretation of Islam. The growing number of people taking up this position, and the growth of queer Muslim organizing in the Netherlands, undermines the notion that homosexuality and Islam are mutually exclusive (Aydemir 2011; Jivraj & De Jong 2011).

Civil Islam's positions on LGBTQIA rights and tolerance, however, are not separate from sexual nationalism, for proponents of civil Islam tap into sexual nationalist discourse by assuming normative, essentializing notions of gayness. But before I turn to the relations between civil Islam and sexual nationalism, I shall look at civil Islam's discourse on sexuality. As I shall show, LGBTQIA issues and the question of sexual autonomy create "moments of ethics" (Zigon) for liberal Muslims and proponents of civil Islam like Ahmed Marcouch (see also, Peumans 2014). According to Zigon, moral attitudes are not unreflective but can come into being in moments of "moral breakdown," creating what Zigon calls an "ethical moment." As he believes, one's ethics are "a conscious acting on oneself either in isolation or with others so as to make oneself into a more morally appropriate and acceptable social person not only in the eyes of others but also for oneself" (Zigon 2008, 165). His notion of moral breakdown should be understood broadly as applying to events in a person's everyday life that force him or her "to reflect upon the appropriate ethical response" (Zigon 2009, 262).

The narrative of Ahmed Marcouch offers an example of the role of ethical moments in the construction of liberal Muslim subjectivity. I first heard Marcouch speak in September 2010, when he had left his position in New West after a dispute within the local chapter of the PvdA and had just been elected as a member of parliament for his party. Marcouch spoke at one in a series of expert meetings, called Being Yourself in Slotervaart, that had been initiated under his leadership. His presentation was straightforward and he spoke with conviction, trying to get across how important lesbian and gay rights and tolerance toward lesbians and gays were for him.

In Marcouch's eyes, culturalists are right when they maintain that sexuality in general, and lesbian and gay sexuality in particular, are broadly taboo in Dutch Muslim communities. In an interview on Amsterdam's local television station, he pointed out:

> Take into account that there is hardly a positive vocabulary to speak about lesbians and gays in Dutch Muslim circles. I was recently at a school and I asked children there what would happen if they were to talk about gayness at home. They said: "The first thing that would happen is that we would get slapped." It is a dirty word that you are not supposed to use in public.
>
> (Marcouch 2010)

Why did Marcouch choose to pursue gayness in these ways? He is a practicing Muslim who has been active in his community for decades. Before becoming a politician, he was a police officer, one of the founders of a network of Dutch-Moroccan police officers. Though not gay himself – he is married to a woman with whom he has had two sons – he became interested in gay emancipation in 2001, during the so-called "El-Moumni affair," in which a conservative *imam* in Rotterdam, Khalil El-Moumni, stirred controversy in a television interview when, commenting on the introduction of gay marriage laws in the Netherlands, he said, "What Islam says about homosexuality is known among all Muslims. It is a sin."[3] The affair forced Marcouch to reflect on the appropriate ethical response, which began his refashioning of his moral self. That is to say, sexuality and lesbian and gay rights have become part of a politics of ethical formation, the formation of a particular kind of moral Muslim, self-structured by liberal ethics (Fadil 2011, 86). More broadly speaking, lesbian and gay issues in the Netherlands offer ethical grounds for the formation of liberal Muslim moral selves, articulations of Muslim subjectivity that have come to play an important role in the Dutch civil sphere and in political debates.

Making homosexuality "bespreekbaar"

After the El Moumni affair, it became clear to Marcouch that "young Dutch-Moroccans played a relatively big role in (often violent) homophobic incidents" in Dutch cities, including Amsterdam (Buijs et al. 2012).[4] This worried him, and he wanted to understand why it was the case. So, he started to discuss these issues in the Muslim community. As he was active in the Moroccan religious community as a board member of an organization [*koepelorganisatie*] of Amsterdam mosques, he was in a position to take the lead on this matter.

> But it was not just because of my work in the religious community. I also saw it in my circles. You just know, coming from that community, that homosexuality is something that is not talked about. There is no language, no vocabulary, and to talk about something you need a language. A lot of Moroccan, Muslim gays – and I have met many of them in the last couple of years – cannot talk with their parents, family, or friends. And throughout the community, this is the core problem. So I tried to explore how we could develop a language to discuss these issues within Moroccan and Muslim circles.
> (Marcouch 2011)

Marcouch's initiatives to bring the issue of homosexuality to the table attracted some support but, more often, anger and frustration. In 2003, other members of the organization of mosques filed a motion of no confidence, against which he had to defend himself, because of Marcouch's argument that homosexuality should be made "discussible." Marcouch told me:

> For me, that experience showed me more than ever how necessary it was to talk about these issues. And after the murder of Van Gogh[5] this became even more urgent. I felt, we have to do something about these taboos – to discuss sexuality, to discuss homosexuality. Yes, Muslims did speak out against violence, but that was not enough, that was banal. We had to do more. So I tried to contribute to discussing these issues within the religious community. And another thing had to be brought to the table – the position of lesbians and gays within our own communities.
> (Marcouch 2011)

Marcouch remained convinced, he declared, of the importance of the topic of homosexuality. His words express the centrality of lesbian and gay issues in creating those moments of ethics in which Marcouch refashioned his moral self in relation to his more orthodox fellow Muslims and conservative family members and friends, who disagreed with him. In engaging with these issues, Marcouch developed a political discourse focused on changing the Muslim community in order to make deeper cultural integration possible. He was also concerned, he said, with countering white Dutch suspicions of Dutch-Moroccans and Muslims and thereby countering the rise of right-wing culturalism:

> Often we would discuss the rise of Wilders' populism. This also worries me of course – I am a Dutch Muslim. But I said, look, as long as the Muslim community keeps silent about sexuality and lesbian/gay rights, etcetera, we will be vulnerable. People will start "guessing," they will start thinking we condone misconduct toward gays, that we think it is OK. That it is our standard [*een gedragen norm*]. We cannot say: this is not our priority, this is not our concern.
>
> (Marcouch 2011)

Marcouch made waves in the Dutch-Moroccan and Muslim communities. He pointed out to me that his "provocative style" had "at least" made people discuss sexuality and LGBTQIA visibility. While many supported him, he was also ridiculed, for instance, in a popular video on YouTube that depicted Marcouch as gay and suggested that he was interested in young boys (Anon, 2012). He also told me that many young Dutch-Moroccans write to or tweet him, complaining that homosexuality is the "only" thing he ever talks about.

> It says something about the emotionality of this topic. I feel I do not talk about gays that often, not more than I talk about good education, integration of Muslims, and the right of Muslims to have their own identity, the right of orthodox people to express their views. You see, for me these questions are connected. But when it comes to homosexuality, it hits people like a wave and they become emotional.
>
> (Marcouch 2011)

When, in 2006, Marcouch became the district chairman of Slotervaart, his public profile grew, and he felt that he should use his position to increase awareness of the issue. He wanted homosexuals to be seen differently, as normal people wanting to live in safety and be able to exercise their freedom.

Marcouch's approach to LGBTQIA issues is grounded, in my view, in three interconnected discourses. The first, which is on what he calls "Dutch norms," is "a humanist approach, an approach based on human rights." As he told me, "That is our common idiom in the Netherlands, what I refer to as 'the Dutch' 'moral Esperanto.' So that has nothing to do with theology." In Marcouch's view, Dutch norms are equivalent to human rights and humanist ideals. Second, Marcouch's support for LGBTQIA rights is grounded in a particular interpretation of Islam, and here we see the central role that questions of sexual freedom play in fashioning a moral self *vis-à-vis* "orthodox figures" [*orthodoxe figuren*]:

A post-progressive nation 31

> Islam advocates individuality and freedom of religion. Sexuality is the domain of people themselves. And sexual morality in Islam is highly progressive. Yes, there are guidelines, but there are hardly any rules for punishment. Even in the case of adultery – in Islamic law there must be four witnesses before an adulterer can be punished. That makes it almost impossible, theologically, to punish people for adultery – if Muslims really did follow the law, it would not be possible. There is a lot of *humaniteit* [humanism/humanitarianism] in Islam. [...] Moreover, there is the obligation of Muslims to behave decently to other people, to let them be.
> (Marcouch 2011)

Marcouch thus links his interpretation of Islam, which he sees as full of "*humaniteit*," with Dutch norms, which, in his view, are central to humanist traditions and human rights. In this way, he sees a place for Islam within, not outside of, the Dutch national moral community. At the same time, he promotes his view of Islam as a disciplinary practice that focuses on shaping Muslim individuals and practices to be more in line with ideals of sexual democracy:

> There is another topic that is important to me. I introduced a term, the "Muslim gay" [*de homo-moslim*]. It was very interesting to see what happened when I used that term. Even the most progressive religious people told me: "We are with you all the way, but this is not possible: to be Muslim and gay." But it *is* possible. They exist. I told them: "Is it your right to deny someone the right to be both gay and Muslim? Who am I? That is something that belongs to that person and to the Creator." And I said the same thing to the homo-network within the Labor Party. We had a discussion about the "contradiction" between article 1 [the anti-discrimination article] and freedom of religion. I said: "there is no contradiction". You are doing precisely what some orthodox religious people do who deny lesbians and gays the right to be religious. But there is no contradiction. If you are gay, you are gay. If you are a Muslim gay, you are that. You, and no one else, decides about that. I enjoy article 1 just as much as I enjoy the freedom of religion.
> (Marcouch 2011)

The third discourse in which, in my view, Marcouch's approach is grounded is contemporary social-democratic thought. Echoing accusations of the Left's uncritical multiculturalism, Marcouch argues that social democrats have "too long" had the feeling that they had to "choose" between supporting cultural minorities and supporting LGBTQIA people. He believes that social democracy has to refashion itself in relation to these cultural and sexual issues and has a key role to play in "teaching Muslims." Social democrats must stand for the right of Muslims, including orthodox Muslims, to "be there" and be visible, but that means, in his opinion, that there should be no taboos against "criticizing Muslims." Though Marcouch prefers pragmatic dialog, he says, "What Wilders [and, hence, the populist right] does is not forbidden." Echoing Scheffer's plea for a new moral-cultural offensive, he argues:

> Social-democracy has always been based on a kind of moral, civilizational politics [*een morele verheffingspolitiek*]. We mustn't think this is a dirty notion. Paternalism is part of this tradition. But it must be in balance. And that's what makes it complex. We no longer know how to show leadership. [...] What we need are institutions – the police for instance – that guarantee safety. Safety is fundamental to freedom and to human existence. And these institutions must be vital – the political sphere, the juridical sphere, and education. These spheres must play a role in building personalities. So that young people, who are sixteen or seventeen and happen to be lesbian or gay, can stand up to their parents and say: this is who I am.
>
> (Marcouch 2011)

In review, Marcouch combines a defense of Islam against culturalist attacks with a politics of sexual and gender emancipation and safety and, in this way, attempts to bridge the gap between pragmatists and culturalists. Like culturalists, he insists that homophobia among Muslims should be uncompromisingly countered. His political agenda is rooted in his belief in the necessity of a strong moral state. He thereby links classic social-democratic passions with important elements of culturalist discourse. At the same time, he counteracts the secularist imperative in sexual-nationalist discourse by transcending the contradiction, which is taken for granted, between religious, and especially Muslim, subjectivity and ideals of sexual progress. For Marcouch, defending gay rights is a matter of being a good Muslim in the contemporary Dutch context. He says, "We as Muslims are not barbarians, we can talk about homosexuality. The right of a Muslim to be Muslim is the right of a homosexual to be a homosexual." Thus, he opposes the essentialization of Muslim communities as static without fully rejecting the culturalist framework.

Conclusion

The role of sexuality and desire – and of knowledge of the sexuality of Others – in shaping modern subjectivity has been a central topic in scholarly inquiry into modernity and bourgeois nationalism (e.g. Foucault 1985; Mosse 1985; Stoler 1995; McClintock 1995; Van der Veer 2006). Sexuality has always been structured by desires and discourses that were never about sex alone (Stoler 1997, 43). For, the production of desire and sexuality has always been closely tied up with the production of other social and cultural classifications: class, gender, race and, especially important today, religion. And the formation of modern national subjectivity has been contingent upon the construction of alterity, both at home and in the colonial encounter. This discursive field, concerning ideas and images of and writings about the sexual Other, in which modern sexuality has come into being through assumptions about the alterity of racialized Others, is still in place today (Dudink 2011). The construction of modern sexuality and desire always involves discourses and fantasies about the sexuality of racialized Others, and this provides an excellent starting point to discuss the entanglements of sexuality, culture, and race in contemporary discourses on gay rights, sexual freedom, and multiculturalism (Balkenhol et al. 2016). In this chapter, I have focused on the culturalist production in the Netherlands of gayness as progressive, secular, and modern. As a result of these dynamics, gayness has, like progress in more general terms, become associated with white Dutchness, while homophobia has become associated with allegedly conservative post-immigrant communities, most notably young men whose parents or grandparents were born in Morocco and who are often read as Muslim.

As I have argued, the post-progressive construction of Dutchness goes hand in hand with the construction of immigrant, and especially Muslim, culture as "pre-progressive." In other words, whereas white Dutch citizens are increasingly seen to have arrived in the post-progressive present, LGBTQIA migrants are framed as in need of self-emancipation. This explains the strong focus on Dutch discourse on the visibility and speakability of homosexuality in minoritized communities. Migrants must *become* a particular kind of individual, and that "requires a particular standard of inhabiting one's sexual identity that replicates the dominant recognizable Western model" (Jivraj & De Jong 2011, 153). As Jivraj and De Jong (2011) argue, this paradigm allows LGBTQIA Muslims who come out of the closet, speak out, and make themselves visible to be included in Dutchness and absorbed into the national community.[6] The paradigmatic status of this articulation of LGBTQIA sexual identity and the emblematic status of visible, out, queer Muslims is not always or only inclusionary. Such homonormative conceptions of lesbian and gay identities also have exclusionary effects, for "non-emblematic queers of color become invisible, nonexistent, or perceived of as 'not quite there yet,'" a kind of "gay in progress for whom the closet door still needs to be opened fully" (Jivraj & De Jong 2011, 153).

These conceptions of contemporary homosexuality ground a construction of non-performative, non-visible gayness as lagging behind and pre-progressive, a construction that is central to the culturalist discourse. Moreover, many proponents of this discourse, including Marcouch, partake, to a certain extent, in a temporal and racialized understanding of homophobia. Indeed, Marcouch seems to accept the analysis of Muslim communities as pre-progressive, and he thereby reinforces policies focused on regulation, discipline, and emancipation. This focus on integration and discipline goes hand in hand with one on security and policing that is characterized by a strong faith in "the right hand of the state" (Bourdieu 1994) and which, Marcouch argues, is necessary for protecting LGBTQIA people against homophobic violence and harassment. Some spaces need to be made safe for LGBTQIA people, he argues.

34 *Paul Mepschen*

In my view, in the context of today, this approach may unfortunately lead to increased policing of already targeted young post-immigrant men, who are construed and read as homophobic (Haritaworn 2013).

Within the dominant discourse in the Netherlands, we see different articulations of Islam and homosexuality emerge. Culturalists frame them as incompatible, as do some Muslims (Rahman 2014). Pragmatists are drawn to the "homonationalist" (Puar 2007) position, while the positions of lesbians, gays, bisexuals, Trans people, and women within Muslim communities have become a rallying point for liberal Muslims, like Ahmed Marcouch, for whom LGBTQIA issues create ethical moments in which to refashion their moral and political selves. What holds these different articulations of the relationship between homosexuality and Islam together is a homogenizing culturalism. Within culturalist representations, homosexuality is a singular and universal category. This stands in stark contrast to Foucault's analysis, according to which sexuality, including homosexuality, is "the set of effects produced in bodies, behaviors, and social relations by a certain deployment deriving from a complex political technology" (Foucault 1990, 127). Thus, sexuality is not singular but plural and asymmetrical, and the same can be said about heterosexuality and homophobia. This insight, it seems to me, is crucial for the analysis of LGBTQIA practices and identities in a globalizing world. However, the culturalist framework ignores these complexities. Contemporary struggles for sexual liberation emerge from this modern regime of sexuality, and the effect of this liberation has not only been increased freedom to express our sexuality but a *requirement* to do so. In other words, from a Foucauldian perspective, the increase in sexual freedom since the 1960s is a double-edged sword. It has increased the freedom of sexual expression while it has also chained people to the classifications that distinguish truthful sexual expression and identity – the right way to be gay or queer – from articulations that are considered hypocritical in a time of sexual truth. It is precisely this politics of truth, or so it seems to me, that we have to transform, for gayness is not universal.

Notes

1 Thanks to my friend Merijn Oudenampsen for allowing me use his concept of "post-progressive" in the title of this chapter. Many thanks also to professor Peter Geschiere for his many important remarks on an earlier version of the chapter. And thanks to the copyeditor, Greg Sax.
2 Frits Bolkestein, the leader in the 1990s of the free-market, conservative liberals mentioned above (the VVD), criticized an existing discourse on ethnic minorities as too permissive. Bolkestein presented himself as a politician who voiced, unjustly, marginalized popular discourses that could, he argued, be encountered in the country's churches and bars. He said, "A representative who ignores the people's concerns is worth nothing" (Prins 2004). In his important assessment of the transformation of Dutch society and politics in the 2000s, the internationally renowned sociologist Ian Buruma quotes Bolkestein as saying, "You should never underestimate how deeply Moroccan and Turkish immigrants are hated by the Dutch. My political

success rests upon the fact that I have listened to these feelings" (Buruma 2006, 58). See, for example, Mepschen (2016).
3 For an elaborate analysis of the El-Moumni affair, see Mepschen et al. (2010) and Uitermark et al. (2014).
4 The issue of homophobia and anti-gay violence among young post-immigrant men, especially those of Moroccan descent, is central in debates on safety and gay emancipation in the Netherlands. The sociologist Laurens Buijs and colleagues (2012) have done extensive research on anti-gay violence in Amsterdam, interviewing perpetrators and analyzing data. Buijs et al. argue that some aspects of male homosexuality are widely considered undesirable. Despite the liberal reputation of the country, four issues are widely rejected: anal sex, feminine behavior, the public display of homosexuality, and attempts to seduce (i.e. the fear of becoming a sex object of homosexual men) (Buijs et al. 2012). In short, norms of gender and sexuality are key issues in the explanation of homophobia and anti-gay violence. These norms are irreducible to cultural background or ethnicity but are intimately connected to a wider culture of hetero- and gender-normativity. Nonetheless, Buijs et al. (2012) argue that the data show an "over-representation" of young Moroccan-Dutch men among the perpetrators of anti-gay violence. If the data Buijs et al. (2012) have analyzed are correct, this may contribute to the notion among the men to whom I spoke that cultural background – somatically signified – is connected to homophobia. However, the authors do not take into account habits of policing, especially ethnic profiling (Cankaya 2015), while relying on police data. Moreover, the data show that while Moroccan-Dutch young men are "over-represented," white Dutch men are not "under-represented." That is to say, from the perspective of the everyday, homophobia also cannot be reduced to ethnicity or cultural background, a conclusion for which Buijs et al. also argue. It seems to me that the common-sense way in which this connection is nevertheless drawn in everyday discourse is imaginary – it is connected to a particular distribution of the sensible (Rancière 2004) in which homophobia is perceived through a racialized lens.
5 Filmmaker Theo van Gogh was killed in Amsterdam by a self-proclaimed radical Islamist.
6 See the contribution of Deniz Akin and Stine Helena Bang Svendsen in this book.

References

Ahmed, L. 1992. *Women and Gender in Islam. Historical Roots of a Modern Debate*. New Haven, CT: Yale University Press.

Anonymous (Comedy Squad TV). 2012. Ahmed Marcouch: Ik ben homo en trots... [video online]. Available at: www.youtube.com/watch?v=lHlqdIAzzzY [Accessed October 27, 2016].

Aydemir, M. Ed. 2011. *Indiscretions. At the Intersection of Queer and Postcolonial Theory*. Amsterdam: Rodopi.

Balkenhol, M., Mepschen, P. and Duyvendak, J.W. 2016. "The Nativist Triangle: Sexuality, Race and Religion in the Netherlands." In *The Culturalization of Citizenship. Belonging and Polarization in a Globalizing World*, eds. J.W. Duyvendak, P. Geschiere and E.H. Tonkens, 97–112. New York: Palgrave Macmillan.

Beekers, D.T. 2015. *Precarious Piety. Pursuits of Faith among Young Muslims and Christians in the Netherlands*. Dissertation. VU University Amsterdam.

Bourdieu, P. 1994. "Rethinking the State: On the Genesis and Structure of the Bureaucratic Field." *Sociological Theory* 12, 1: 1–19.

Bracke, S. 2012. From "Saving Women" to "Saving Gays". Rescue Narratives and their Dis/Continuities." *European Journal of Women's Studies* 19, 2: 237–252.
Brown, W. 2006. *Regulating Aversion. Tolerance in the Age of Identity and Empire.* Princeton, NJ: Princeton University Press.
Buijs, L., Duyvendak, J.W. and Hekma, G. 2012. "As Long As They Keep Away From Me. The Paradox of Antigay Violence in a Gay Friendly Country." *Sexualities* 14, 6: 632–652.
Buruma, I. 2006. *Murder in Amsterdam.* New York: Penguin Press.
Butler, J. 2008. "Sexual Politics, Torture, and Secular Time." *British Journal of Sociology* 59, 1: 1–23.
Cankaya, S. 2015. "Professional Anomalies. Diversity Policies Policing Ethnic Minority Police Officers." *European Journal of Policing Studies* 2, 4: 383–404.
Castells, M. 1993. European Cities, the Information Society and the Global Economy. *Journal of Economic and Social Geography* 84, 4: 247–257.
Drucker, P. 2015. *Warped. Gay Normality and Queer Anti-Capitalism.* Leiden: Brill.
Dudink, S. 2011. "Homosexuality, Race, and the Rhetoric of Nationalism." *History of the Present* 1, 2: 259–264.
Fadil, N. 2011. "Not-/Unveiling as an Ethical Practice." *Feminist Review* 98, 1: 83–109.
Fassin, E. and Salcedo, M. 2015. "Becoming Gay? Immigration Policies and the Truth of Sexual Identity." *Archives of Sexual Behavior* 44, 5: 1117–1125.
Foucault, M. 1985. *The History of Sexuality, Volume 2: The Use of Pleasure.* New York: Random House.
———. 1990. *The History of Sexuality. Volume 1: An Introduction.* New York: Vintage Books.
Geschiere, P. 2009a. *The Perils of Belonging. Autochthony, Citizenship and Exclusion in Africa and Europe.* Chicago, IL: The University of Chicago Press.
Geschiere, P. 2009b. "Autochtonie, Cultuur en Geschiedenis. Het glibberige pad van de identiteit." *De Gids* 8, 180, December, 901–991.
Haritaworn, J. 2013. "Beyond 'Hate'. Queer Metonymies of Crime, Pathology and anti/Violence." *Jindal Global Law Review* 4, 2: 44–78.
Jivraj, S. and de Jong, A. 2011. "The Dutch Homo-Emancipation Policy and its Silencing Effects on Queer Muslims." *Feminist Legal Studies* 19, 2: 143–158.
Lentin, A. and Titley, G. 2011. *The Crises of Multiculturalism. Racism in a Neoliberal Age.* London: Zed Books.
Marcouch, A. 2010. Personal interview. Interviewed by Paul Mepschen. May 31. Amsterdam.
———. 2011. Personal interview. Interviewed by Paul Mepschen. January 11. Amsterdam.
McClintock, A. 1995. *Imperial Leather. Race, Gender, and Sexuality in the Colonial Contest.* New York: Routledge.
McRobbie, A. 2004. "Post-Feminism and Popular Culture." *Feminist Media Studies* 4, 3: 255–264.
Mepschen, P. 2016a. *Everyday Autochthony: Difference, Discontent and the Politics of Home in the Netherlands.* PhD-thesis. University of Amsterdam.
———. 2016b. "Sexual Democracy, Cultural Alterity and the Politics of Everyday Life in Amsterdam." *Patterns of Prejudice* 50, 2: 150–167.
Mepschen, P. and Duyvendak J.W. 2012. "European Sexual Nationalism: The Culturalization of Citizenship and the Sexual Politics of Belonging and Exclusion." *Perspectives on Europe* 42, 1: 70–76.

Mepschen, P., Duyvendak, J.W. and Tonkens, E. 2010. "Sexual Politics, Orientalism and Multicultural Citizenship in the Netherlands." *Sociology* 44, 5: 962–979.

Meyer, B. 2012. "Mediation and the Genesis of Presence. Towards a Material Approach of Religion." *Inaugural lecture*. October 19. Utrecht University.

Mosse, G.L. 1985. *Nationalism and Sexuality: Respectability and Abnormal Sexuality in Modern Europe*. New York: Howard Fertig Pub.

Oudenampsen, M., 2013. "Postprogressive Politics: On the Reception of Neoconservatism in the Netherlands." Unpublished working paper. Available at: www.academia.edu/3256524/The_conservative_embrace_of_progressive_values_neoconservatism_and_the_rise_of_the_Dutch_New_Right [Accessed October 22, 2016].

Peumans, W. 2014. "Queer Muslim Migrants in Belgium: A Research Note on Same-Sex Sexualities and Lived Religion." *Sexualities* 17, 5–6: 618–631.

Prins, B. 2004. *Voorbij de Onschuld: Het Debat over Integratie in Nederland*. Amsterdam: Van Gennep.

Puar, J.K. 2007. *Terrorist Assemblages. Homonationalism in Queer Times*. Durham, NC: Duke University Press.

———. 2013. "Rethinking Homonationalism." *International Journal of Middle East Studies* 45, 2: 336–339.

Rahman, M. 2014. *Homosexualities, Muslim Cultures and Modernity*. Basingstoke: Palgrave Macmillan.

Rancière, J. 2004. *The Politics of Aesthetics. The Distribution of the Sensible*. London: Continuum.

Scheffer, P. 2000. "Het Multiculturele Drama." *NRC Handelsblad*, January 29.

———. 2006. "Terug naar de tuinstad. Binnen en buiten de ringweg van Amsterdam." *Inaugural lecture*. Amsterdam: University of Amsterdam.

Schinkel, W. and Van Houdt, F. 2010. "The Double Helix of Cultural Assimilationism and Neo-Liberalism. Citizenship in Contemporary Governmentality." *British Journal of Sociology* 61, 4: 696–715.

Scott, J. 2009. "Sexularism: On Secularism and Gender Equality." *RSCAS Distinguished Lectures*, 1. Available at: http://cadmus.eui.eu/bitstream/handle/1814/11553/RSCAS_DL_2009_01.pdf?sequence=1 [Accessed October 27, 2016].

Sears, A. 2005. "Queer Anti-Capitalism. What's Left of Lesbian and Gay Liberation?" *Science & Society* 69, 1: 92–112.

Stoler, A. 1995. *Race and the Education of Desire: Foucault's History of Sexuality and the Colonial Order of Things*. Durham, NC: Duke University Press.

———. 1997. Educating Desire in Colonial South Asia. Foucault, Freud, and Imperial Sexualities. In *Sites of Desire, Economies of Pleasure*, eds. L. Manderson and M. Jolly, 27–48. Chicago, IL: University of Chicago Press.

Swierstra, T. and Tonkens, E. eds. 2008. De beste de baas. Prestatie, respect en solidariteit in een meritocratie. Amsterdam: Amsterdam University Press.

Uitermark, J. 2010. *Dynamics of Power in Dutch Integration Politics*. Dissertation. University of Amsterdam.

Uitermark, J. 2012. *Dynamics of Power in Dutch Integration Politics. From Accommodation to Confrontation*. Amsterdam: University of Amsterdam Press.

Uitermark, J., Mepschen, P. and Duyvendak, J.W. 2014. "Progressive Politics of Exclusion. The Populist Framing of Islam in the Netherlands." In *European States and their Muslim Citizens. The Impact of Institutions on Perceptions and Boundaries*, eds. J.R. Bowen, C. Bertossi, J.W. Duyvendak and M.L. Krook, 235–256. New York: Cambridge University Press.

Van den Hemel, E. 2014. "Proclaiming Tradition. The 'Judeo-Christian' Roots of Dutch Society and the Rise of Conservative Nationalism." In *Post-Secular Publics. Transformations of Religion and the Public Sphere*, eds. R. Braidotti, E. Midden and B. Blaagaard, 53–76. London: Palgrave Macmillan.

Van der Veer, P. 2006. "Pim Fortuyn, Theo van Gogh, and the Politics of Tolerance in the Netherlands." *Public Culture* 18, 1: 111–124.

Van Rooden, P. 2004. "Oral History en het Vreemde Sterven van het Nederlands Christendom." *BMGN – Low Countries Historical Review* 119, 4: 524–551.

Verkaaik, O. 2009. *Ritueel burgerschap: een essay over nationalisme en secularisme in Nederland*. Amsterdam: Aksant.

Verkaaik, O. and Spronk, R. 2011. "Sexular Practice. Notes on an Ethnography of Secularism." *Focaal* 59: 83–88.

Wekker, G. 2009. "Van homo nostalgie en betere tijden Multiculturaliteit en postkolonialiteit." *George Mosse Lecture*. Universiteit Utrecht. Available at: www.let.uu.nl/~gloria.wekker/personal/PDFOnlineMosselezingGl09.pdf [Accessed October 22, 2016].

———. 2016. *White Innocence. Paradoxes of Colonialism and Race*. Durham, NC: Duke University Press.

Zigon, J. 2008. *Morality: An Anthropological Perspective*. Oxford and New York: Berg.

———. 2009. "Within a Range of Possibilities. Morality and Ethics in Social Life." *Ethnos* 74, 2: 251–276.

2 Becoming family
Orientalism, homonormativity, and queer asylum in Norway

Deniz Akin and Stine Helena Bang Svendsen

Introduction

In a heated debate in the spring of 2015 over the number of Syrian refugees Norway should accept, an openly gay politician from the Conservative Party (Høyre) pointed out that Norway could cut the cost of integrating refugees by prioritizing LGBT (lesbian, gay, bisexual, transgender) asylum seekers rather than letting the UNHCR (United Nations High Commissioner for Refugees) select the refugees to fill its UN quota. LGBT refugees, Vegard Rødseth Tokheim argued, would be more beneficial for Norway than others because they are more likely to embrace life in Norway wholeheartedly (Bjørndal 2015). And, importantly, they would be cheaper for the state because they are less likely to request family reunification, partner with people of their own ethnic group, and produce second-generation refugees. Tokheim's argument shows how issues of sexuality, family, and reproduction form a significant political subtext to the issue of LGBT[1] asylum in Norway.

Tokheim's statement drew on discursive resources similar to those used to call attention to the threat of public Islam by other openly gay political and public figures, such as the American author Bruce Bawer, who lives and publishes in Norway, and the far-right Dutch politician Pim Fortuyn, who had been a key representative of the opponents of multiculturalism (Long 2009; Mepschen, Duyvendak, and Tonkens 2010). Commenting on the anti-immigration sentiment voiced by openly gay conservative public figures, Scott Long points out that their gayness obscures the xenophobia in their message: "… gayness veneers prejudice with respectability. How can a victim victimize?" (2009, 131). What is particularly interesting about Tokheim's argument is that he draws both on the idea that LGBT refugees are less threatening than other refugees, because of their presumed compatibility with Norwegian culture, and the presumption that they would not reproduce. In a political climate of white anxieties about racial and cultural "drowning" in the imagined "flood" of refugees from the south (Ahmed 2004), a queer immigrant who rejects "reproductive futurism" (Edelman 2004, 2) can be construed as a political resource for nationalist immigration agendas.

In this chapter, we discuss a case from Norway in order to show how a cultural and affective form of what we call "kinning" can be at work in the adjudication of asylum cases involving LGBT applicants in Norway. That is, various forms of familiarity and interaction with the local LGBT community and its culture can influence whether or not a gay applicant is granted asylum. The case we explore involves a queer Iranian asylum seeker whose application was rejected by both the Norwegian Directorate of Immigration (UDI) and the Norwegian Immigration Appeals Board (UNE). In the end, the applicant was granted asylum as the result of his appeal to the district court of Norway (Tingrett). Paying close attention to the period between the UDI and UNE verdicts, we discuss the kinds of reasons given to justify the persecution and the protection of a member of a sexual minority in the light of changes in the asylum regulations in 2012, on the one hand, and of strategies that the applicant used to increase his chances of winning asylum, on the other. We also consider this case in terms of the "homonationalism" (Puar 2007) that Tokheim, the gay, Conservative politician, illustrates above, and we draw parallels to a number of other cases in which presenting LGBT asylum seekers as members of the international LGBT "family" seems to have been crucial to the success of their claims.

In what follows, we analyze the aesthetic and cultural adjustments that the applicant made to his life in preparing to enter the imagined LGBT family. We read these adjustments as attempts to be recognized as a homosexual in Norwegian society. We also compare the adjudication of asylum cases with cases of marriage immigration, and use our case to illustrate how the cultural politics of marriage immigration can also be found in Norwegian LGBT asylum adjudication.

Scholars have shown that, in addition to the local resident's ability to provide financially for her or his partner, marriage immigration in Norway depends on officials' heteronormative understanding of what a real marriage is (Eggebø 2013). For a marriage to qualify and not be rendered *pro forma*, that is, entered into just for the sake of obtaining a residence permit, the marriage should, preferably, be entered into on romantic grounds and involve sexual intimacy, and it should seem probable that the couple will fit in with society at large (Muller Myrdahl 2010). Research conducted in this field has revealed a tendency toward suspicion of marriages in which the foreign spouse is perceived to be more financially and socially independent than the local resident. Specifically, marriages between white Norwegian women and younger non-Western men are considered suspicious in this way, and they are looked into. In such cases, the men are considered likely to trick the women in order to obtain Norwegian residency (Hagesæther 2008). However, it is not considered suspicious when Norwegian men marry younger foreign women, not even when the women marry for economic reasons. Such marriages are not seen as duplicitous or a threat to the integrity of the nation's borders (Mühleisen, Røthing, and Svendsen 2012). Furthermore, a recent increase in the income requirement to apply for family reunification has made family reunification even less attainable for many women, who are over-represented in low income and part time jobs also in Norway. In short, marriage immigration requires that the local resident with sufficient means to provide for the spouse enter into an implicit contract with the state to take responsibility for the spouse, and, for this to be convincing, the spouse can display only limited agency.

In theory, the adjudication of asylum cases differs fundamentally from cases of marriage immigration, as immigration regulations do not apply to the institution of asylum, the granting of which relies solely on the need for protection. This separation seems to blur, however, when industrialized societies do not consider immigrants as economic resources, but, rather, as burdens on their welfare systems and wealth. In many European countries, this framing of immigration has led to "asylum being viewed as subsidiary to immigration and human rights as secondary to policing logics" (Fassin 2013, 53).

The contemporary anxiety over the increased numbers of refugees voiced in many European countries, including Norway, is a public expression of the suspicion that economically motivated immigrants apply for entry under the guise of being refugees or the spouses or family members of residents. For instance, in an interview with the Norwegian newspaper *Morgenbladet* on December 24, 2015, Sylvi Listhaug, the Norwegian Minister of Immigration and Integration, expressed concern that people whose family reunification applications in Norway are rejected go back to their countries, change their identities, and then take another shot at it as asylum seekers. As Listhaug's concern makes clear, both the asylum institution and the practice of family reunification fall under suspicion when immigrants are suspected of either having economic motivations or manipulating the system for their own benefit.

In this chapter, we argue that sexual orientation-based asylum claims are rendered not credible through a process that is similar to the process that renders certain marriages *pro forma*. The "pro forma" and "not credible" decisions are not based on definitions of "true," "authentic," or "real" marriages or asylum needs but result, rather, from officials' judgments about whether a potential immigrant will make a good participant in Norway's neoliberal capitalist democracy (Luibhéid 2008). Normative understandings of an ideal LGBT immigrant seem closely tied to the changed relationship between the state and its LGBT citizens in many Western countries, including Norway (Svendsen 2014). In the following section, we outline the theoretical insights that inform our discussion of queer asylum adjudication.

Theoretical underpinnings: Nordic homonormativity

Sexual minorities have gained substantial visibility as asylum seekers over the last decade as a wide consensus has been reached that sexual orientation and gender identity can be reasonable grounds for seeking asylum (Berg & Millbank 2009; Spijkerboer & Jansen 2011). The plight of sexual minorities in many countries is not a new phenomenon. Rather, it is the solidification of sexual minorities into particular social groups eligible for protection under the UN Refugee Convention's category "membership of a particular social group" that is new. For instance, though sexual minorities could be denied entry and deported as sexual deviants in the United States until the 1990s, the country currently offers asylum on the basis of sexual orientation (Cantú 2009; Luibhéid 2002; Randazzo 2005). "What has changed?" one might ask. First and most importantly, the advocacy of LGBT organizations and various human rights institutions has contributed to a raised awareness of the plight of sexual minorities worldwide. A second notable change is "homonationalism" (Puar 2007), which celebrates tolerance for gays and lesbians as a cultural distinction of the West, which, in turn, casts non-accepting cultures as the intolerant Other (Brown 2006). The strategic mobilization of gender and sexuality in the construction of the new politics of national identity has brought sexual minorities to the forefront of politics in Europe and North America (Haritaworn 2008, 2012; Mepschen et al. 2010; Mühleisen et al. 2012).

Western LGBT lobbying efforts and equal-rights advocacy have resulted in increased visibility and acceptance of minority sexual identities and practices in accord with Western ideals of coupledom and love. However, alternative ways of doing queer sexuality and identity have received only limited attention. At the same time, scholars in queer studies have taken on the job of interrogating, in discussions on multiculturalism and immigration politics, the politics of what Lisa Duggan described as "the new homonormativity," that is:

> politics that does not contest dominant heteronormative assumptions and institutions, but upholds and sustains them, while promising the possibility of a demobilized gay constituency and a privatized, depoliticized gay culture anchored in domesticity and consumption.
>
> (Duggan 2003, 50)

The new homonormativity is seen as a constituent of "homonationalism" (Puar 2007), "sexual democracy" (Fassin 2010), and "queer liberalism" (Eng 2010). What Jasbir Puar and Eric Fassin have in common is their approach to the new politics of national identity, which strategically mobilizes the acceptance of the full range of gender and sexuality as a mark that distinguishes White Western people from immigrants of color, who are considered to be intolerant of sexual diversity and to have pathologized minority sexualities. Fassin bases his conclusions mainly upon the French context but extends them to many other European destinations for immigrants. He argues that "sexual democracies" (2010, 513) are significant for the defense of Europe's actual and symbolic cultural borders against non-European immigrants, whereas the USA utilizes the trope of the so-called "sexual clash of civilization" to legitimize its overseas military interventions (Fassin 2010). Similarly, David

Eng, who coined the term "queer liberalism" (Eng 2010, 2) to refer to the legal recognition and granting of rights to those gay and lesbian people who are willing to take on a homonormative queer identity and lifestyle, points to the absence of considerations of race in American queer-liberation politics in arguing that queer liberalism's success has produced an image of progress toward social justice while obscuring racism, poverty, and citizenship (issues of great significance for many LGBT people) from view (ibid., 49).

All communities that extend beyond the people whom we meet and know are, to use Benedict Anderson's term, "imagined communities" (Anderson 1991). Western nations imagine themselves, specifically, to be extended families, as such metaphors as "motherland," "fatherland," and the description of the nation's population as a "brotherhood" show. These metaphors of kinship point toward the centrality of reproductive sexuality and the nuclear family in Western national imaginaries. To be included in the fold of the motherland, however, one must renounce one's other mother (so to speak): there is only room for one motherland or fatherland in the structure of feeling that governs the Western politics of belonging (Eng 2010).

Love holds a privileged position in this structure, as it constitutes what is taken to be the only legitimate reason to transition from one family to another. Love is a force for "affective assimilation," as Lene Myong and Mons Bissenbakker have argued (Myong & Bissenbakker 2014). It is often believed that romantic love is free from all social constraints, a necessity for the realization of the modern individual, and independent of other forms of affective attachment, such as desire or lust (Povinelli 2006, 177). And it is imagined to produce self-governing, civilized individuals who are liberated from the constraints of all forms of social determinism and to differ from any other sort of intimacy (Luibhéid 2008, 299); therefore, it strongly informs studies of immigration (Mai & King 2009). Conceived in this way, love is a trope that can render the immigrant both less suspect and more desirable to the nation.

In the case of Norway, previous studies have shown that tolerance of sexual minorities is often considered constitutive of "Norwegianness," while negative attitudes toward sexual diversity are considered a symptom of poor integration and the lack of modernity (Bangstad 2012; Gressgård & Jacobsen 2008; Røthing & Svendsen 2011). The following is an extract from the speech of the Conservative Norwegian Prime Minister, Erna Solberg, opening the Pride Park Oslo in 2014, which illustrates the homonationalist cultural politics that the authors cited above have discussed in their work:

> The efforts of many organizations, the commitment of individuals and cross-party unity on this issue have brought our society forward. In Norway we have a single Marriage Act for all, and we have anti-discrimination laws. Special attention is being paid to improving the situation for young gays and lesbians in towns and rural areas. There is still a long way to go in many countries: We know of the difficulties and dangers faced by LGBT people in Uganda. We know about the

brutality that Russian LGBT activists, and LGBT activists in many other countries, meet every day. We know of the struggle of LGBT people in most countries of the world. We all agree that we need to do our share to improve the situation.

(Solberg 2014)

Solberg highlights the recent legal and policy changes regarding sexual minorities in Norway, which are formal markers of Norwegian "homonormalization" (Roseneil, Crowhurst, Hellesund, Santos, and Stoilova 2013). Anti-discrimination laws and the 2009 Equal Marriage Act are important achievements for the Norwegian gay and lesbian liberation movement. In Solberg's speech, it is evident how these landmark events have constituted a national "we" that includes the LGBT population and which, at the same time, is mobilized as a humanitarian agent who directs its efforts at those who fail to uphold these new national values.

Providing asylum on the basis of sexual orientation can be considered a part of this broader sexually informed humanitarian project. Solberg's speech is made more meaningful by the fact that she was the author of strict immigration measures, which earned her the nickname "Iron Erna," when she served as Minister of Local Government and Regional Development from 2001 to 2005 (Gudbrandsen 2010).

Our hypothesis is that homonormalization deeply informs asylum adjudication for LGBT people in contemporary Norway. Below is an overview of Norwegian immigration policies and practices regarding the selection of the "right kind" of queer individuals for asylum.

An overview of asylum regulations in Norway

The Norwegian Directorate of Immigration (UDI), the central executive administrative agency for immigration and refugees in Norway, has been granting asylum on the basis of sexual orientation since 1997 (ILGA Europe 1997). Two chief criteria of evaluation are whether the applicant is genuinely homosexual and whether she has a well-founded fear of persecution on that basis. Previous studies concluded that the UDI had often distinguished between sexual inclination and sexual practice, and they argued that this distinction allowed them to turn down certain applications on the grounds that sexual inclination need not be dangerous as long as the applicant does not practice it (Mühleisen, Rothing, and Svendsen 2012). This policy, which is called "discretion reasoning," had been widely applied among asylum-granting countries and widely criticized for reducing sexual orientation to sexual acts (Spijkerboer & Jansen 2011). Since 2012, discretion reasoning is no longer valid, at least in theory, following the verdict of the Norwegian Supreme Court, which, citing an earlier verdict from the UK,[2] ruled that if a person has to hide his homosexuality upon returning to his home country, then he has a well-founded fear of persecution (Skjeggestad 2012).

However, there are discrepancies between theory and practice. There are still cases in which adjudicators are convinced that the claimant is homosexual but deny her asylum because they believe she would hide her sexual orientation and not live it out in her home country for reasons other than fear of persecution. In an example from 2014, the Court of Appeal in Norway rejected the appeal of an Iranian applicant, noting, "He will adapt his behavior in public spaces because of fear of bullying, harassment, discrimination and ostracism in the community – not because of fear of persecution from the government."[3] In support of their decision, the judges pointed out that during the time that the applicant had been in Norway he had not expressed his sexual orientation in the Norwegian gay community, and he had engaged in sexual intercourse only in the privacy of his room in an apartment (Beskyttelse & asyl 2014). That is, the applicant had not made his homosexuality public. The distinction between voluntary and involuntary closeting, which the Court of Appeal applied in this case, is commonly applied in Europe. The legal scholar Thomas Spijkerboer (2013) described it as a mutated version of discretion reasoning.

In this case, as well as the case we shall discuss in depth later in this chapter, the court not only considered whether the applicant was in fact gay but also the cultural style in which he performed his sexual identity. This question of style is a matter of recognizability, that is, is the applicant recognizable as a homosexual to Norwegian adjudicators? The frame of understanding that adjudicators apply is constructed from what they know of lesbian and gay culture and practice in Norway. This is evident in their frequent references to the local community in adjudications. Being recognizably homosexual, then, depends on one's similarity with, or at least assimilability into, the local gay and lesbian community. In short, it is crucial to perform the right kind of queerness. Queer individuals who can demonstrate such a sexual identity, regardless of their practice of sexuality, are favored in comparison to those who merely engage in same-sex practice and fail to manifest a recognizable sexual identity (Akin 2015).

This prompts the question of which feelings, thoughts, and practices are understood to be inherent and integral to possessing a sexual identity (Hathaway & Pobjoy 2011). As the legal scholars James Hathaway and Jason Pobjoy ask: "Is refugee status owed to gay claimants whose risk follows only from holding hands, kissing in public? To those at risk because they cohabit, marry, or decide to raise children?" (Hathaway & Pobjoy 2011, 334). Or, should asylum be granted to those who are recognizably LGBT precisely because of the shame that could prevent them from doing any of the above?

We now address what recognizable sexual identity amounts to in Norwegian LGBT-asylum practice. Drawing on the work mentioned above, we suggest that a particular sort of LGBT asylum seeker is construed in Norwegian political discourse and law as especially assimilable into Norwegian society as a part of the imagined Norwegian gay community. Considered as belonging to this imagined community, and thus being recognized as assimilable into

Norwegian society, entails conforming to particular styles of queerness. These are the issues we will explore through the case study that we now present.

The case

Samet, as we shall call him, came to Norway from Iran in 2010 and applied for asylum. His application was turned down by both the UDI and the UNE. He then took his case to the district court of Norway. The first part of our data is extracted from the district court's verdict that granted him asylum. Samet communicated the verdict to those who had been involved in his legal battle against the immigration authorities, and the court's decision was later communicated to one of us, *viz.*, Akin, by one of the queer organizations with which her research involves her. Akin got in contact with Samet via Facebook and got his permission to obtain a copy of the verdict and use it in her research. However, Samet denied Akin's request for a formal interview on the grounds that his story and the court's verdict had already been covered in a local newspaper, and he wanted to move on with his life and leave the asylum-seeking process behind him. We have extracted the following background story from court documents and strictly anonymized all information concerning Samet's identity.

In the initial interview for his application for asylum in 2010, Samet stated that he was homosexual. Adjudicators often consider early disclosure of one's sexual identity favorably. During the interview, Samet told Norwegian authorities that he had had an intimate relationship in Iran with a friend from school. They often had sex in his friend's apartment. One day, a teacher caught them having sex in an empty classroom. The teacher reported it to the principal, who stated that he would make an example of them for the other students. They were punished physically (probably beaten) and expelled. The principal had also immediately informed both the morals police and the students' mothers. Before the morals police had arrived, Samet and his friend had run away. The rest of his story was about his flight to Norway.

Neither the UDI nor the UNE found his story credible. They denied Samet asylum for two reasons. First, they did not believe his story about getting caught in a classroom. They stated in their verdict that they did not believe that the applicant would take such a big risk as having sex in a public place, especially since homosexual conduct is punishable by death in Iran. They also stated that in an overwhelmingly patriarchal society the school's principle would have informed the students' fathers, not their mothers. Second, they argued that there was no evidence that the applicant would be persecuted upon his return to Iran. In accord with the discretion reasoning, they judged that the applicant would be safe upon his return, granted that he kept a low profile and did not engage in behavior that challenged the norms of his society.

Samet's lawyer appealed the decision to the district court of Norway in 2012, which ruled in 2013 that the applicant had a well-founded fear of persecution, for the Iranian authorities would by then have become aware of his sexual orientation. Furthermore, the judges noted in their decision that Samet had appeared in court with "dyed blond hair and with ear rings" and his appearance "will have to be changed if he had to return to Iran." They believed that he would have to make these changes to his appearance because of "fear of punishment and violence" and, hence, that he would be prevented from living out his sexuality openly and without fear of persecution.

In order to learn more about the case and understand how changes in Norwegian asylum practices had influenced the court's decision, Akin interviewed a key person involved in Samet's case. Maria, that is the pseudonym we give her, who is an LGBT activist and also from Iran, had helped Samet prepare his oral testimony for the district court. Maria identifies as lesbian and volunteers for one of the queer-rights organizations in Norway. After his initial asylum application was rejected but before appealing the verdict to the district court, Samet had gotten in touch with the queer organization where Maria works and asked for assistance. Maria said that her organization was familiar with similar cases and they knew how to prepare applicants for their interrogations by the immigration office by styling their gay image.

Maria told how they had helped Samet fine tune his performance for his interview before the court:

> He looked very shy and innocent, like someone who has just come out of the closet. He needed some tips on his appearance because he is one of those not-very-effeminate gays. I know the feeling as no one believes that I am a lesbian either; look at me. [*Author's comment: she is femme and fond of dresses and high heels.*] [...] He can be as masculine as he wants after the appeal, but he needed to look like a *bottom* [our emphasis] for the next interview. [...] Bottoms are risking their life in my country, and you can hardly hide if you are passive.

Maria told how adjudicators were usually eager to hear romanticized versions of being homosexual. She said:

> Everyone is in danger in my country. Being homosexual does not make you special. What makes you special is your look, your longing for a liberated life in Norway. Norwegians really enjoy hearing that they have something that you lack, which they can offer you.

During his time in Norway, Samet had engaged in a romantic relationship with another man from the same organization. They recorded a support video that depicts the couple holding hands. Samet's boyfriend is crying in the video, and he asks people to follow the case and pressure the government if necessary so that Samet would not be sent into a dangerous future in Iran. Samet is silent and rests his head on his boyfriend's shoulder toward the end. Samet's case had been made public before the legal hearing in 2012, and activists had circulated petitions online. Samet had also marched in the Gay Pride

Parade in Trondheim, Norway, carrying his nation's flag. When the district court found in his favor, queer networks spread the happy news via social media, and his story was covered in a local newspaper.

Analysis: wedding the queer nation

Maria's narrative suggests that Samet and the local LGBT community collaboratively tried to influence the outcome of the case by performing a recognizable style of homosexuality, which would also more effectively cast Samet as a victim of persecution in Iran. It is difficult to say to what extent his performance succeeded. It is a fact, however, that the district court did not doubt Samet's story, as the UDI and UNE had. This was pivotal for the outcome of the case. By taking a closer look at the stage where Samet's appearance was being crafted to fit his claim to need protection, we can identify some of the lenses through which the actors involved (including Samet) made him appear as a recognizable homosexual from Iran who was deserving of asylum.

For his appearance before the district court, Samet was made to look, and presented, as a vulnerable Muslim gay man who longed for a committed relationship, and, preferably, a family, neither of which his country would permit him to have. The success of the presentation confirms that a certain conventional ideal of a good couple in a romantic union predominates in Norway. The support video, in which Samet and his boyfriend hold hands, illustrating their intimate bond, functions as a plea to save their union. Samet is silent in the video; the Norwegian boyfriend speaks on behalf of them both. This arrangement suggests that Samet's Norwegian partner will take care of him and assimilate him into Norwegian society. As a silent figure, the video portrays Samet as lacking agency and in need of saving. As a symbolic damsel in distress, Samet is dissociated from Muslim masculine agency, which European cultural imaginaries link to terrorism, and instead aligned with the feminine Muslim woman who, it is imagined, needs White men to save her from Brown men (Spivak 1988). The discursive construction of Samet as the vulnerable partner in the same-sex union speaks against the hegemonic notions of romantic love that are "consistent with a highly individualized and neoliberal model of society, celebrating the expression of individual autonomy and gender equality" (Mai & King 2009, 300). To the contrary, by downplaying Samet's self-governance because the host society perceives them as indicators of an agency that it finds threatening, the video creates the expectation that Samet will engage in a different norm of romantic love.

When considered through the framework of Orientalism (Said 2003), Samet's reworked image appears as a strategy partly designed by Maria. Her origins are in the same imaginative geography of the Orient as Samet's, but she currently resides in the imaginative geography of the Occident and is well aware of its representations of their country of origin. Maria realized that a homosexual's claim of persecution would not be adequate for the court; one's claim should underscore one's desperation to be saved, aspiration to liberty, and admiration for the sheltering country of Norway.

As we've said, the district court overthrew the previous rejections and granted Samet asylum. And the court did not base its judgment on Samet's testimony about being caught having sex; rather, it stated that he would risk persecution if he were forced to practice his sexual identity in secret.

Norwegian authorities used to believe that homosexuality was inherent, and they believed that it could be practiced safely in the closet. They argued that sexual identity and sexual practice were private matters, and the need to keep them private did not amount to persecution. Since 2012, sexual identity has been considered more broadly to include its public display. Currently, not being able to act out one's sexual identity is considered a form of persecution and a violation of one's self. In other words, in addition to a risk of persecution, officials look for a recognizable identity the recognizability of which depends on Norwegian norms.

We want to shed light on the relationship between the state, LGBT organizations, and the applicant in cases such as Samet's, where the LGBT community vouches for the sexual identity of the applicant. It seems to us that the change in regulations in Norway in 2012 has modified the concept of asylum as it applies to LGBT people in ways that need to be understood.

We think that contemporary LGBT asylum cases like Samet's blur the difference between the asylum institution and marriage immigration, and that the blurring results from the homonormative and Orientalist presumptions of homonationalism. In preparing Samet's appeal, Maria and her organization reworked him politically and aesthetically. He was supposed to look like a "bottom," as she said. However, the reason may not only have been to make persecution seem more likely; they may also have wanted Samet to look like someone who did not have the necessary agency to take advantage of the Norwegian state. Furthermore, Maria, Samet's new boyfriend, and their LGBT organization vouched in effect for his legitimacy as a homosexual. In addition, the display of a committed union in jeopardy of being torn apart deepened the appearance of victimhood that is considered decisive in the asylum context (Giametta 2014; Murray 2014).

In our view, the role of Maria, the boyfriend, and their organization in Samet's case was not only to offer practical advice to help Samet pass as gay, but, more fundamentally, they conducted a symbolic process of accepting him as kin. The representation of Samet's case mimics the heteronormative elements of a successful claim for family reunification: a spouse who can provide for the claimant, a community willing to integrate the claimant, and a symbolically feminine claimant. By publicly including Samet in the LGBT family, they represented him as their dependent. Including him in the nation through such a public act of kinning, however, required that he be presented symbolically as without agency, as someone who both needed to be saved by the Norwegian nation and could not take advantage of his new family.

Samet's relational subjectivity

Chávez (2010) discusses how queer rights and immigrant rights organizations produce a script of cultural citizenship. On the basis of her reading of a human-rights report on bi-national same-sex couples, Chávez states that foreign immigrants are usually depicted in terms of their relationships with their partners as if they had only "relational subjectivity" (2010, 142). This relational subjectivity establishes "hybrid familiarity," which erases a person of color's difference through his relationship with a White partner (ibid.). This process seems to have been at work in Samet's case, even though his status as an asylum seeker should have rendered his relationships irrelevant. Samet's relational subjectivity was determined by his relationship to his new boyfriend, which also underscored his membership in the extended family of the Norwegian LGBT community. The video of Samet and his boyfriend mimicked the public vow of love witnessed by friends and family in the symbolic sphere of the wedding.

Love played an important part in the depiction of Samet's case as an affective force mobilizing support for him. In the depiction of Samet's relationship with his White Norwegian boyfriend, love also had the performative effect of showing both Samet's ability to love Norway and Norway's ability to love him. This aspect of the depiction ties in with what Lene Myong and Mons Bissenbakker have called "white transraciality," through which depictions of "love across borders" confirm White colorblindness as both real and good (Myong & Bissenbakker 2016). In this light, Samet's relational subjectivity also produces what Sara Ahmed (2004) called a "hybrid whiteness," which "confirms the nation's white racial hegemony through its ability to incorporate the non-white into itself" (Myong & Bissenbakker 2016, 139).

Conclusion

Maria's involvement in Samet's case prompts the question of which asylum seekers should be entitled to the support of an organization? Organizational vouching for a queer couple's heartfelt union was previously seen in the case of an Iranian lesbian couple that had been publicized with a focus on how their love had helped them survive exile and the asylum process (Engesbak 2012). Did Samet deserve the support of Maria's organization because he is identifiable as queer, or did he deserve their advocacy on the grounds that he was able to perform a kind of queer that fit the organization's policies and politics? In Samet's involvement with the queer organization, one can see queer liberalism's normative politics of family and kinship (Eng 2010) and its attentiveness to "tacit subjects" (Decena 2008) who need assistance in appropriating a public sexual identity. To become "proper gays" (El-Tayeb 2012), that is, autonomous queer individuals who are not only recognizable as such but who will also be assimilable citizens, such subjects need the help of already homonormative queer liberal subjects. Nevertheless, we cannot determine whether Samet's videotape, his participation in a gay pride parade, and the refining of his case stemmed from a pure asylum strategy or an organizational agenda. However, homonationalism has been naturalized to the extent that it is difficult for LGBT activists to prevent their work from being understood in its terms, even if they are aware of the problems that that involves (Svendsen 2014).

The ability of LGBT persons and communities to vouch for applicants in the way we have described depends on their inclusion in state-sanctioned sexual structures and, specifically, their inclusion into the institution of marriage. Drawing on the work of David Eng, we can say that the Nordic LGBT movement's ability to privatize sex has, paradoxically, made queer intimacy recognizable in the public sphere (Eng 2010). The pervasive influence of homonationalism in the Nordic context makes the blurring of the distinction between marriage immigration and LGBT asylum particularly significant. Put simply, the inculcation of homotolerance as a national and regional virtue, and the converse projection of homophobia onto racialized people through Orientalist discourse, gives the kinning of queer foreigners racial dimensions. Depictions of love and its public display in Samet's case showed him symbolically wedded to, and adopted by, the Norwegian queer community. In this sort of imaginary, the asylum applicant is symbolically saved from homophobia in the non-West through "affective assimilation" into the nation (Myong Petersen 2009). However, he is also transformed from a racialized Other into a protected charge of Norway's homonormative citizenry.

One might ask: Isn't this what asylum is all about? Juridically, it is. Culturally, however, asylum seekers and those who have been granted asylum are criticized in the Norwegian public sphere as potential abusers of the welfare state and not even remotely included in the national community. Kinning is the key symbolic route to cultural citizenship in the Nordic context (Myong Petersen 2009). In Samet's case, it was conducted through an elaborate public display of his belonging not only to Nordic culture but to specific people within that culture. Indeed, kinning is used to challenge the denial of asylum on all grounds. For example, local communities sometimes rise to vouch for their immigrant inhabitants and oppose the decisions of the state, like the LGBT community did in Samet's case, arguing that those residents are one of them. What such campaigns reveal, however, is the local community's power to decide who deserves asylum on the basis of its own judgment of whether an asylum seeker fits in. Whenever such judgments inform asylum adjudication, they implicitly challenge the principle of the right to protection from persecution. The blurring of the distinction between queer asylum and marriage immigration that we have diagnosed in this chapter suggests that access to the institution of asylum is unequal. Only asylum seekers who, like Samet, can credibly be depicted as harmless dependents can enter into symbolic kinning processes like the one we have traced here. Furthermore, only nationals who are deemed proper subjects have the power to kin others. In the case of

Norway, this suggests that the efforts of queer liberalism to protect its own kind from injustice sustain a culture of White hegemony.

Notes

1 Throughout this chapter, we refer to people with non-conforming sexual orientation and/or gender identity as LGBT, following how that is the abbreviation most commonly used in public discourse in Norway. Our analysis, however, leaves out the "T" as our main focus is placed upon sexual orientation rather than gender identity. Another reason is that our material does not provide sufficient information to analyze the lived experiences of transgender asylum seekers. We also use the term "queer" as an umbrella concept to refer to people with non-conforming sexual orientation, even though not all such persons necessarily identify as queer.
2 HJ (Iran) and HT (Cameroon) v Secretary of State for the Home Department (2010).
3 Our translation. The Norwegian original reads: "Han vil tilpasse sin opptreden i det offentlige rom på grunn av frykt for mobbing, trakassering, diskriminering og utfrysning I nærmiljøet- ikke på grunn av frykten for forfølgelse fra det offentlige."

References

Ahmed, Sara. 2004. *The Cultural Politics of Emotion*. Edinburgh: Edinburgh University Press.
Akin, Deniz. 2015. "Assessing Sexual Orientation-Based Persecution: A Closer Look at the Norwegian Practice of Asylum Evaluation of Gay and Lesbian Claimants." *Lambda Nordica* 20, 1: 19–42.
Anderson, Benedict. 1991. *Imagined Communities* (2nd ed.). London: Verso.
Bangstad, Sindre. 2012. "En norsk sekularisme?" In *Sekularisme – med norske briller*, edited by Sindre Bangstad, Oddbjørn Leirvik, & Ingvill Thorson Plesner, 47–66. Oslo: Unipub.
Berg, L., & Millbank, J. 2009. "Constructing the Personal Narratives of Lesbian, Gay and Bisexual Asylum Claimants." *Journal of Refugee Studies* 22, 2: 195–223.
Beskyttelse, & asyl. 2014. Homofili som forfølgelsesgrunn. Iran. Utl. § 28 1 a. [17 September]. LB-2012-162219. Available at: http://udiregelverk.no/no/rettskilder/underrettsavgjorelser/lb-2012-162219/ [Accessed October 30, 2016].
Bjørndal, Bente. 2015, June 20. Vil hente 8000 homoflyktninger. Available at: www.dn.no/nyheter/politikkSamfunn/2015/06/20/1003/Flyktninger/vil-hente-8000-homoflyktninger [Accessed March 7, 2017].
Brown, Wendy. 2006. *Regulating Aversion: Tolerance in the Age of Identity and Empire*. Princeton, NJ: Princeton University Press.
Cantú, Lionel. 2009. *The Sexuality of Migration: Border Crossings and Mexican Immigrant Men*. New York: New York University Press.
Chávez, Karma R. 2010. "Border (In)Securities: Normative and Differential Belonging in LGBTQ and Immigrant Rights Discourse." *Communication and Critical/Cultural Studies* 7, 2: 136–155.
Decena, Carlos Ulises. 2008. "Tacit Subjects." *GLQ: A Journal of Lesbian and Gay Studies* 14, 2–3: 339–359.
Duggan, Lisa. 2003. *The Twilight of Equality? Neoliberalism, Cultural Politics, and the Attack on Democracy*. Boston, MA: Beacon Press.

Edelman, L. 2004. *No Future: Queer Theory and the Death Drive*. Durham, NC: Duke University Press.
Eggebø, Helga. 2013. "A Real Marriage? Applying for Marriage Migration to Norway." *Journal of Ethnic and Migration Studies* 39, 5: 1–17.
El-Tayeb, Fatima. 2012. "'Gays Who Cannot Properly Be Gay': Queer Muslims in the Neoliberal European City." *European Journal of Women's Studies* 19, 1: 79–95.
Eng, David. 2010. *The Feeling of Kinship. Queer Liberalism and the Racialization of Intimacy*. Durham, NC: Duke University Press.
Engesbak, Reidar. 2012. Overlever på kjærlighet. *Blikk*. Available at: http://blikk.no/index.php/2012/01/04/overlever-pa-kjaerlighet/ [Accessed March 7, 2017].
Fassin, Didier. 2013. "The Precarious Truth of Asylum." *Public Culture* 25, 1: 39–63.
Fassin, Éric. 2010. "National Identities and Transnational Intimacies: Sexual Democracy and the Politics of Immigration in Europe." *Public Culture* 22, 3: 507–529.
Giametta, Calogero. 2014. "The sexual politics of asylum: lived experiences of sexual minority asylum seekers and refugees in the UK." London Metropolitan University, PhD Dissertation.
Gressgård, Randi, & Jacobsen, Christine. 2008. "Krevende Toleranse. Islam og Homoseksualitet." *Tidsskrift for kjønnsforskning* 32, 2: 22–39.
Gudbrandsen, Frøy. 2010. "Partisan Influence on Immigration: The Case of Norway." *Scandinavian Political Studies* 33, 3: 248–270.
Hagesæther, Pål Vegard. 2008. *Uekteskap. En studie av proformaekteskap i Norge*. Oslo: Unipub.
Haritaworn, Jin. 2008. "Loyal Repetitions of the Nation: Gay Assimilation and the 'War on Terror.'" *Darkmatter Journal* 3. Available at: www.darkmatter101.org/site/2008/05/02/loyal-repetitions-of-the-nation-gay-assimilation-and-the-war-on-terror/ [Accessed March 7, 2017].
———. 2012. "Women's Rights, Gay Rights and Anti-Muslim Racism in Europe: Introduction." *European Journal of Women's Studies* 19, 1: 73–78.
Hathaway, James C., & Pobjoy, Jason. 2011. "Queer Cases Make Bad Law." *New York University Journal of International Law and Politics* 44, 2: 315–389.
ILGA-Europe. 1997. The European Region of the International Lesbian and Gay Association. *ILGA Euroletter 54*. October. Available at: www.france.qrd.org/assocs/ilga/euroletter/54.html [Accessed October 26, 2016].
Long, Scott. 2009. "Unbearable Witness: How Western Activists (Mis)recognize Sexuality in Iran." *Contemporary Politics* 15, 1: 119–136.
Luibhéid, Eithne. 2002. *Entry Denied: Controlling Sexuality at the Border*. Minneapolis, MN and London: University of Minnesota Press.
Luibhéid, Eithne. 2008. "Sexuality, Migration, and the Shifting Line between Legal and Illegal Status." *GLQ: A Journal of Lesbian and Gay Studies* 14, 2–3: 289–315.
Mai, Nicola, & King, Russell. 2009. "Love, Sexuality and Migration: Mapping the Issue(s)." *Mobilities* 4, 3: 295–307.
Mepschen, Paul, Duyvendak, Jan Willem, & Tonkens, Evelien H. 2010. "Sexual Politics, Orientalism and Multicultural Citizenship in the Netherlands." *Sociology-the Journal of the British Sociological Association* 44, 5: 962–979.
Mühleisen, Wencke, Røthing, Åse, & Svendsen, Stine H. Bang. 2012. "Norwegian Sexualities: Assimilation and Exclusion in Norwegian Immigration Policy." *Sexualities* 15, 2: 139–155.
Muller Myrdahl, Eileen. 2010. "Legislating Love: Norwegian Family Reunification Law as a Racial Project." *Social & Cultural Geography* 11, 2: 103–116.

Murray, David A. B. 2014. "Real Queer: Authentic LGBT Refugee Claimants and Homonationalism in the Canadian Refugee System." *Anthropologica* 56, 1: 21–32.
Myong, Lene, & Bissenbakker, Mons. 2016. "Love Without Borders? White Transraciality in Danish Migration Activism." *Cultural Studies* 30, 1: 129–146.
Myong Petersen, Lene. 2009. *Adopteret: fortællinger om transnational og racialiseret tilblivelse*. Aarhus: Danmarks Pædagogiske Universitetsskole, Aarhus Universitet.
Povinelli, Elizabeth A. 2006. *The Empire of Love: Toward a Theory of Intimacy, Genealogy, and Carnality*. Durham, NC and London: Duke University Press.
Puar, Jasbir K. 2007. *Terrorist Assemblages: Homonationalism in Queer Times*. Durham, NC: Duke University Press.
Randazzo, Timothy J. 2005. "Social and Legal Barriers: Sexual Orientation and Asylum in the United States." In *Queer Migrations: Sexuality, U.S. Citizenship, and Border Crossing*, edited by Eithne Luibheid & Lionel Cantu Jr., 30–60. Minneapolis, MN: University of Minnesota Press.
Roseneil, Sasha, Crowhurst, Isabel, Hellesund, Tone, Santos, Ana Cristina, & Stoilova, Mariya. 2013. "Changing Landscapes of Heteronormativity: The Regulation and Normalization of Same-Sex Sexualities in Europe." *Social Politics: International Studies in Gender, State & Society* 20, 2: 165–199.
Røthing, Åse, & Svendsen, Stine H. Bang. 2011. "Sexuality in Norwegian Textbooks: Constructing and Controlling Ethnic Borders?" *Ethnic and Racial Studies* 34, 11: 1953–1973.
Said, Edward W. 2003. *Orientalism*. London: Penguin.
Skjeggestad, H. 2012. Enklere for homofile asylsøkere å få asyl i Norge. *Aftenposten*. [online]. Available at: www.aftenposten.no/norge/Enklere-for-homofile-asylsokere-a-fa-asyl-i-Norge-151179b.html#.UiX1F21YWDA [Accessed October 26, 2016].
Solberg, Erna. 2014. Norwegian Prime Minister Opening Speech for Pride Park Oslo, Norway, 25 June. Available at: www.regjeringen.no/en/aktuelt/Opening-speech-Pride-Park-in-Oslo/id764437/ [Accessed on October 26, 2016].
Spijkerboer, Thomas. 2013. "Sexual Identity, Normativity and Asylum." In *Fleeing Homophobia: Sexual Orientation, Gender Identity and Asylum*, edited by Thomas Spijkerboer, 217–238. London: Routledge.
Spijkerboer, Thomas, & Jansen, Sabine. 2011. *Fleeing Homophobia: Asylum Claims Related to Sexual Orientation and Gender Identity in the EU*. Amsterdam: Coc Nederland/Vu University Amsterdam.
Spivak, Gayatri. 1988. "Can the Subaltern Speak?" In *Marxism and the Interpretation of Culture*, edited by Cary Nelson & Lawrence Grossberg, 271–314. London: Macmillan.
Svendsen, Stine Helena Bang. 2014. *Affecting Change? Cultural Politics of Sexuality and "Race" in Norwegian Education*. Trondheim: Norwegian University of Science and Technology.

3 Homophobia as identity politics and a tool for political manipulation in the former Yugoslavia[1]

Hana Ćopić

This chapter discusses LGBTQI issues in the Croatian and Serbian contexts from the broader perspective of state manipulation of human rights. I enhance this perspective with a brief history of Yugoslavia's emancipatory policies, practices, developments, and its human rights traditions and achievements prior to its violent dissolution into its successor states.

The non-existent LGBTQI history of Yugoslavia: (de-)criminalization and the break-up

Before analyzing the post-conflict situations in Croatia and Serbia, we need to go back and take a brief look at the development of the LGBTQI movement in the former Yugoslavia, a state with a much greater liberal tradition than its successor states with their nationalistic, ethnicity-driven policies. First, let us take a closer look at the political preconditions of the Yugoslav state in order to understand how radically the new Yugoslavia differed from the old Yugoslavia (1929–1941) and from the Kingdom of the Serbs, Croats, and Slovenes (1918–1929). After almost three years of armed struggle against fascism, the Antifascist Council of the People's Liberation of Yugoslavia (AVNOJ), meeting in the small town of Jajce in central Bosnia, issued a declaration during its second session, on November 29, 1943, on re-establishing the state and the principles that it would follow "in accordance with the true will of all nations of Yugoslavia, demonstrated during the course of the three-year long common peoples' liberation struggle that has forged the inseparable fraternity of the Yugoslav nations" (Pupovac 2006).[2] In thus establishing a completely new, indeed, a revolutionary, tradition, the AVNOJ put an end to all of the political traditions that Yugoslavia had maintained between the two world wars. That is, the new state would not be based on ethnic principles; for the brotherhood and unity that those who had fought, and would win, the war against fascism embraced clearly superseded ethnic-nationalist causes. Rather, the people of Yugoslavia, organizing themselves into different committees, councils, and fronts, would set up their new political traditions.

One of the most important committees for the struggles for emancipation in Yugoslavia after World War II was the Women's Antifascist Front (AFŽ).

The AFŽ was established by 166 delegates from across the country, meeting in Bosnia in 1942, the same year that the AVNOJ was formed. Immediately after World War II, its members, who were fighting on Yugoslavia's battlefields, would fight for the rights of women and, hence, the emancipation of Yugoslavian society. At the founding assembly, President Tito addressed women throughout Yugoslavia:

> Women, my comrades, have passed the maturity test; they have shown that they are capable, not only to run households, but to fight with guns in their hands, to rule and hold power in their hands.
> (Dugandžić 2015)

This spirit of equality between men and women was further implemented by the widespread participation of female combatants in the partisan movement in the course of the next three years (1941–1943). But, more importantly, it was inscribed into the new Yugoslav Constitution of 1946 and, thence, the laws established on its basis. For example, under Article 920 of the Serbian Civil Code of 1844, which was valid until 1945, women were considered minors, but, according to Article 24 of the new Constitution,

> Women are equal to men in all spheres of state, economic, and sociopolitical life; women are entitled to the same pay as men for equal work and to enjoy special protection concerning employment; the state protects the interests of mothers and children by establishing facilities such as childbirth and childcare centers and children's homes; mothers have the right to paid leave before and after childbirth.

Yugoslavian women, who had already become economically independent, were granted the right to vote in November 1945. In addition, the constitution introduced civil proceedings (guaranteeing the same rights and obligations for men and women) to replace religious marriage registration and social insurance for all workers. In 1951, abortion was made legal, and wearing headscarves in public was abrogated by law as part of a broader campaign of emancipation. Courses to eliminate women's illiteracy were offered throughout the country (Zaharijević 2008, 433–435). In general, then, the law finally began to treat women as full citizens. A commitment to women's rights in socialist Yugoslavia was a feminist litmus test for politicians, and it would be a pre-condition for emancipatory movements in the future.

During its first ten years, the new, socialist Yugoslavia[3] developed an authoritarian sort of modern sexual ideology on the basis of its socialist puritanism. Sexuality, that is, heterosexuality, was supposed to promote health and cleanliness; hence, homosexuality was seen as a decadent bourgeois practice deriving from "perverted capitalism," and it was supposed that the only persons inclined to such unhealthy practices were "decadent intellectuals," members of the (upper) middle class, and "priests and slackers" but by no means socialist youth or workers. Working under that ideological presumption and wanting to demonstrate its commitment to fighting capitalist decadence, the state tried many male homosexuals throughout Yugoslavia in 1949 (Dota 2015). Accordingly, in 1951, Article 186 of the Criminal Code made male homosexuality (which it called "deviant sexual intercourse") punishable by up to two years' imprisonment, which was reduced two years later to up to one year. That was the first step in a process that led to the invisibility of non-heterosexuals. Interestingly, the AFŽ, the feminist branch of the Yugoslav partisan movement, was dissolved the same year. By simultaneously criminalizing (male) homosexuality and closing down AFŽ institutions, a mere six years after the establishment of a new, progressive state and society, the government essentially halted the emancipatory process which had only just begun in earnest. It was as though the potential tectonic changes indicated by the struggle against patriarchal, heteronormative gender roles were nipped in the bud. Sexual relationships between women were not recognized as criminal and, accordingly, were not made illegal (Kahlina 2013).[4] Based on provisions of the SFRY Penal Code, some 500 men were convicted of (male) "lewdness against the order of nature," that is, homosexual acts, in the period between 1951 and 1977. Half of them received suspended sentences, while others were sentenced to short prison terms. Some 300 men were convicted in Croatia and Serbia, whereas 200 were convicted in the other Yugoslav republics. For the sake of comparison, the number of convicted men in Western Europe was much higher during that period: 100,000 in West Germany, 70,000 in Great Britain, 30,000 in Italy, and 12,000 in Austria (Dota 2016). It is also important to emphasize that party membership for gays and lesbians was out of the question.

The non-heterosexual population was to remain invisible until the 1980s. Two conditions permitted liberalization and the emergence of LGBTQI groups and initiatives in Yugoslavia: the American Psychiatric Association's elimination of homosexuality as a psychiatric disorder in 1973 and constitutional changes in Yugoslavia in 1974 that transferred legislative authority to the republics and autonomous provinces. The process of decriminalizing (male) homosexuality then began in 1977 in the Republics of Croatia, Montenegro, and Slovenia and the Autonomous Province of Vojvodina; Serbia did not follow suit until 1994 (Kahlina 2013, 6).[5] In the mid-1980s, Ljubljana and Zagreb became centers of the new gay culture and the LGBTQI community and its political initiatives.

New initiatives in the feminist movement emerged at the same time. In 1978, feminists from Belgrade, Sarajevo, and Zagreb, most notably Žarana Papić and Dunja Blažević, organized the conference Comrade Woman: The Women's Question: A New Approach? (Drug-ca žena. Žensko pitanje. Novi pristup?). Participants spoke in the language of feminist criticism of the existing system and the future of feminism. Women from Italy, Germany, France, England, Poland, and Hungary attended. It was the first feminist conference held in a socialist country that included feminists from so many

European countries. Discussions were dedicated to different facets of the women's movement: sexuality, identity, emancipatory politics, and so on. Because of its criticism of Yugoslav socialism, the authorities severely condemned Drug-ca žena, self-confidently claiming that "the women's question" had been resolved, and, therefore, there was no need for feminism in Yugoslavia. Harboring no such illusions, Yugoslav feminists came up with the conference's motto: "Proletarians of the World, Who Washes Your Socks?" (Bonfiglioli 2008).[6]

After the conference, feminists founded new women's groups that attracted activists and theorists from all over Yugoslavia. The Woman and Society section of the sociology departments at Zagreb University and Belgrade University organized discussions on the social role and status of women, sexuality, and equality and on violence against women. As Yugoslavia began to dissolve in the late-1980s, LGBTQI people organized the first such informal group in Serbia, despite the war and the fact that everything was then subordinated to it and the republic's omnipresent nationalism.

States without societies and the resulting backlashes

Yugoslavia's break-up into small ethnic states was in no way idiosyncratic for the Balkans. But, by manipulating the endemic hatreds among the ethnicities of Yugoslavia, which the communist government had supposedly suppressed, with promises of fulfilling their dreams of independent ethnic states, nationalistic leaders and their henchmen triggered a mass hysteria of "us" against "them" and, thereby, produced the worst bloodbath in Europe since World War II (Buden 2013a).

In addition to ethnic nationalism, the war resulted in a notable normalization of violence in daily life and impeded the emergence of a peace that meant more than the sheer absence of organized fighting. Patriarchal norms were re-established and declared as traditions of the "good old days," which the supposedly evil communists had abandoned. With the return of this old set of values, people who did not adopt the victimized attitude of the nationalists were easily labeled as traitors. The most obvious were the loud and visible "queers" – feminists (starting in the 1990s) and the LGBTQI community (starting in the 2000s) – but any transgressors of the new normality were condemned as potentially endangering the majority. The mainstream nationalist, phobic discourse made the direction that Serbian society would continue to take, clear to all of its members. Having revived the simplistic pattern of ideals of the white, Roman Catholic (Croatia)/Orthodox (Serbia), heterosexual male, *viz.*, unity and uniformity, it became convenient to identify minority groups with external Others, especially if such a group took on a higher public profile and attempted to enter the sphere of politics.

The break-up of Yugoslavia in the 1990s, which precipitated the dissolution of its emancipatory traditions, clearly illustrates the lessons of feminist history. The Socialist Federal Republic of Yugoslavia's (SFRY's) self-management system, which had created and maintained these traditions, was characterized by an

> inbuilt anti-authoritarianism, which made Yugoslav socialism so fundamentally different from the USSR's brand, deeply humanist in its core, and, therefore, ever more disposed to the emancipation of women. ... [It] was not understood to be perfect or complete but as perfectible and completable. It was firmly believed that "inherited" social divisions based on sex may be eradicated only through institutionalization and further development of socialist self-management and material productive forces, which would, in turn, ensure improvement of various social, educational, cultural, health-related, and other humanitarian factors.
>
> (Zaharijević 2016)[7]

But the Civil War and its nationalist order quickly reduced life to key oppositions: us versus them, chetniks against ustashi/balije, or simply, normal against abnormal. These categories were applied within national borders, where ossified patriarchal modes of operation for dealing with internal enemies, and with women and bodies that are perceived as female, came back to life. The revival of defunct traditions quickly produced a widespread reversal of social norms: What only yesterday was on the verge of becoming customary, was almost normal, today is suspicious, decadent, urban, unpatriotic, debauched, and increasingly less permissible in the public sphere. The revived patriarchal, hetero-normative discourse intensified rapidly. Yugoslavia was to be abandoned, swiftly and in every way. As quickly as possible, nationalists and the churches forged an alliance in order to install a system that quickly became hegemonic. Their control has lasted to this day. The moral authority of the churches of the traditional religious communities (*viz.*, Roman Catholic, Orthodox, and Muslim), as the nations' authentic representatives, became incontestable almost overnight; indeed, these institutions began to enter public space as the voice of reason, offering solutions for the problems of all walks of life. Given "freedom, from privacy into public life, media, schools and army barracks, into political parties, ministry and parliament lobbies, into the art and cultural scene and, finally, into the market" (Buden 2012, 122), the churches (and through them God) have become political players. They have re-socialized themselves, re-establishing their social influence by means of their dogmatism and by carefully marking certain elements of society as enemy and agitating against them. Both nationalist organizations and the churches, neither of which have ever distanced themselves from the public statements and actions of their most problematic members, continue their political manipulations.[8]

While the members of Western LGBTQI communities, after their long struggle for full civil rights, were gradually becoming first-class citizens, their Serbain and Croatian peers, once equal citizens of the SFRY, faced a deterioration of their status and were increasingly marked as radically different

"Others" in their newly established, small, poor, and war-torn countries. In such circumstances, coming out, which is always a long and complex process, was a life challenge *par excellence*. This is where LGBTQI people found themselves in the period from the early 1990s to the 2000s as the former Yugoslavian republics began their new lives as independent states.[9]

The promised land of Europe

Having fostered hostile discourse for more than 20 years, homophobia was, despite democratic changes in Serbia, the backlash of the 1990s. Serbian society came apart into frustrated, poor people, manipulative and manipulated by the structures of power. In such an atmosphere, it is futile to explain that one's feminism or sexual orientation is not a matter of identity politics but, rather, a political statement. Rejecting such identities as not "ours," not part of the polity's genuine habitus, and, worse, as imposed by the West, Serbia's politicians in effect brought the Civil War back home to its citizens, who were made pawns in their state's bio-political game.

That was the other side of the post-Civil War power struggle in Serbia, the side where Serbian nationalists manipulated the country's citizens on a daily basis. Politicians in power at the time embraced the term "transitology" as a synonym for taking no responsibility for social problems, and, at the same time, they encouraged the conservatives and right-wing youth who posed as alter-globalists,[10] particularly after the assassination of Serbian Prime Minister Zoran Đinđić in 2003. In these ways, they allowed the Church to emerge as a counterweight to Western NGOs. In the present debate on human rights, both state and Church authorities still constantly point to LGBTQI rights as an example of the extremes to which the West goes in Europeanizing what it considers the backward East, democratizing it, and helping it to overcome its repressive past (Buden 2010). The state takes this as an insult and sees itself as a victim of the West. According to Belgrade, the EU imposes democratic policies on Serbia that are not natural for Serbian citizens.

A good example of this attitude is a statement that Ivica Dačić, Serbian Prime Minister from July 2012 to April 2014, made in an interview in October 2013, five days before banning the Pride Parade in Belgrade. Asked whether he would attend the march, he said that he would not because, although everybody has the constitutional right to express their diversity, "one should not go from one extreme to the other, we shouldn't adulate all of them [homosexuals]." He then asked, "Should I become gay now because it's pro-European?" Shortly later, he added that Serbians would not allow their country to be colonized by homosexuals in order to satisfy the EU's demands.[11] Again, producing the enemy in one's own backyard brought the war back home.

In Croatia, on the other hand, the discourse on homosexuality has been different. In light of its Roman Catholic tradition, Croatia sees itself as a bulwark against the East. There has been no substantial discussion about the appropriateness of European norms with regard to LGBTQI. Rather, there is a national consensus that Croatia is European, an identity with which the population distances itself from the rest of the Balkans. At the same time, both the Roman Catholic Church in Croatia and the Serbian Orthodox Church share the same standpoint with regard to the issue of abortion. Both regard procreation to be a first-rate national interest – albeit primarily in terms of rhetoric – and both condemn abortion out of hand. Regardless of both states' constitutionally defined secularity, conservative and retrograde movements continually challenge the right to abortion.[12] While Croatia has redefined itself as a Central European state, Serbia has divided its socio-political affinities between the West and the East so as to play the EU and Russia off against each other (Kahlina 2013, 11).

Traitors and scapegoats

As mentioned above, in the 1990s, during the Yugoslav wars, Albanian, Croatian, and Serbian feminists were denounced as traitors, witches, and the like.[13] In the 2000s, the LGBTQI community experienced similar hostility. Its attempts to influence politics through protest made it dangerous for mainstream politicians. During the 1990s, the Yugoslavian feminist movement was an umbrella for the "always disobedient" (i.e. the *Women in Black*), anti-state and anti-war groups, and a part of the LGBTQI community. There were, and still are, numerous epithets to discredit the *Women in Black*, a loose network of feminist, anti-militarist peace activists established in Serbia in 1991, and their political protests. Their informal political power has made the *Women in Black* a thorn in the side of nationalist groups.

Over the last 25 years, they have established themselves as an impressive political force because, to quote Heinrich Böll (1952, 62), their political stances have been "human and unbribable," or, in their own words, because they made nonviolent resistance effective; built a women's solidarity network, peace coalitions, and other alliances; demanded a continuous confrontation with Serbia's past; produced an alternative, feminist history of the Civil War; and organized peace education within their network. The common denominator among nationalists of all stripes opposed to the feminist solidarity of the *Women in Black* and their demand that the Serbian state accept responsibility for all of its actions is indignation over the fact that the *Women in Black* have always been firm anti-nationalists. They have been routinely accused, on the basis of a despicably selective choice of facts, of aiding "the enemy" and of ignoring "their own." Many of their protests were attacked in the 2000s, and they still take place under police protection.

The long march of changes

With two or three official bans and one *de facto*[14] ban on Pride marches, Serbia has been trying to trace a path between the EU's demands and the Serbian elite's desire to introduce more Russian-style laws banning what is called homosexual propaganda, like the recent law protecting minors from propaganda for non-traditional sexual relations. Following street clashes in Belgrade during the Pride Parade in March 2010, in which three rings of police protected some 1,000 participants from a crowd of counter demonstrators seven times as large, that included rioters who were ready to lynch them, the government decided that a ban would be much cheaper. "Security first" became the authorities' slogan. The question is how the authorities allowed approximately 1,000 hooligans in 2001 (at the first Pride Parade attempted in Belgrade) to increase to around 7,000.[15]

The recently successful Pride marches do not indicate victory for liberal, tolerant society; however, they do powerfully illustrate the present social climate. In 2012, the 10-year anniversary of the Zagreb Pride March was celebrated without incident, and subsequent parades have needed substantially less police presence. Zagreb's largest Pride Parade took place in 2013, with more than 10,000 people in attendance. The Serbian government organized the Pride parades in Belgrade in 2014 and 2015, which were held almost without incident. In addition, Belgrade's first Trans Parade took place in 2015 alongside the Pride Parade. Does this mean that the struggle for visibility, or even acceptance and equality, in Serbia has ended happily with the LGBTQI community there able to show its many faces? Or, has the state, by taking responsibility for Serbia's Pride parades, demonstrated unequivocally, in case anybody was wondering, that it is in full control of the situation? There may be no unambiguous answer. But its handling of the issue of Pride parades in recent years has surely helped the Serbian government to score human rights points in the EU. In a further symbolic move in this direction, in 2016 Serbian Prime Minister Aleksandar Vucic nominated an openly gay woman, Anna Brnabic, as minister of public administration and local government (Bertinchamps 2016).

The Serbian LGBTQI community has changed with the passage of time, as it has been both provoked by the repressive actions of the Serbian government and inspired by international support and solidarity. Although the Pride Parade is the community's most visible activity, it also conducts many other visible activities throughout the year, most of them for the general public. For example, there are numerous festivals celebrating queer life and exploring the subject of queerness through lectures and art exhibits, and many documentaries show the many facets of LGBTQI life.[16]

A Croatian initiative aptly called *In the Name of Family* (*U ime obitelji*), which proposed a ban on gay marriage and a constitutional definition of marriage limiting it to heterosexual couples, passed by referendum (with 65% of the vote) in 2013. However, in 2014 the legislature adopted the Life Partnerships Act, and within a year around 80 same-sex couples had exercised their new right. In 2015, the Slovenian parliament passed a law allowing same-sex marriage and adoption. Together the Croatian and Slovenian laws constitute an immense improvement in LGBTQI civil rights.

To parade, and how to parade?

Identity politics in the former Yugoslavia, whose arguments reveal its homophobia, pretends to protect citizens by defending the traditional values of the majority against foreign, more specifically, Western, influences, which, ironically enough, it characterizes in the old, well-known anti-feminist terminology as "too aggressive," "obsessed with identity," coming from "outside," and "too progressive" for "our circumstances" and the "immaturity of our society," and, of course, it accuses LGBTQI organizations of politicizing the issue. Such allegations are commonplace in the media landscape in former Yugoslavia.

Over the last 25 years, and especially since its social coming-out (i.e. getting the public, through its activism, to recognize its existence) the LGBTQI community has been excluded, suppressed, and exposed to violence. This history has to be incorporated into the public's common knowledge; it must be written, communicated, and, above all, mainstreamed in all of its complexity, without manipulation, and without imposing a tragic fate on those who don't fit into the majority.

Starting to fight openly and visibly for its rights in 2001, with its attempt to stage the first Pride Parade in the former Yugoslavia, not succeeding until 2009 or, rather, 2010, and not holding another until 2014, the LGBTQI community in Serbia has had its ups and downs, which have inevitably influenced its public image and also its own understanding of activism and community. There have been many critics and much self-criticism of the community's development and its needs. The institution of the Pride Parade has been one such sensitive issue, especially after 2009. Summarizing only the constructive criticism, the 2010 Belgrade Pride Parade was a case of pinkwashing the political situation in Serbia at the time; the issue of human rights is being hijacked by neoliberal stakeholders who treat it as a class-neutral ideology; and the Pride Parade is not inclusive and does not arise from the LGBTQI community itself (Maljković 2013).

The Zagreb Pride Parade is also coming of age as an expression of a heterogeneous and inharmonious community that changes and grows each year. The parade's annual staging is certainly an expression of the Croatian government's political resolve; however, it would be meaningless if it did not satisfy a need of the LGBTQI community or was not the result of negotiations within the community. In every year since 2002, the Zagreb Pride Parade has adopted a different theme and slogan pertaining to different political demands. The parade's organizing committee changes every year. The organizers in 2005 almost canceled the parade. The organizers in 2006 made the event international, and 13 countries participated. In the following years, organizers have sought broader support, included the families of LGBTQI people in the march, and supported the initiative to hold a march in the Dalmatian town of Split. These developments have not been easy, inevitable results of history simply unfolding itself over the past 15 years; they have been the outcome of struggles within the community to express its different needs and its subsequent discussions and negotiations.

Conclusion

Nationalism has been a tool of political manipulation in the former Yugoslavia since the 1990s, reaching its peak after 2000. During the processes of transition and democratization in its successor states following the Civil War and recovery from the last world economic crisis, manifold forms of nationalism in both Croatia and Serbia have found expression in the fascistic acts of their governments and societies. This emergence of what is, in effect, the reinvention of normality is a "peaceful reproduction of war" (Ivančić 2014).

Everything that Yugoslavia stood for is now held in contempt in its successor countries, particularly its emancipatory policies and practices and its concept of equality for all ethnicities and classes. And the overwhelming poverty in the majority of the countries of the Western Balkans has produced more ethnicity-driven identity policies than has any mass movement, denying the fact that gaining territory does not feed anyone. So, to quote Boris Buden (2013b), "identity instead of class politics" is still at work, although the precarious living of almost all of the inhabitants of the former Yugoslavia during the last 25 years has begun to change as a multitude of voices, speaking out against an exclusively exploitative way of life, emerge. This emerging attitude was accurately and humorously expressed by graffiti on the streets of Belgrade (and Rijeka and Zagreb) during the Pride Parade in 2014: "You're not being screwed by gays but by capitalism." In other words, don't be another victim of capitalism, for the ultimate consequence of capitalism is that one is deprived of even the notion that one can be a political agent in one's society. In Judith Butler's words:

> Once groups are marked as vulnerable within human rights discourse or legal regimes they become reified as definitionally vulnerable, fixed in the political position of powerlessness and lack of agency. All the power belongs to the state, the NGOs, the international institutions that are now supposed to offer them protection and advocacy. Such moves tend to underestimate or actively efface modes of political agency and resistance that merge in so called vulnerable populations. To understand how those extra-juridical modes of resistance work we would have to think about how resistance and vulnerability work together, something that paternalistic moment cannot possibly do.
>
> (Butler 2015)

This chapter elaborated upon the historical background, contemporary geopolitical manifestations, and emancipatory culture of the former Yugoslavia,

Homophobia as identity politics 65

and it reviewed related developments in the independent states of Croatia and Serbia, which can at best be termed ambiguous with regard to the inclusion and emancipation of LGBTQI groups in society. True emancipation will occur when the outcast and marginalized come together and make a political statement of a new kind, calling for the displacement of a society controlled by ethnic identity politics, by a society that includes the deprived, where the gap between "us" and "them" is left open and "no nationalist compromise would be possible anymore" (Buden 2013b).

Notes

1 Although the title refers to Yugoslavia, I primarily discuss Croatia and Serbia, as I consider them to be the starting points, and their discourses are transferable to the other ex-Yugoslav states (excluding Slovenia).
2 For the text of the Declaration, see www.arhivyu.gov.rs/active/en/home/glavna_navigacija/leksikon_jugoslavije/konstitutivni_akti_jugoslavije/deklaracija_drugog_zasedanja_avnoja.html [Accessed October 26, 2016].
3 In 1943, the name of Yugoslavia was Democratic Federal Yugoslavia. After World War II, in 1946, it was renamed the Federal People's Republic of Yugoslavia, and then the Socialist Federal Republic of Yugoslavia in 1963.
4 The 1959 Criminal Law, Act no. 186, Art. no. 2, called lesbian relationships "wanton acts" Kahlina (2013, 6)
5 According to Dota (2015), criminologists, doctors, and lawyers were in favor of the complete decriminalization of homosexuality. After 1974, their debates with opponents became increasingly frequent and public; accordingly, we can assume that the subject was no longer taboo by the 1980s.
6 For more about the work of Žarana Papić, see www.rwfund.org/wp-content/uploads/2014/09/%C5%BDarana-Papi%C4%87-To-je-moj-izve%C5%A1tajvama.pdf [Accessed October 26, 2016].
7 The author has courteously given me access to this work prior to publication.
8 I refer primarily to the church's role in the wars of the 1990s and the simultaneous and ensuing process of the clericalization of society. For more on the role of the Serbian Orthodox Church, see http://pescanik.net/zasto-se-u-crkvi-sapuce-full/ [Accessed October 26, 2016].
9 The break-up of the SFR Yugoslavia began in 1991 with a series of armed conflicts of differing proportions and intensities that would culminate in civil war, mass relocation, ethnic cleansing, and genocide. Its disintegration would be complete in 2006, when Montenegro left the last remaining alliance of former socialist republics. However, here I refer to the ten years of intensive conflicts in different parts of the former SFRY, the last of which occurred in Kosovo, which ended with the bombing of Serbia in 1999 and the removal of Slobodan Milošević from power in October 2000.
10 International sanctions during the 1990s, NATO's bombing in 1999, and the EU's policies toward Kosovo have influenced the anti-Western discourse in Serbia (Kahlina 2013, 11).
11 After equating being gay with being pro-European, the Serbian Prime Minister went on to elaborate the benefits of organizing Pride Parades as a way to signal to the EU, Serbia's willingness to enter into the initial accession negotiations in January 2014.
12 For more on the conservative movements and/or political parties in Croatia and Serbia, see "U ime obitelji" and "Dveri Srpske": http://uimeobitelji.net/ and http://dverisrpske.com/ [Both accessed February 26, 2017]. For more on politics of

reproduction in Serbia, see the work of Rada Drezgić: www2.warwick.ac.uk/fac/arts/theatre_s/current/postgraduate/maipr/staffcurrent/drezgic/ [Accessed February 26, 2017].

13 The term "witches" comes from a Croatian newspaper's attack of five Croatian feminists and writers (Jelena Lovrić, Rada Iveković, Slavenka Drakulić, Vesna Kesić, and Dubravka Ugrešić) in December 1992. The persecution of feminists as anti-nationalists at the beginning of the war, when all of the nationalists focused on creating bodies of citizens who would not question their respective national causes, carried out in the press by their colleagues and other intellectuals, made brutal use of all of the resources of patriarchal and abusive language, which fueled the nationalist fire. This history is a paradigm of journalistic malice in the service of state-sponsored nationalism:www.women-war-memory.org/index.php/hr/povijest/vjestice-iz-ria [Accessed October 26, 2016].

14 The 2009 Pride Parade was not explicitly banned, but rerouting it had the same effect, as it did with all of the Pride marches in the following years. The Serbian Constitutional Court ruled that both the rerouting in 2009 and the ban in 2011 were unconstitutional: www.ustavni.sud.rs/page/view/sr-Latn-CS/0-101820/usvojena-ustavna-zalba-udruzenja-parada-ponosa-beograd?_qs=parada [Accessed October 26, 2016].

15 Slobodanka Macanović, the head of the Autonomous Women's Center, posed the question during a hearing in the Serbian Parliament in 2014.www.womenngo.org.rs/sr/vesti/363-kako-je-drzava-dozvolila-da-700-postane-7000-huligana [Accessed October 30, 2016].

16 See, for example, Queer Zagreb Festival, 2003–2013: www.queerzagreb.org/sample-page/history/;Merlinka International Queer Film Festival, in Belgrade since 2009 and travelling through Serbia and the rest of the former Yugoslavia: http://merlinka.com/; LGBT magazine *Optimist*, since 2010 with 15,000 unique visitors to its web portal: www.optimist.rs/; and the Center for Queer Studies, founded in Belgrade in 2010: www.cks.org.rs/ [All accessed October 26, 2016].

References

Banović, Damir and Vasić, Vladana. 2012. "Seksualna orijentacijai i rodni identitet u kontekstu ljudskih prava u Bosni i Hercegovini [Sexual Orientation and Gender Identity in the Context of Human Rights in Bosnia and Herzegovina]." In *Čitanka LGBT ljudskih prava (drugo, dopunjeno izdanje)*, eds. Spahić, Aida and Gavrić, Saša, 141–159. Sarajevo: Sarajevski otvoreni centar, Heinrich Böll Stiftung.

Bertinchamps, Philippe. 2016. "Ana Brnabic, Ministre Lesbienne d'une Serbie aux Penchants Homophobes." *Libération*, August 17. Available at: www.liberation.fr/planete/2016/08/17/ana-brnabic-ministre-lesbienne-d-une-serbie-aux-penchants-homophobes_1473042 [Accessed March 7, 2017].

Böll, Heinrich. 1952. *Bekenntnis zur Trümmerliteratur [Commitment to Rubble Literature]*. Ed. Árpád Bernáth and Gyurácz, Annamária. Vol. 6. 58–63. Köln: Kiepenheuer & Witsch.

Bonfiglioli, Chiara. 2008. *Remembering the Conference "Drugarica Zena. Zensko Pitanje – Novi Pristup?" ["Comrade Woman. The Women's Question: A New Approach?" Thirty Years After]*. MA thesis. Utrecht University. Available at: http://dspace.library.uu.nl/handle/1874/31158 [Accessed October 26, 2016].

Buden, Boris. 2010. "Children of Postcommunism." *Radical Philosophy. A Journal of Socialist and Feminist Philosophy* 159: 18–26.

———. 2012. *Zona prelaska. O kraju postkomunizma. [Zone of Transition. On the End of Post-Communism]*. Beograd: Fabrika knjiga.

———. 2013a. Interview, September 16. Available at: http://arhiva.portalnovosti.com/2013/09/boris-buden-slucaj-cirilice-pothranjuje-ugodne-iluzije/ [Accessed October 30, 2016].

———. 2013b. Interview, December 2. Available at: http://pescanik.net/2013/12/boris-buden-intervju-2/ [Accessed October 26, 2016].

Butler, Judith. 2015. "Vulnerability/Resistance." Keynote Lecture at the Conference "How to Act Together?" Belgrade Institute for Philosophy and Social Theory, November 20, 2015. Available at: http://media.rcub.bg.ac.rs/?p=4818 [Accessed October 26, 2016].

Dota, Franko. 2015. "Once Upon a Time There was a 'Deviant Sexual Intercourse' – Homosexuality in the Yugoslav Socialist Criminal Law." Lecture held on May 13 at the Institute for Philosophy and Social Theory in Belgrade. Available at: http://instifdt.bg.ac.rs/franko-dota-filozofski-fakultet-sveucilista-u-zagrebu/ [Accessed October 25, 2016].

———. 2016. "Once Upon a Time There was a 'Deviant Sexual Intercourse.'" Lecture held on June 8 at the book club Booksa during Zagreb Pride Week.

Dugandžić, Danijela. 2015. "Life Woven into Revolution: A Look into a Forgotten Women's Movement in Former Yugoslavia." Creative Time Reports, October 12, 2015. Available at: http://creativetimereports.org/2015/10/12/struggle-given-us/ [Accessed October 25, 2016].

Durkalić, Masha. 2011. "Analiza medijskog izvještavanja o seksualnim manjinama u BiH" [Analysis of Media Reporting on Sexual Minorities in BiH]. In *Rozi izvještaj: Stanje LGBT ljudskih prava u BiH u 2011*, eds. Huremović, Lejla, Durkalić, Masha, Banović, Damir and Bošnjak, Emina, 16–48. Sarajevo: Sarajevski otvoreni centar.

Ivančić, Viktor. 2014. Interview, January 30. Available at: http://pescanik.net/viktor-ivancic-intervju-2/ [Accessed October 26, 2016].

Jurčić, Marko. 2012. "Povijest LGBTIQ aktivizma u Hrvatskoj" [The History of LGBTIQ Activism in Croatia]. In *Čitanka LGBT ljudskih prava (drugo, dopunjeno izdanje)*, eds. Spahić, Aida and Gavrić, Saša. Sarajevo: Sarajevski otvoreni centar, Fondacija Heinrich Böll.

Kahlina, Katja. 2013. "Contested Terrain of Sexual Citizenship: EU accession and the changing position of sexual minorities in the post-Yugoslav context." *Working Paper 33*. University of Edinburgh, School of Law. The Europeanization of Citizenship in the Successor States of the Former Yugoslavia (CITSEE). Available at: www.citsee.ed.ac.uk/working_papers/files/CITSEE_WORKING_PAPER_2013-33.pdf [Accessed October 26, 2016].

Knežević, Nenad. 2014. "'Out and Proud': LGBT zajednica i politike posle 2000. godine." In *Među nama. Neispričane priče gej i lezbejskih života*, eds. Blagojević, Jelisaveta and Dimitrijević, Olga, 348–357. Beograd: The European Commission and Heinrich Böll Stiftung Southeastern Europe.

Maljković, Dušan. 2013. "Čiji je naš Prajd? Konkretna analiza Prajda u Srbiji 2010–2012" [To whom belongs our Pride? Concrete Analysis of the Pride Parade in Serbia 2010–2012]. *Parada i politika – Debata u kulturnom centru Rex 26. februara 2013. Doprinosi učesnika/ca* [*Pride Parade and politics – Debate in cultural centre Rex*, February 26, 2013]. Beograd: Fond B92/ Kulturni centar Rex.

———. 2014. "To radi u teoriji, ali ne u praksi – Identitetski (LGBT) aktivizam protiv kvir aktivizma" [It Works in Theory, Not in Practice – Identity (LGBT) Activism Against Queer Activism]. In *Među nama. Neispričane priče gej i lezbejskih života*, eds. Blagojević, Jelisaveta and Dimitrijević, Olga, 360–369.

Beograd: The European Commission and Heinrich Böll Stiftung Southeastern Europe.
Mladenović, Lepa. 2005. "Prvo je stiglo jedno pismo" [A Letter Came in First]. In *Prvo je stiglo jedno pismo: 15 godina lezbejskog i gej aktivizma u Srbiji i Crnoj Gori 1990–2005*, ed. Živković, Ljiljana, 7–8. Beograd: Labris.
Pantelić, Ivana. 2011. *Partizanke kao građanke. Društvena emancipacija partizanki u Srbiji 1945–1953* [Partisan Women as Citizens. Social emancipation of Partisan Women in Serbia 1945–1953]. Beograd: ISI i Evoluta.
Pupovac, Ozren. 2006. "Project Yugoslavia: The Dialectics of the Revolution." *Prelom. Journal for Images and Politics* 8: 9–22. Available at: www.prelomkolektiv.org/pdf/prelom08.pdf [Accessed October 26, 2016].
Višnjić, Jelena. 2014. "'I'm Coming Out': Medijsko delovanje i strategije otpora LGBT aktivista i aktivistkinja u Srbiji." In *Među nama. Neispričane priče gej i lezbejskih života*, eds. Blagojević, Jelisaveta and Dimitrijević, Olga, 370–383. Beograd: The European Commission and Heinrich Böll Stiftung Southeastern Europe.
Višnjić, Jelena and Lončarević, Katarina. 2011. *Politike reprezentacije LGTTIQ populacije u medijima Srbije* [Policies of Representation of the LGBTIQ Population in Serbian Media]. Beograd: Labris.
Zaharijević, Adriana ed. 2008. *Neko je rekao feminizam? Kako je feminizam uticao na žene XXI veka* [Somebody Said Feminism? How Feminism Affected Women in XXI Century], 2nd revised edition, Heinrich Böll Stiftung, Belgrade.
———. 2016. "What Does Eastern Feminism Stand For? Feminism and Socialism in Yugoslavia." In *Cultural Life of Capitalism: Yugoslavia's (Post)Socialism and Its Other*, eds. Jelača, Dijana, Kolanović, Maša and Lugarić, Danijela. New York: Palgrave.

4 Contemporary art versus homophobia
Selected Eastern European cases

Pawel Leszkowicz

In this chapter, which is inspired by my own curatorial work, I consider some recent art works that thematize homophobia. I focus on Central Eastern Europe in a transnational comparative context to raise and elucidate questions about the character of visual homophobia and strategies to oppose it. The first part interprets art created to oppose homophobia. The second part investigates cases of what I will call "homophobic art" and discusses its history, implications, and some ethical problems that it poses with respect to the fight against today's inequalities.

A new wave of opposition to equality, which also targets LGBTQ rights, has arisen over the last several years in Europe. Against this ultraconservative movement, which is particularly strong in Eastern Europe, the queer counterculture's resistance continues to grow. In my work, I study the activist and artistic forms of this oppositional democratic movement. The post-Communist transition has included an era of rapid and often dramatic developments in LGBTQ issues in Central and Eastern Europe, which have proceeded, along with international trends in visual culture and human rights, toward a more open expression of diverse sexual identities and legalization of same-sex unions. In my analysis, I will take into consideration these oppositional forces.

Art against homophobia in Poland

The art works I shall discuss tackle different aspects of Central Eastern European homophobia and its everyday and political praxis, for in many parts of the region queer rights and representations spark cultural tensions, political conflicts, and acts of censorship and violence.[1] The 1989 transition has given rise to a new dissidence of love and sexuality against the legacy of the totalitarian system, religious fundamentalism, the complacency of society, and the new far-right governments. Therefore, despite European Union (EU) protection, LGBTQ citizens live in a volatile climate of culture war, and openly homophobic discourse is part of their political realm. In the new united Europe, a diversity of love intermingles with the old hatreds as both visions of the continent are simultaneously acted upon in a number of the region's countries.

My own curatorial work started as a personal and professional reaction to Polish political homophobia in the first decade of the twenty-first century. In 2005, I had the feeling that Poland's political transition had gone terribly wrong. LGBTQ citizens were leaving the country in a wave of queer emigration. The situation had begun a decade before, in the 1990s, when the Communist system, which had collapsed in 1989, gave way to national and religious fundamentalism instead of genuine democracy. As a result, there have been free elections and travel abroad, which was restricted under Communism, without the granting of full civil rights to women and sexual minorities. More generally, the Polish state has chosen misogynist and homophobic sexual politics for itself. Although homosexuality was decriminalized in Poland very early, in 1932, some high-school textbooks still, in the twenty-first century, teach that homosexuality is an illness, and abortion, legal under Communism, was criminalized in 1993. From that time onward, as the state has increasingly fallen under the influence of a Catholic pseudo-religious ideology, it has forcefully promulgated the concept of the reproductive family.

On May 7, 2004, one week after Poland joined the European Union, members of one of the ruling parties and the ultra-conservative League of Polish Families and its youth organization, the All-Polish Youth, brutally attacked the Krakow Feminist and Gay Parade of Equality with acid. At the time, official media channels broadcast anti-gay arguments involving the religious prohibition of sin, medical pathology, and unnatural behavior. Earlier, in order to scare Poles into voting against EU membership, the League of Polish Families had argued that Western liberalism promotes homosexuality, and the far right had unleashed a highly visual anti-gay campaign with posters appearing in the far-right and nationalistic press and featuring homophobic representations – for example, an image of a same-sex couple with a child, to symbolize Western Europe's moral depravity. At the same time, the heterosexist system of representation completely dominated official Polish popular and commercial visual culture.

In 2005, the anti-gay, Catholic former mayor of Warsaw, Lech Kaczyński, won the presidential election, and his conservative Law and Justice Party, headed by his twin brother Jarosław Kaczyński, won a majority of seats in the nation's parliament. The result was a dramatic shift to the far right in a country already dominated by the fundamentalist Polish branch of the Catholic Church. The brothers announced the beginning of a moral revolution. During the presidential campaign, they had publicly denounced homosexuality, including a call for gays to be barred from teaching in primary and secondary schools. As the mayor of Warsaw, Lech Kaczyński had twice banned, unconstitutionally, gay pride parades in the city. As a consequence, equality parades in Poznań, Krakow, and Gdańsk were frequently banned or attacked until 2007, when the Law and Justice Party/League of Polish Families coalition lost power. In 2015, the Law and Justice Party, now led by Jarosław Kaczyński, won the elections on a wave of anti-refugee prejudice. Once again, it has unleashed a torrent of xenophobia, anti-Semitism, homophobia, and censorship that could result in even more dire social consequences than in 2005–2007 (Solomon and Polish Pen Club 2016).

As the new far-right government firmly controls public cultural institutions and media, it has banned all forms of queer expression from them. It promotes only nationalistic and patriotic themes related to Polish history. Moreover, the government has significantly reduced funding for contemporary art, and it sponsors only exhibitions portraying its tightly controlled version of Polish history, which incorporates the Law and Justice Party's pernicious ideology of resentment and hatred. This policy caught international attention, when the Polish government dismissed several directors of Polish Cultural Institutes across Europe as well as those in New York and New Delhi in 2016, because they did not promote Polish culture in a way that reflected the government's ideological line (Michalska 2017; Pawlowski 2016). The effect has been that all queer culture in Poland is now an active oppositional counterculture that exists outside of the state-funded and -controlled network, as in Russia.

In hindsight, it is clear that Poland's entry into the EU in 2004 unleashed a conservative backlash to protect the country from supposedly un-Polish Western liberal influences. Fundamentalist nationalists resisted the anti-discriminatory attitude that was part of the European legal system by directing their bigotry at every type of minority, with populist homophobia and anti-feminism at the forefront of their conservative movement. Consequently, this inspired a strong coalition between these two demonized and marginalized groups, *viz.*, feminist women and gays in revolt against post-Communist patriarchy (Kitliński & Lockard 2004).

In this oppressive ideological environment, art pioneered sexual and political dissidence, creating an alternative visual sphere. Thus, I turned to contemporary art to discover and help create an alternative and subversive visual culture of love and sexuality. Poland is a country of ambivalences. On the one hand, it is hostage to homophobia with the power of the far right increasing and neither protection against anti-gay speech and violence nor recognition of same-sex unions; one the other hand, parts of Polish society have become hospitable to queer activism and culture. This has made the country a hub of effervescent civic, artistic, and educational campaigning in which visible actions and visual art, literature, theatre, and humanities intensively explore queer issues and contribute to social change. Contemporary art is an especially rich field of queer explorations and promising material for scholarly and curatorial research.

I decided to base my curatorial strategy on this premise of queer visual culture as counterculture in order to challenge homophobic and heteronormative visual culture by an influx of queer and feminist images. Hence, I organized *Love and Democracy* (2005 and 2006), a socially oriented exhibition of contemporary Polish gay and feminist art. The exhibition concerned amorous pluralism and freedom in opposition to the nationalist homophobia and censorship that ruled Poland at the time. My curatorial concept emphasized relations between the democratic culture and plural erotics of pioneering feminist art and a new wave of gay art. The artists followed two subversive strategies, each with both a sexual and a social dimension. On the one hand, they visualized a diversity of love and erotic stories, relationships, and identities in opposition to the exclusively heteronormative constructions of gender and sexuality in the public and private spheres. On the other hand, they shot and used documentary footage of the homophobic violence in the Polish public space at the time (Leszkowicz 2006).

The films of Aleksandra Polisiewicz, Ewa Majewska, and Joanna Rajkowska, which show the battles surrounding marches for equality and those against the counterculture club Le Madame, directly document the social conflicts on the streets of Poland in 2005 and 2006. Polisiewicz's film *The Reanimation of Democracy – the March for Equality Moves On* (2005) documents the demonstration in Warsaw in support of the banned equality march in Poznań that was brutally suppressed on November 19, 2005. This was one of the year's events most covered by the media, and it had great social significance. It echoed all around the world, especially because the march was constitutional and the ban issued by city authorities unlawful. On November 27, the demonstration in solidarity with Poznań continued as a march for equality in the capital's Constitution Square. Another documentary, made by the feminist collective TV Sirens, consisting of Ewa Majewska, Aleksandra Polisiewicz, and Ell Southern, was about the march for equality in Warsaw, which the authorities had banned, on June 11, 2005. Another part of the same trend of spontaneous social protest for a free public and alternative space was the defense of the club *Le Madame* in April 2006, whose last dramatic phase is documented in Joanna Rajkowska's film *Le Ma!* (2006). The club was the center of the culture of political and moral opposition in Warsaw; it was a multi-sexual place, friendly toward customers of all sexual orientations. It became the symbol of the new, young left in a city ruled by the extreme right and was, therefore, closed on an administrative pretext. In protest, young people barricaded themselves in the club. Their eviction by the police was an ominous example of the new totalitarian state's use of violence against the peaceful acts of civil disobedience of people who were not part of the national Catholic culture.

The banning of marches for equality and suppression of an independent club indicated that the authorities were trying to govern by subjugation. In the attacks on citizens' pro-democratic initiatives, which the aforementioned films documented, the homophobic violence of ultra-right street gangs, teenage hooligans, and armed policemen in bulletproof vests dominated. Through the media of video and film, these artists registered the homophobic oppression of the state and populist neo-fascist youth gangs that again thrive in Poland in 2015 and 2016. In general, art in opposition to homophobia plays the role of witness but also of citizens' journalism, which is so potent in contemporary global social struggles.

Ars Homo Erotica is a show that I organized at Poland's National Museum in Warsaw in the summer of 2010 (Leszkowicz 2010). The director of the Museum at the time, the well-known Polish leftist art historian Piotr Piotrowski, commissioned and supported the project. This queer exhibition in the National Museum reflected his concept of a critical and socially engaged museum involving itself in burning social questions, such as the culture war being fought in new Eastern European democracies over gender/sexuality politics and queer rights as human rights (Piotrowski 2011, 2012).

Given its prestigious and highly visible location in the Polish capital's biggest museum, the controversies surrounding *Ars Homo Erotica* massively mainstreamed queer culture. So, it was a very successful case of art for social change. The invited artists came from Eastern Europe, where amorous diversity sparks cultural tensions, political conflicts, and acts of censorship and violence. *Ars Homo Erotica* gave me the opportunity to deal with the artistic, sexual, and political implications of queering the art collection of a conservative country's national museum. In general, national museums have an enormous, yet neglected and often forbidden, queer potential hidden in their vast archives, and, as my exhibition exemplified, the national museum can be a treasury of homoerotic heritage when its collection is displayed from a queer perspective. *Ars Homo Erotica* opposed the marginalization of queer-themed art in the museum's display. The selection of works according to transgender and lesbian/gay homoerotic iconography reached into the museum's unconscious; it involved the discovery of many forgotten objects that were once considered to be of only minor importance and emphasized homoerotic pieces that the permanent display had silenced or marginalized. The selection was a chance to rethink the authoritarian concept of the museum and its collection, to reconsider what is in and what is out, to bring out what had been hidden or suppressed, and to remove the heteronormative filter that had been imposed on the cultural institution but also on the concepts of personal and national identity. The show's most important aspect was that it was a transnational and queer project at the national museum that subverted an institution so strongly intertwined with national values. This is an example of the political impact of queer curating as it works against the dominant, and usually homophobic, narratives of major museums. Queerness in the national museum opens the traditional concept of the national up to the diverse contemporary, international, and pluralistic values of hospitable democratic societies, which go beyond the narrow official borders of the nation, gender, and the erotic (Davies 2013).

Ars Homo Erotica presented over 200 artworks from antiquity to the twenty-first century: Greek vases illustrated with Sappho and frolicking youths, male nudes by the old masters and mistresses of early-modern and nineteenth-century sculpture and painting, and contemporary queer art. The exhibition took a homoerotic perspective on the entire collection of the National Museum in Warsaw and, more broadly, of the art of Central and Eastern Europe. Works from the collection of the National Museum as well as those of invited contemporary artists surveyed cultural history from a LGBTQ point of view. *Ars Homo Erotica* involved itself in the revision of the

National Museum's collection but also in the volatile and polarizing queer politics of Eastern Europe.

The exhibition began in the museum's main hall with the contemporary section "The Time of Struggle," whose artworks and visual campaigns reflected the turbulent world of LGBTQ politics and struggle in the region. This section included some powerful works dealing with the impact of homophobia on individuals. I'd like to discuss two examples. A Croatian artist, Igor Grubic (2008), documented the murderous aspect of homophobia. His photographic series *Monument and Flowers* portrayed the dark side of Croatian gay reality. The images commemorate the place in a park in central Zagreb where skinheads beat a gay man to death. There is a figurative monument near that place, a grouping of powerful soldiers commemorating the Heroes of World War II who gave their lives fighting the Nazis. Grubic lays flowers on the spot where the man died and on the chest of one of the statues and photographs them. It is an alternative gesture of commemoration to the one inscribed in the nation's official historical narrative. A similar approach to sacrifice can be ascribed to the heartbreaking video performance *Tears are Precious* (2008) by the Romanian artist Alex Mírutziu. The video presents a slow-motion close-up of the face of a crying author and his falling tears. The piece is open to many interpretations, but, as the artist is gay and often deals with queer themes in his art, a reading of it as about homophobia is certainly one of them. Romania, which has a long history of criminalizing homosexuality, was the last country in Europe to decriminalize it (in 2000), and its transition to the embrace of human rights has been painful. Therefore, the video can be read as an allegory of a young gay man's suffering. Representations such as this deal emphatically with the cruelty of homophobia and the power of art and images to document, but also heal, its violence and to create compassion. Grubic's (2008) and Mírutziu's (2008) works presume that the viewer has enough compassion and understanding to receive their message of tolerance.

Art installations interrogate homophobia

There is also a different strategy for dealing with prejudices based on sexual orientation, a paradoxical and more immersive strategy that goes deeper into the complex and conflictual nature of contemporary society. To illustrate it, I have selected art installations which, first, feature homophobic behaviors and discourses within their spaces and, then, interrogate them, thereby transforming themselves into critical reflections on homophobia. These works were not in the show at the National Museum in Warsaw.

The explosive video installation *East Side Story* (2006/08), another piece by Igor Grubic, portrays the constant and dramatic fight for LGBTQ rights (see Figure 4.1 and 4.2).

The installation, which won an award at the 11th Istanbul Biennial in 2009, is a two-channel video that juxtaposes documentary footage with a

Contemporary art versus homophobia 75

Figure 4.1 Igor Grubic, *East Side Story*, video installation (2006–2008)
Source: Photo by Pawel Leszkowicz

re-enactment of the events filmed through the medium of dance. The documentary footage shows the brutal neo-Nazi attacks on the Gay Pride Parades in Belgrade (Serbia) (2001) and Zagreb (Croatia) (2002).[2] The artist combined this document of the real events with film of a dance that recreates some of its scenes. There are four dancers each of whom gives his or her own interpretation of events by mimicking certain movements and postures visible in the documentary footage. They dance in the same place in Zagreb where the parade was attacked. On one wall of the installation, we see the disturbing scenes of homophobic violence; on the other, the dancers' re-enactment. *East Side Story* brings the brutality of the documentary, music, and the poetic vision of the dance together into a reflection on nationalist and sexual hatred.

The same hatred had previously produced the bloody ethnic conflicts in the former Yugoslavia before it was directed against queer-rights activists and supporters. As the critic Dejan Stretenovic explained,

> The dramaturgic structure of the work focuses on the media representation of real events, foregrounding distressing and frightening scenes of violence, which constitute a warning that extreme nationalism, in the absence of an immediate "threatening" ethnic Other, finds a new victim in the shape of an "internal enemy," embodied by sexual minorities in this case.
>
> (McDonald 2010)

Figure 4.2 Igor Grubic, *East Side Story*, video installation (2006–2008)
Source: Film still by Igor Grubic

The slow movements of the dancers on the second screen manage to produce an effect that seems almost to heal the trauma of past events, which the brutal scenes on the first screen represent. The critic Shamita Sharmacharja (n.d.) wrote that the work constitutes an argument for the redemptive properties of art and its power to educate. I argue that through art and contemporary dance Grubic recorded homophobic violence but, more importantly, transformed it into something different – a healing catharsis. Although art in and of itself does not prevent homophobic violence, this is an excellent example of how art can help sublimate the dark drives of hatred and destruction. The two screens are like an enactment of the mythical struggle between the forces of good and evil.

Igor Grubic's work deals with the contemporary illegal homophobic violence of far-right organizations and gangs of hooligans. The persistent threat of violence from far-right extremists confirms Zillah Eisenstein's diagnosis that post-Communist nationalism in Eastern Europe and its masculinist borders are the products of racialized and sexualized hatreds (Eisenstein 1996, 15). The next example shows that homophobic speech is still a part of Central Eastern European politics and media. Liisi Eelmaa's and Minna Hint's *Heard Story* (2011) is a video installation that was shown in the exhibition *Untold Stories* (2011) curated by Rebeka Põldsam, Airi Triisberg, and Anders Härm at Kunstihoone in Tallin (see Figure 4.3).

Contemporary art versus homophobia 77

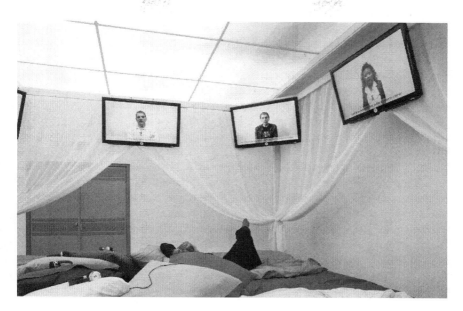

Figure 4.3 Minna Hint and Liisi Eelmaa, *Heard Story*, video installation (2011)
Source: Photo by Anna-Stina Treumund

The project was organized at a time of increased debate on LGBTQ rights in Estonia, but it reflected broadly on the everyday experiences of queer people in Central Eastern Europe. Many of the artworks in the exhibition took a documentary approach, directing attention to the alliances between the queer struggle and other social movements against discrimination and injustice.

Heard Story (2011) features a big colorful, comfortable canopy bed on which viewers are invited to lie. Suspended above the bed are eight TV monitors showing prominent Estonian politicians and public intellectuals expressing homophobic opinions. The artists shot the videos while interviewing these opponents of homosexuality. For example, we hear the leader of the Estonian National Movement, the senior inspector of the Estonian Health Board's Supervision Department, the director of the Tallinn Art Secondary School, and professors of psychology and theology at the University of Tartu. One of their prevailing arguments is that, since sexuality belongs exclusively in the private sphere and, so, is not a matter of civil rights, homosexuality is tolerable only as long as it takes place in private spaces, and there is no demand for its representation in the public sphere (Põldsam, Triisberg, & Härm 2011, 5). Through these voices, the installation suggests that it is homophobia that has the right to the public space. Lying on the bed, the viewer listens, through headphones, to the voices while safe in its enclosed privacy. Yet, the intimacy of the setting is shattered by the menacing views of the pundits obsessed with homophobia to which the viewer is subjected. In this way, the piece questions the conservative opinion that homosexuality belongs only in the private realm when it is obviously and aggressively discussed in society and politics and, as the installation shows, such public voices forcefully invade the intimate sphere.

As we see in this installation, there is no simple way to reject homophobia, but the artists have fully appropriated homophobic discourse into their piece and transformed it from the inside out into something else. At the same time, the homophobic language that is recorded, preserved, and disseminated, but also subtly questioned, destroys the domestic coziness of the space. The artwork encourages viewers to hear these stereotypical prejudices from a critical distance and with discomfort or even disgust. The contrast between the private and the public is made radical; yet, the spheres merge into one another. So, the artists make homophobia work against itself; they reverse its message by disrupting the illusion of a strict division between the public and the private. In essence, the artists multiplied and intensified what citizens experience in the privacy of their homes as they watch the talking heads on TV who encourage discrimination.

Another work goes beyond the Eastern European framework. I have chosen it as an illustration of the danger that, in projecting homophobia onto formerly Communist Eastern Europe, Western European academic and journalistic discourse tends to portray the region as a reservoir of the old prejudice that is supposedly no longer alive in the West. This tendency is a smoke screen that hides the persistence of homophobia, which, like racism and xenophobia, exists in all national and cultural contexts. It is present everywhere, and its local specificity, agency, and scale depends on regional constructions of gender, sexuality, and nationality.

The sound installation *The Shower of Homophobic Insults* (2013) was presented at the exhibition *The Gender Bazaar: Feminine/Masculine in the Mediterranean* (2013) curated by Denis Chevallier at MUCEM – Musée des Civilisations de l'Europe et de la Méditerranée. The huge show concentrated on the changes in gender and sexual identities in European and African Mediterranean societies. *The Shower*, which the show's organizers created, was one of a group of works about homophobia. Located in one of the exhibition's transition spaces, viewers had to pass through it to get to the next part of the exhibition.

The Shower of Homophobic Insults recreates the shape of a real shower. It is a translucent enclosure separated from the outside by loosely hanging plastic strips with speakers in the shape of showerheads inside, but, instead of water, a stream of multilingual homophobic abuse and derogatory terms pours out onto the individual alone inside. As a consequence, each viewer entering the installation, regardless of her sexual orientation, is subjected to homophobic abuse. The loud, hateful swearing and insults make the installation aggressive. Through the variety of Mediterranean languages it employs, the work documents the everyday homophobic vocabulary of Mediterranean countries. Thus, the shower of insults is like a dictionary of homophobic expressions in those languages. It testifies to the tenacious character of homophobia across the Mediterranean countries despite the enormous legal differences in LGBTQ rights among them.

When inside, one experiences verbal abuse, but one can also study it; so, homophobia is, again, displaced, turned against itself, and dissected. As with the bed in the Estonian installation, homophobic prejudice and aggression invade a domestic space whose security and safety evaporate. In both works, we are inside falsely secure private spaces that are broken down by the external public discourse of discrimination. As both works manifest psychic and domestic interiority, they emphasize how homophobia is both imposed on a subject from outside and internalized psychically. The strategy of both for grappling with homophobia is, first, to record it and, then, intensify it to a disturbing level so that the bombarded viewer, driven to escape its violence, turns against it. Though they verge on black humor, both works are difficult to enjoy because of the toxic intensity of hatred of which they make critical use.

As a final illustration of the strategy, I conclude with an American example, as this type of reflection on homophobia is international. Timothy Gabriel's conceptual public sculpture *Love Does Not Harm* (2014) depicts an androgynous silhouette, an allegory of the LGBTQ community/subjectivity, covered with spiteful words and hanging on a cross. Behind the crucifixion stands a rainbow banner declaring, "Love Does Not Harm." The sculpture was displayed in front of St. Mark's Episcopal Church in Grand Rapids, Michigan. According to the artist, its purpose is to raise awareness of the impact that homophobic rhetoric has on LGBTQ people in Russia and African countries like Uganda, and to draw attention, specifically, to the role that American Evangelical groups play in this very real persecution. Significantly, vandals splashed the sculpture with red paint, but it was later restored (Artprize 2016).

In all of these examples, the artists rework homophobic arguments and statements through the not very subtle strategy of repeated direct quotation so as to undermine them within the space of their art. In these examples, art functions as a dissecting table upon which to study homophobic ideologies, language, and actions. As homosexuality is an object of obsessive attention for the homophobic psyche and its politics, the art installations I have discussed take their oppositional stand by moving away from homosexuality and concentrating on homophobia. That is, these artists take homophobia, instead of homosexuality, and display it. As in many countries homophobic language and images are considered normal and, hence, are diffused into the mainstream and thereby visibly made invisible; putting them under the magnifying glass of art reveals the perversity, hatred, absurdity, and irrationality of the thought behind them. Through such magnification via incorporation, art takes possession of homophobia, exorcising it by devouring it. Psychoanalytic metaphors are particularly useful here. Artists put homophobia on the couch so that the viewer can listen to it and analyze what it says from the analyst's disengaged perspective. Indeed, such art sublimates the homophobic death drive to annihilate sexual difference. It is a talking, and visual, cure.

It is important that these installations are enveloping, immersive, visual, and sonic environments, which the viewer has to enter and which force her personally to experience homophobic utterances by surrounding her with them. The experience of such art is traumatic, as it shows us the individual and social trauma caused by hatred and violence from both the victim's and the perpetrator's points of view. The political impact of these paradoxical and moving works may be that they expose life dominated by homophobic hate speech as a constant trauma for all involved. Both the queer and the homophobic subjects are in crisis. The trauma of queerness is abjection, discrimination, and subjection to violence, and the trauma of homophobia is constant anxiety over the irreversible reality of a multi-sexual society. In a homophobic society, queer citizens are always subject to institutional or physical violence, and homophobic citizens are neurotically obsessed with utopian heteronormativity and sexual violations of it. All suffer. Thus, this art is about suffering.

Strategies of subversion

We deal here with the strategy of a "reverse discourse," as Michel Foucault (1980) theorized in the Introduction to *The History of Sexuality*. He writes about how homosexual subjects restaged the criminal, medical, and perverse statuses to which they were assigned in order to distance themselves from them and find new forms of self-expression, visibility, and counter-representation. To utilize the negative terms and images is not to endorse them but, rather, to question and even ridicule them, to expose and transform them. Restaging them in a different mode of representation – in this case, art – opens homophobic imaginings to further inquiry (Meyer 2002, 11–12). This approach has a long tradition in contemporary art.

Some queer artistic movements and theorists[3] have already employed the disruptive power of negativity to confront oppressive cultural and social heteronormativity, especially in American culture. Wallowing in abjection is an established twentieth-century strategy of subversion that at one point almost became a queer and feminist norm, as the international movement of abject art in the 1990s exemplifies. This strategy employs transgressions and negative attitudes for the purpose of comic, political, or erotic emancipation. For example, analyzing the history of homosexuality in American art in the twentieth century, Richard Meyer demonstrated how major gay artists – Paul Cadmus, Andy Warhol, Robert Mapplethorpe, David Wojnarowicz, and Holly Hughes – incorporated censorship, homophobic stereotypes, and other elements of oppression to create groundbreaking confrontational queer art. The negative image of homosexuality, as crime and sin, constitutes the pictorial language on which these artists have drawn (Meyer 2002, 8). This tradition of negativity will always have a seductive artistic and intellectual potential, but it is the product of a homophobic culture and society, and, as we move away from homophobic regimes in many parts of the Western world, more and more things become possible, and a variety of strategies are needed to counter the traumas and exclusions of the past and advance the continuing global struggle.

What are the social and political implications of these meta-homophobic works, that is, works that employ homophobia to combat it? Clearly, they are educational and informative. But does their aesthetic of intensification, their magnified and concentrated display, help us to go beyond homophobia, to overcome its ideology and psychology, or is it just a repetition of what we already know very well and are more or less often forced to endure? In the cases that I have selected, art doesn't have an answer; it mainly poses the question and strives to sensitize viewers to the language and images of hatred.

But there is also another way to use such homophobic disgust without being captivated by the abject. The way out was explored by Martha C. Nussbaum in her book *From Disgust to Humanity: Sexual Orientation and Constitutional Law*. She showed how disgust can be transformed into legal reforms aimed at more equality and respect for human rights (Nussbaum 2010). Many artists struggle aesthetically to enact this potent idea, and their work constitutes an ongoing project to move from disgust to humanity by creating images of love, sensuality, and the humanity of the Other, that is, the sexual, ethnic, racial, and national Other. The project consists mainly of affirmative and humanizing portrayals instead of denigration. In my curatorial work in Poland and other parts of Europe, I have been involved with this project through exhibitions like *Love and Democracy* (Leszkowicz 2006), *Ars Homo Erotica* (Leszkowicz 2010), and *Love is Love. Art as LGBTQ Activism: from Britain to Belarus* (Leszkowicz 2011). Contemporary art and culture have played a significant role in opening up our vision of human sexuality, love, and identities. The subsequent emancipatory political changes wouldn't have been possible without this pioneering cultural work.

Homophobia and art history

Art has played an enormous role in establishing and promoting the politics of identity, plurality, and freedom. But, since freedom of expression is one of the main principles in contemporary art, one might ask if there is homophobic art, art that incites hatred. This is the question that I now pose. In *The Dictionary of Homophobia* edited by Louis-Georges Tinin, Karim Ressouni-Demigneux optimistically writes in his entry on art that there has never been a homophobic art movement: "...homophobia as such has never been an artistic issue. Unlike Nazi or colonial art, there has never been a homophobic art form whose formal expression coincided with the will to propagate a certain ideology" (Ressouni-Demigneux 2008, 64–66). He suggests, rather, that there is a tradition of homophilic art. Yet, he acknowledges that there have been homophobic art works and gives examples of some early-modern religious paintings that depict gay people in insulting or ridiculing ways, but, he argues, because of the changing character of insults in different historical contexts, their homophobic intent is debatable. For instance, the representation of effeminate men and male couples in certain religious Renaissance images (e.g. in Bronzino's paintings) might have symbolized the supposed perversity of the pagan world before Christianity, but, on the other hand, art historians have argued that proto-gay artists created these works for a gay (*avant la lettre*) audience as depictions of homosexuality. Thus, effeminacy can be interpreted as a homophobic rendering of homosexuality or as a known sign, a code, for same-sex lovers of these historical periods (Saslow 1999, 84–85).

Nevertheless, there are clear examples of the homophobic ideological imagination in history. These include the representations of tortured sodomites in scenes of the Last Judgment, such as those in Taddeo di Bartolo's fresco *The Last Judgment* (1363–1422) in the Collegiata, San Gimignano, Italy; in the scene "Sodomite and Adulterer," a devil inserts a rod into the anus of a naked man that comes out through his mouth and then goes into the mouth of another naked man. There are also depictions of punishments for sodomy, for example, burning at the stake, as in the illustration *Sodomite Richard Puller and his Page, Zurich* (1482) from Diebold Schilling's manuscript *Die Grosse Burgunder-Chronik*. Of the most drastic character is the illustration *Balboa Feeding Indian Sodomites to the Dogs* in Theodore de Bry's book *America* (1590), representing the massacre of effeminate Panamanian Indians by Vasco de Balboa, the conqueror of Panama, in 1513. This type of image was part of colonial propaganda. It depicted historical facts but also sought to justify the brutality of the conquest of the new lands in terms of the religious mission to bring Catholicism to eradicate the sin of sodomy there (Fone 2000).

Moreover, visual/textual mockery, denigration, and cruelty are very much present also in modern and contemporary art discourses. For example, in the U.S. there has been a long debate in art history over homophobia in the discipline and in museological practice. It began with the publication of James M. Saslow's (1979) seminal text *Closets in the Museum: Homophobia and Art History* and has continued through years of discussion about the downplaying or silencing of the queer dimension of the works and lives of such major artists as Robert Rauschenberg, Jasper Johns, and Cy Twombly (Katz 2015). Despite the fact that a number of LGBTQ exhibitions had been organized since the 1970s, it took more than 40 years for a big museum to mount a major queer show: *Hide/Seek: Difference and Desire in American Portraiture* at the Smithsonian's National Portrait Gallery in 2010 (Katz & Ward 2010). Yet – and this is very important – the exhibition was censored (Kennicott 2010). Thus, homophobia in many national art histories is a well-established fact and a well-researched subject.

Art for homophobia?!

Furthermore, homophobic ideas, impulses, and ambiguities seem to be a new frontier in supposedly progressive global contemporary art. In contemporary art and visual culture, there are artists, designers, writers, and filmmakers who collaborate with, are financed by, or are members of nationalistic, far-right, or fundamentalist groups and actively create powerful images with negative or offensive messages about queer people, politics, and community. This occurs in many countries, including the U.S. and in Europe, and it can easily be turned into a global movement by an exhibition collecting such pieces together. There are even formal similarities in these works in their uses of the grotesque and the abject and of the technique of juxtaposing text and image. I shall give two examples, the first from Poland and the second from the U.S.

Wojciech Korkuc is a popular and controversial Polish poster designer who, in 2000, co-organized the *Movement for Moral Hygiene* against progressive, liberal sexual politics, especially the LGBTQ and feminist movements, in Poland. The purpose of his posters is to promote his vision of so-called "moral hygiene." He specializes in political posters advocating conservative and ultranationalist values, and his art has been displayed in public spaces as well as many international poster and art exhibitions. He has been awarded prizes in Europe and the U.S. He closely collaborates with Polish far-right political parties and runs a successful commercial design studio. His posters use derogatory stereotypes of gender and sexuality. One conflates homosexuality, pedophilia, and sexual addiction: the slogan "You are homo (gay) – OK, but don't queer (faggot) the youth. Especially for money" accompanies a crude drawing of a brain in a penis. Another denigrates feminist women: the slogan "You are mean, ugly and lazy – become a feminist. Or go to a psychologist" is juxtaposed with an image of three monstrous, half-animal women. Though the artist advocates visual hate speech, he has been shown in many public art institutions in Poland in a variety of curatorial contexts, some of which criticize his art, some of which affirm it.

The American example gives a surprising new twist to the story of the relationship between contemporary art and the queer community, which usually work together against conservatives and censors. But the absurdist performance piece *The Art Guys Marry a Plant* (2009) by the straight duo The Art Guys (Michael Galbreth and Jack Massing) created conflicts between some members of the LGBTQ and the art communities in Houston. In the performance, The Art Guys are two men in suits who wed an oak tree in a public ceremony in the Sculpture Garden of the Museum of Fine Arts in Houston followed by a reception in the Contemporary Arts Museum. In 2011, they donated the piece to the Menil Collection in Houston, an act that reignited discussion around the piece.

Some critics considered the performance too provocative, insensitive, offensive, opportunistic, and an artistic gift to the religious right at a time when gay marriage was hotly discussed and contested and the media was reporting an increase in suicides of bullied queer teens. It did not help that the Art Guys called their gay critics "unhappy homosexuals" and stated that they did not care about the issue of gay marriage but were happy that it was an issue because it generated interest in their work. According to their critics, though, the work reinforced the argument that gay marriage would lead to the legalization of marriage between people and animals and inanimate objects as well as between adults and children and thereby destroy the integrity of marriage (Payne 2011).

Polish and American artists are at different points on the "homophobic continuum," to use Didier Eribon's (1999, 14) term; their levels of hatred differ. Therefore, there is a diversity of homophobia in art. Korkuc is a typically Polish programmatic conservative ideologue; the Art Guys seem to be provocative pranksters who crave fame and use a very American strategy, similar to some types of stand-up comedians and politically incorrect entertainers, to get it. Yet, in both cases, the works are in conflict with queer equality and deliver openly or potentially homophobic messages.

In thinking about such works of art, we must acknowledge that according to the cherished artistic tradition of rebellion it is perfectly fine for artists to be outrageous, offensive, and provocative. Contemporary art has developed a very libertarian culture of limit testing. The artists' freedom of expression licenses them to create works that oppose equality or even human rights. But this freedom, including the right to discriminate and denigrate, poses a difficult curatorial question for art institutions and individual curators. It is a problem with which I often grapple. Homophobic as well as racist and xenophobic messages are more and more often present in contemporary art and visual culture more broadly.[4] Thus, to display such art, for example, art advocating or ambiguously playing with homophobia, in a group show is to promote it, to publicize the artists and the tendency, and to enforce the power of their discriminatory ideology. Should we do that? It is an ethical dilemma. Art historians and curators face a responsibility to document and analyze a plurality of artistic developments and not only tendencies that correspond with one's own world view. Therefore, it is important to devise a strategy for putting art works of any ideological inclination at critical display. This is a form of platforming and no platforming at the same time with regard to homophobic images, which defends the freedom of speech.

We deal here with the other side of the homophobic discourse in contemporary art, not culture against homophobia and other prejudices but art for homophobia and against social equality. I am not saying here that all queer art or art about queerness is or must be compassionate or progressive, but since the 1960s, the power of the visual message to change, to democratize the world was expressed by radical artists but also critics, academics, and curators. Yet in the current global conservative climate, what about the power of visuality to maintain the status quo and to spread prejudice and discrimination? This is a movement that needs to be addressed critically, not silenced or ignored. Thus I propose that visual homophobia become a subject of study, a field in which contemporary art (with its vast freedoms and privileges) has a role to play. Regarding the ethical curatorial question, hardly anyone wants to be a censor, and, thus, perhaps the sensible way to display discriminatory and derogatory messages in contemporary art is to put them in a critical context, that is, juxtapose and question them with oppositional pieces or well-researched contextual background.

I began with Central and Eastern Europe, and I now conclude with it. There is one powerful image which is brutal, crude, and direct but very effective and omnipresent in the Eastern European public sphere. Far-right militants and ultranationalists across Eastern Europe who attack and protest queer pride events invented it. Based on prohibitory traffic signs, it is composed of the silhouettes of two male figures involved in anal sex with a slash through them and the slogan "Stop the fags" or "Stop the queering" in one or another Eastern European language. The image is as present at queer events in the region as the rainbow but, of course, on the opposite side of the police cordon. One can see it in many documentaries and art projects about the culture war over LGBTQ rights. In Poland, for example, it cannot be banned, despite its vulgarity, because it is legally protected as a symbol of some ultranationalist parties that call themselves patriotic (Kitlinski 2011). The sign exemplifies how homophobic images can permeate and poison the social space and how they require constant visual, critical, and curatorial creativity to counter their pernicious ideology.

Notes

1 Because of the official sanctioning of homophobia in Russia, where it is part of state policy and legislation, I excluded from my chapter Russian culture and society, which I believe requires a separate analysis, even though publications about queer rights and culture in Russia inspired my thinking about Central Eastern European homophobia.
2 Thus, the installation is based on two events which happened a long time ago. Croatia's recent negotiations to join the EU have significantly improved the queer-rights situation and official political attitudes (Butterfield 2013).
3 Two exhibitions of abject art in the U.S. established the trend: *Dirt and Domesticity: Constructions of the Feminine*. 1992. New York: Whitney Museum of American Art, and *Abject Art: Repulsion and Desire in American Art*. 1993. New York: Whitney Museum of American Art. Julia Kristeva's concept of the abject was used in the construction of the exhibitions (Kristeva 1980).
4 See recent case of London's gallery LD50 exhibition promoting far right ideology: Jonathan Jones, No one should demand the closure of galleries – even for far-right artworks, www.theguardian.com/artanddesign/jonathanjonesblog/2017/feb/22/art-galleries-free-speech-ld50-dalston [Accessed February 23, 2017].

References

Abject Art: Repulsion and Desire in American Art. 1993. [Exhibition]. (New York: Whitney Museum of American Art).
Artprize. 2016. *Love Does Not Harm* [online]. Available at: www.artprize.org/timothy-gabriel/2014/love-does-not-harm [Accessed December 1, 2015].
Butterfield, N. 2013. "Sexual Rights as a Tool for Mapping Europe: Discourses of Human Rights and European Identity in Activists' Struggles in Croatia." In *Queer Visibility in Post-socialist Cultures*, eds. N. Fejes and A.P. Balogh, 11–35. Bristol: Intellect.

Davies, J. 2013. "Towards an Intimate Democracy in Europe: Paweł Leszkowicz's Queer Curating." *Journal of Curatorial Studies* 2, 1: 54–69.

Dirt and Domesticity: Constructions of the Feminine. 1992. [Exhibition]. (New York: Whitney Museum of American Art).

Eelmaa, L. and Hint, M. 2011. *Heard Story* [video installation] (exhibited in *Untold Stories*, 2011, curated by Rebeka Põldsam, Airi Triisberg, and Anders Härm at Kunstihoone in Tallin).

Eisenstein, Z. 1996. *Hatreds: Racialized and Sexualized Conflicts in the 21st Century*. Abingdon/New York: Routledge.

Eribon, D. 1999. *"Ce que l'injure me dit. Quelques remarques sur le racisme et la discrimination." In L'Homophobie, comment la définir, comment la combattre*. Paris: Editions ProChoix.

Fone, B. 2000. *Homophobia. A History*. New York: Metropolitan Books.

Foucault, M. 1980. *The History of Sexuality, Volume I: An Introduction*. Translated by Robert Hurley. New York: Random House.

Grubic, I. 2006/08. *East Side Story* [video installation].

———. 2008. *Monument and Flowers* [photographic series]. (Exhibition in Ars Homo Erotica).

Katz, J.D. 2015. *Committing The Perfect Crime: Sexuality, Assemblage and the Postmodern Turn in American Art* [online]. Available at: www.queerculturalcenter. org/Pages/KatzPages/Crime1.html [Accessed December 1, 2015].

Katz, J.D. and Ward, D.C. 2010. *Hide/Seek. Difference and Desire in American Portraiture*. Washington, DC: Smithsonian Books.

Kennicott, P. 2010. "'Fire' man: Wojnarowicz, censored by Smithsonian, sounded an alarm in dire times." *Washington Post* [online]. December 10. Available at: www. washingtonpost.com/wp-dyn/content/article/2010/12/09/AR2010120905895.html [Accessed December 10, 2015].

Kitlinski, T. 2011. "Post-Communist Blues." *Souciant Magazine* [online], November 29. Available at: http://souciant.com/2011/11/post-communist-blues/ [Accessed December 10, 2015].

Kitliński, T. and Lockard, J. 2004. "Sex Slavery and Queer Resistance in Eastern Europe." *Bad Subjects* [online]. June 2004, Issue 69. Available at: http://bad.eserver. org/issues/2004/69/kitlinski_lockard.html [Accessed September 10, 2013].

Kristeva, J. 1980. *Pouvoirs de l'horreur: essai sur l'abjection*. Paris: Éditions du Seuil.

Leszkowicz, P. 2006. *Love and Democracy*. Exhibition Catalogue. Gdańsk: Center for Contemporary Art Bathhouse.

———. 2010. *Ars Homo Erotica*. Exhibition Catalogue. Warsaw: The National Museum.

———. 2011. *Love is Love. Art as LGBTQ Activism from Britain to Belarus*, The City Gallery of Contemporary Art – Labirynt, Lublin [Exhibition]. (Co-curated with Tomasz Kitliński).

McDonald, K. 2017. *Igor Grubic – East Side Story 2006–8* [online]. London: Tate. Available at: www.tate.org.uk/art/artworks/grubic-east-side-story-t13651/text-summary [Accessed October 29, 2015].

Meyer, R. 2002. *Outlaw Representation. Censorship and Homosexuality in Twentieth-Century American Art*. Oxford: Oxford University Press.

Michalska, Julia. 2017. "Poland's Clampdown on its Cultural Institutes." *The Art Newspaper*. January 11. Available at: http://theartnewspaper.com/news/poland-clamps-down-on-overseas-cultural-institutes/ [Accessed January 31, 2017].

Mírutziu, A. 2008. *Tears are Precious* [video performance].
Nussbaum, M.C. 2010. *From Disgust to Humanity: Sexual Orientation and Constitutional Law*. Princeton, NJ and Oxford: Princeton University Press/Oxford University Press.
Pawlowski, Roman. 2016. "Poland: Creative Freedom Undermined in Cultural Revolution." *Artsfex*, December 2, 2016. Available at: http://artsfreedom.org/?p=12992 [Accessed January 31, 2017].
Payne, J. 2011. "Homophobia in the Arts." *Huffington Post* [online], December 20. Available at: www.huffingtonpost.co.uk/james-payne/homophobia-in-the-arts_b_1157343.html [Accessed December 5, 2015].
Piotrowski, P. 2011. Museum: From the Critique of Institution to a Critical Institution. In *(Re)staging the art museum*, ed. T. Hansen, 77–90. Høvikodden: Henie Onstad Art Centre.
———. 2012. *Art and Democracy in Post-Communist Europe*. London: Reaktion Books.
Põldsam, R., Triisberg, A. and Härm, A. eds. 2011. *Untold Stories*. Tallinn: Tallinna Kunstihoone.
Polisiewicz, A. 2005. *The Reanimation of Democracy – the March for Equality Moves On* [Film]. Poland.
Rajkowska, Joanna. 2006. *Le Ma!* [Film]. Available at: www.rajkowska.com/pl/filmy/168 [accessed October 19, 2016].
Ressouni-Demigneux, K. 2008. Art. In *The Dictionary of Homophobia: A Global History of Gay & Lesbian Experience*, ed. T. Louis-Georges, 64–66. Vancouver: Arsenal Pulp Press.
Saslow, J. 1979. "Closets and the Museum: Homophobia and Art History." In *Lavender Culture*, eds. K. Jay and A. Young, 215–228. New York and London: New York University Press.
———. 1999. *Pictures and Passions. A History of Homosexuality in the Visual Arts*. New York: Viking.
Sharmacharja, S. n.d. *Postcards from Istanbul – Through Crimson Tinted Glasses* [online]. Available at: www.artvehicle.com/postcard/40 [Accessed December 10, 2015].
Solomon, A. and the Polish PEN Club. 2016. "Stop Racist Violence in Poland!" *The New York Review of Books* 63, 1 [online]. Available at: www.nybooks.com/articles/2016/01/14/stop-racist-violence-in-poland/ [Accessed October 19, 2016].

5 "How gay is Germany?"
Homosexuality, politics, and racism in historical perspective

Claudia Bruns

In July 2004, the headline on the front page of *Bild*, Germany's largest daily tabloid, posed the question "How gay is Germany?" (see Figure 5.1).[1] The article underneath was prompted by the fact that Guido Westerwelle (1961–2016), head of the Free Democratic Party (FDP) and the German Minister of Foreign Affairs between 2009 and 2013, had presented his partner at a reception in Berlin, a gesture with which he publicly acknowledged himself as homosexual.

In addition to Westerwelle, the article named the openly gay mayors of Berlin and Hamburg, as well as some gay comedians, to underline its message that homosexual men were more and more often becoming prominent representatives of the nation. The *Süddeutsche Zeitung*, an important daily newspaper in Germany, described the article as a silly story meant to fill the summer news lull – a *Sommerlochgeschichte* – but, nonetheless, took the trouble to respond to the question, asking, ironically, whether an entire country could be gay and mocking the tabloid's sensationalistic style: "Quite formidable. So much, at least, is certain."[2]

That response to the *Bild's* puzzling connection between male sexual orientation and the German nation reveals that the article was more than just a way to get through the summer news slump. The article and the *Süddeutsche Zeitung*'s reaction to it reveal a certain unease that the alleged relationship arouses, a feeling that is difficult to understand. The vacillation between humor and seriousness in the *Süddeutsche Zeitung*'s response to the tabloid's suggestive question shows, in particular, how politically loaded and symbolic the relationship between the state and notions of normative sexuality and masculinity still is. A homosexual man in a political leadership role can be perceived as a threat to the masculinity of a state and a sign of its weakness (Heilmann 2011). The headline "How gay is Germany?" suggests that a few homosexuals in leading positions might be sufficient to change the character of a whole nation regarding its sexual preferences and by implication, its "normality," its masculinity and health. The linkage between sexuality and the nation-state has a long tradition, one that leads us back to the nineteenth century and its discussions of gender, sexuality, nation, and race within the discourse on homosexuality. As I will briefly

"How gay is Germany?" 89

Figure 5.1 "Wie schwul ist Deutschland?", *Bild*, July 22, 2004, p. 1

demonstrate at the end of this chapter, some of these discussions continue to affect public dialog today.

The masculinity of the state and the discourse on (homo)sexuality

In Germany, as elsewhere in Europe, it was a common *topos* in the discursive system of the long nineteenth century that the state was an exclusively masculine domain (Dudink, Hagemann, and Tosh 2004; zur Nieden 2005a). The dominant gender regime of bourgeois society associated women with the private domestic field and men with the public sphere (Hausen 1977). In the German Empire, a strong, militarily powerful state was considered a sign of healthy and Germanic masculinity. By contrast, national degeneration was connected with sexually abnormal, racially deviant, and feminized men (Mehlmann 1998; Oosterhuis 2000; Schmersahl 1998). Thus, the political and social order of the German Empire was built on an unequal division of political and social privileges and rights between men and women and also necessitated a hierarchization of men and of different conceptions of masculinity (Brunotte & Herrn 2008; Bruns 2011a; Müller 1991). The preservation of social hierarchies in the German Empire was no longer legitimized primarily through caste and corporate privileges but, rather, through biologically marked sexual and racial differences (Puschner 2001; Sigusch 2008; Weingart, Kroll, & Bayertz 1996).

Following the emergence of the social and biological sciences, sexuality became a dominant means of explaining social behavior. Contemporary social scientists used conceptions of sexuality not only to analyze the personality of the individual but also to predict and explain his or her biologically based, gender-coded (and racialized) ability to forge bonds with family and society. Increasingly, they explained the attachment of the individual to society, his or her productivity and usefulness, in terms of his or her sexuality (Bruns 2011b). Therefore, the debate in the German Empire over male homosexuality can be read as an illustration of the fundamentally biological explanation of the political-social order. That is to say, power struggles in the political sphere, for instance in parliamentary debates, were often framed as battles between different conceptions of masculinity and between the sexes (and races). This discourse was also visible in the sexual sciences and in social movements (Schmersahl 1998; zur Nieden 2005a; Bruns 2011b).

In the following, I examine connections between sexuality, gender, race, and social order in discourses on homosexuality in Germany around 1900. Although scholars have drawn *parallels* between discourses on sexual and racial difference and issues of intersectionality have increasingly become topics of theory,[3] German historiography has rarely explored the relationships between these discourses and their potentially reciprocal effects. Therefore, I am interested in interrogating how negotiations of homosexual identity shaped, and were shaped by, notions of race. Furthermore, I shall argue that the figure of the male homosexual was divided into good and bad, normal and abnormal, subjects according to a gendered hierarchy (between effeminate and masculine homosexuals), a division that was reinforced by racial characteristics that were ascribed to the effeminate homosexual.

Intersections of political discourses: (masculinist) homosexuality and race

At the end of the nineteenth century, the discourse on sexual pathology became interwoven with an evolving discourse on degeneration. Physicians and sexologists tried to define the normality and abnormality of different patterns of sexual behavior that determined a person's biopolitical usefulness to society in general and the nation-state in particular (Foucault 1999, 276–305; Planert 2000).

The figure of the male homosexual, especially, challenged that notion of normal masculinity that was seen as a sign of a healthy race and a precondition for maintaining a strong nation-state. One of the first racial hygienists in Germany, Ernst Rüdin (1874–1952), argued that it did not matter whether a homosexual was sick or healthy since the only issue of relevance was whether he served "by and large the vital needs of the race" (Rüdin 1904a, 107). In accord with the discursive logic of bio-politics, nothing less than the survival of the nation, or, in Rüdin's words, "the dying down of mankind or the defeat of one people (nation) against another," was at stake (ibid.).

At the turn of the century, a small but well-organized group of homosexual activists sought, in response to this discursive logic, to increase the perceived value of male–male relationships and break the connection that was believed to hold between homosexuality and racial degeneration. The group was affiliated with the Community of the Special Individuals (*Gemeinschaft der Eigenen*), which the writer and publisher Adolf Brand, together with Benedict Friedlaender and Wilhelm Jansen, founded in 1903 and which claimed to foster "the highest values of masculinity within the nation" and proclaimed a "joyful sense of masculinity – for the good and the progress of the state and the culture."[4] These masculinists stressed the special virility and cultural superiority of homoerotic friendships.[5] Their view stood in marked contrast to that of sexual reformers, such as the Berlin-based physician Magnus Hirschfeld. He was one of the founders of the *Wissenschaftlich-humanitäres Kommitee* (Scientific-Humanitarian Committee) (WhK), which was founded in 1897, and he fought for the acceptance of male homosexuals by characterizing them as a "third sex," a feminine soul in a masculine body and vice versa for lesbians (Dose 2005; Herzer 2001; Wolff 1986). From the perspective of the masculinists, it was less important to fight for tolerance of their minority group than to advocate their way of life and to take pride in their masculinity, which they saw as important for the health of the German nation and race. By adopting arguments from racial and bio-political discourses and presenting themselves as the pinnacle of manhood, they challenged the dominant discourse, which characterized homosexuals as perverts and racial degenerates, and tried to integrate male–male sexuality into hegemonic masculinity (Connell 1995; Connell & Messerschmitt 2005), but they thereby also modernized hegemonic structures that discriminated against women. They idealized a "male racially pure culture, as in Greek Sparta," while they regretted that "mankind was markedly getting feminized through contradictory racial instincts" (Mayer 1903, 57).

Other masculinist activists used the discourse on racial hygiene to defend male homosexuality against Rüdin's arguments. For example, the Berlin zoologist Benedict Friedlaender (1866–1908), who had agitated within the *Gemeinschaft der Eigenen* for a break with Hirschfeld, argued that homosexuals were indispensable for the survival and progress of the race. As bisexual men, they were able to start families and hold high positions in the state bureaucracy, and they could also build the sort of male–male relationships upon which the state depended. *The Renaissance of Eros Uranios*, as the title of Friedlaender's book proclaimed, would empower men to meet both their responsibility for biological reproduction and their patriotic duty to the nation, though, in his view, men's familial duties were less important than their contributions to the nation. "Same-sex love, as we understand it," he wrote, "is therefore nearly identical with the social instinct itself" (Friedlaender 1904a, 215). Friedlaender thereby countered the assumption of the nascent racial-hygienist discourse that homosexuals were damaging to the "life process of the race" because they entirely "lacked the drive to preserve the species."[6] He distinguished his "new man," who had been created in an erotic renaissance, from men who were the product of excessive female influence. Thus, the construction of a new, nationwide homo-social male community was to be achieved through the complete rejection of women and femininity.

Friedlaender's theory can be understood as a response to the social changes of his time. Around the turn of the century, women were challenging hegemonic masculinity with unprecedented success. They were gaining access to institutions of higher learning, founding women's clubs and societies, entering the professions, and loudly voicing their emancipatory demands (Gerhard 1990; Planert 1998). The urgent need consequently felt by defenders of the patriarchal order to establish a new, clear social distinction between men and women gave socially and sexually marginalized men a strategic opportunity to reposition themselves in the discourse on hegemonic masculinity. Friedlaender sought to offer both a principled basis upon which to distinguish the sexes and a flexible norm governing male sexual identity. His vehemence in rejecting women's emancipatory claims is symptomatic of his aims: "Nothing is so overwhelmingly stupid and such a great nonsense," he wrote, "as the fanatic belief in gender equality, which is cultivated as the so called women's question" (Friedlaender 1904a, 46, 74). He consigned women, as the "sexus sequior," to the family, a primary social context (ibid., 269–271) that seemed to him uncivilized, disconnected, and primitive:

> The sense for the family is one of the most primitive desires, shared with animals, that could only be praised by Gynaekocrats [men who want to be dominated by women]. Love between the two sexes or between parents is not the only kind of love; rather there is also a third type of love that is primarily social. It has nothing to do with procreation, but is the very foundation of the social principle. If one eliminated this third type of love, which exists between male adults, the state would disintegrate into a mass of individual families.
>
> (Ibid., 213)

The accusation that homosexuals were causing national and racial degeneration was now directed against women: "A people under these influences [of women] must degenerate into an ochlocracy, a gynecocracy, a kleptocracy, and will lose the struggle between the nations. This is one of the few clearly discernible basic laws of the history of nations" (ibid., 278).

In 1912, Hans Blüher (1888–1955), a sexologist and popular chronicler of the *Wandervogel* youth movement who would later become a conservative revolutionary, began to build on Friedlaender's masculinist views.[7] Expelled from the University of Berlin in 1916 without having completed his degree, Blüher called himself a private scholar of the sexual sciences and published numerous psychoanalytic articles in Sigmund Freud's and Hirschfeld's journals. He also worked for a while as a lay analyst (Blüher 1920). Like Friedlander, Blüher argued, on the basis of Freud's new psychoanalytical theories, that sexuality was the very foundation of the social. Specifically, he contended that a man's suitability for political leadership was a function of the degree to which other men found him sexually attractive. Sexual relations between men, as Blüher put it in 1912, are not a pathological deviance from the norm but a manifestation of the biological power that makes a man a "zoon politicon" (a political animal) because it gives him the ability to connect homo-socially to other men (Blüher 1912, 70). His idea of a fundamentally homo-social, state-supporting *Männerbund* – literally, an "alliance of men" – was widely discussed in the first decades of the twentieth century (Geuter 1994, 114, 161–162, 171–185; Widdig 1992, 32, 54).

Also like Friedlaender, Blüher used anti-feminist arguments to break the perceived connection between racial degeneration and homosexuality. He argued that the "required appraisal of women as the sole objects of love and desire" was one-sided and possibly dangerous (Blüher 1912, 112f). Further, he wanted to refute "the former general opinion, which connects same-sex love with the racial question and especially with the decadent parts of the Jewish race" (Blüher 1913a, 20). Blüher stressed that, to the contrary, the homoerotic branch of the *Wandervogel* movement was virile and an "especially German entity" (ibid.). However, he encountered a number of difficulties. In 1913, he was accused of being a Jew (Schmidt 1968, 247f) and of representing Jewish ideas because he held to Freud's psychoanalytic theory and was a member of Hirschfeld's sexual reform movement. These accusations led him to stress his own racial purity and the racial purity of certain types of homosexuals (Bruns 2011a, 179–183).

The gender/race split within the homosexual: feminization versus masculinity

In the years around 1910, the figure of the homosexual underwent a split. It was essentially a split along the lines of gender differences, but, as I shall show, it also involved categories drawn from racial discourse. In 1910, the three representatives of the burgeoning sexual sciences met to exchange ideas: Magnus Hirschfeld, a sexologist who fought for homosexual emancipation; Sigmund Freud, the founder of psychoanalysis; and a member of the younger generation, Hans Blüher. Freud saw Blüher as a possible champion of the psychoanalytic movement and as someone who might bridge the increasing disagreements between the sexual-biological theories of Hirschfeld and the WhK, who defended a hereditary explanation of homosexuality, and psychoanalysts, who held that homosexuality had a social origin. In the course of their discussion over the degree to which homosexuality is healthy and normal, the three bifurcated the figure of the homosexual into the virile, socially useful homosexual, on the one hand, and the neurotic and degenerate effeminate homosexual, on the other, though they disagreed over whether the effeminate male homosexual should be classified as racially deviant. Each integrated, in his characteristic way, the virile homosexual into the spectrum of normality, but this tended to exclude the effeminate gay man from the normal.

While Hirschfeld accepted the entire spectrum of homosexuality as non-deviant, Freud was not yet clear, in 1910, about his assessment of homosexuality. Five years before, in *Three Essays on the Theory of Sexuality*, he had claimed that "inverts" – the term Freud commonly used for homosexuals – were not to be classified as degenerates, for one could find virile individuals among them who "otherwise show no marked deviation from the normal" and whose "mental capacities are not disturbed, who on the contrary are distinguished by especially high intellectual development and ethical culture" (Freud 1938, 556; 2000a, 58). But in his article "Leonardo da Vinci and a Memory of His Childhood" (1910), Freud leaned toward the opinion that inversion was the result of an "individual inhibitor to development" [*individuelle Entwicklungshemmung*] (Freud 1989, 452; 2000b, 87–160). Though he did not believe that the cause of homosexual effeminacy was physiological, he did hypothesize that effeminate homosexuals suffered from a narcissistic over-identification with their mothers that inhibited the development of their masculinity. Homosexuals have a "very intensive erotic attachment to a female person, as a rule their mother," who was, according to Freud, "frequently mannish" [*Mannweiber*]. These mothers were "women with energetic traits of character, who were able to push the father out of his proper place" (Freud 2000b, 125). According to Freud, because such a boy lacks a strong father he identifies with his mother. This identification with the mother causes a "regression" and "narcissism" (a kind of "autoeroticism"), which results in his inability to establish successful relationships, "for the boys whom he now loves as he grows up are after all only substitutive figures and revivals of himself in childhood" (ibid.). Thus, inversion became problematic for Freud when it stemmed from *feminine* identification. At the same time, though, Freud considered Blüher's notion of a homoerotic male alliance (*Männerbund*) to be fundamental for higher cultural development, as I shall show in the following.

Blüher shared Freud's stress on the cultural achievements of homosexuals, especially masculine homosexuals. And, contrary to Hirschfeld, he held that the "complete invert" [*Vollinvertierte*] could not be classified as effeminate on Hirschfeld's scale of the intermediate degrees [*Zwischenstufen*] of homosexuality (Blüher 1912, 59). Blüher also believed that homosexuals could be just as happy as any other healthy human being. In July 1912, Blüher first distinguished three forms of homosexuality: "the latent [*läitent*] one, ... the feminine ... and the normal in the Greek way [i.e. virile]" (Neubauer 1996, 142). He considered the first two of these to be pathological. According to Blüher, the latent and the feminine homosexual needed society's pity and protection, while it must cultivate and foster the virile one. Questioning the credibility of Freud's judgment concerning male homosexuality, Blüher argued that Freud knew of only the pathological individuals who sought treatment. From his own experience in the youth movement, however, Blüher knew of heroic homosexual males who were happy and healthy.

Freud came closest to Blüher's position in 1912 and 1913. In his book *Totem and Taboo*, Freud sought to explain the history of mankind from its origins to his own time in terms of homoerotic male bonding. According to Freud, in prehistoric times, there was a powerful father who was killed by his sons. After the murder, the sons joined together (in a kind of male union or *Brüderclan*) and decided to avoid women in order to save "the organization that had made them strong and which was based upon homo-sexual feelings and activities," as Freud put it (Freud 1938, 917; 2000c, 426–428). According to him, the sons' homo-social feelings for one another were the first step in the development of civilization. Thus, Freud's theory came to incorporate Blüher's masculinist idea of a homoerotic male alliance (*Männerbund*). In fact, Freud had read the work of Blüher and other ethnographic literature prior to writing *Totem and Taboo*. In sum, then, Freud judged homosexual relationships positively when they were the result of identification with the father; it was only when caused by identification with the mother that homosexuality was problematic.[8]

Also in 1913, Blüher posited a closer relationship between the negative, feminized forms of inversion and racial degeneration. He associated *latent* homosexuality with "bad racial mixtures" and saw this form of inversion as a sign of "modern decadence" and "regression," something completely without cultural value (Blüher 1913b, 77–79). Hirschfeld protested his racializing of the effeminate homosexual in comparison to the masculine, but Blüher insisted, for nationalist and right-wing circles were now attacking him by (falsely) claiming he was a Jew and propounding Jewish theories. Displaying his own anti-Semitic worldview, he continued to stress the difference between the masculine hero and the effeminate homosexual [*invertierter Weibling*], claiming that the hero could be like a god to other men and that the cult of the hero stems from homoerotic desire, while an effeminate man was the result of Jewish-liberal degeneration. He further claimed that Jews possessed few of the qualities needed to build a nation because they suffered from a significant lack of homo-social structures [*Männerbundschwäche*] as a result of hypertrophied Jewish family relations (Blüher 1919, 170). As a man bound firmly to his family, the Jew became for Blüher the prototype of the effeminate male and thereby the proper target for the stigma theretofore ascribed to the homosexual. "The associative connection between maleness and Germanness," Blüher wrote in 1922, "and of the effeminate and servile with the Jewish is a direct intuition of the German people, one that becomes more certain day by day" (Blüher 1922, 49). After World War I, then, the signifier of failed masculinity in the masculinist discourse shifted from the effeminate, abnormal homosexual man as described in Hirschfeld's theory of sexual gradations (*Zwischenstufentheorie*) to the Jewish man, who was of a "secondary race."[9]

Conclusions

To conclude, the debates I have discussed show how the figure of the homosexual man was split on the basis of a gender dichotomy. Despite differences in the theoretical approaches of Hirschfeld, Freud, and Blüher, the three sexologists all agreed that the masculine homosexual was culturally more valuable than the effeminate one. Though Hirschfeld defended the effeminate homosexual, his theory also had anti-feminist implications. The gender binary functioned as a cultural marker that either normalized or made undesirable, enhanced or lowered the value of, certain identity constructions. To increase the perceived value of the masculine homosexual, the degradation of the effeminate one was accepted and even promoted.

This discourse also shows how debates about homosexuality were interwoven with racial discourses. The effeminate homosexual was not only categorized as narcissistic, mother-identified, pathological, and degenerate; he was also described with the colonial terms "backward" and "primitive." Specific concepts of race, gender roles, and sexual preferences corresponded to, and mutually reinforced, one another. More specifically, the category of race reinforced the gender gap that existed within the category of (homo)sexual identity. In Friedlaender's work, women and the reproductive realm of the family exemplified the "primitive." Repeating a long-established anti-Semitic trope that depicted Jewish men as effeminate, Blüher and his followers posited a close relationship between Jewishness and what they saw as the degenerate type of homosexuality. After World War I, this combination of homophobia and anti-Semitism became even more pronounced until the Jewish man was not only taken to exemplify the effeminate but came to symbolize a sort of gender undecidability disrupting the dualism of male and female that is crucial for maintaining heteronormativity and, by implication, for maintaining the vitality of the nation at large (Gilman 1991; Hödl 2007; Rohde 2005).

In the terms of racial-homosexual discourse, Blüher was struggling to disengage virile homosexuality from Jewishness. His statements to this effect were part of a general trend in German nationalist discourse to renew the German nation's masculine nature and reinstate its male-defined political order. This explains the appeal of Blüher's ideas, particularly in conservative circles. Inspired by Blüher's theories, some *völkisch* activists of the homosexual movement, including the young physician Karl-Günther Heimsoth (1899–1934), developed the ideal of an Aryan, homoerotic male leader and hero (Bruns & zur Nieden 2006; zur Nieden 2004; zur Nieden 2005a). Ernst Röhm (1887–1934), head of the National Socialist paramilitary (the SA), who openly praised homosexuality and practiced it with SA members, seemed to embody this ideal. Here is the beginning of the influential idea of the homosexual Nazi, which became more influential after World War II and is still important (Zinn 1997; zur Nieden 2005b; Machtan 2001, 2002). The fact that Hitler was well informed about Röhm's sexual preference led masculinists in the early 1930s to assume, falsely, as it turned out, that the Nazi regime would tolerate male–male relationships if they exuded heroic, military masculinity. To the contrary, Röhm's arrest and his execution, together with numerous other SA functionaries during the Night of Long Knives in 1934, was the beginning of the persecution of homosexuality in Nazi Germany, which led to the murder of thousands of men in the 1930s and 1940s (Jellonnek 1990; Hancock 1998; Plant 1986). Contrary to the expectations of homosexuals sympathetic with right-wing politics, Hitler's justification for executing the SA's leaders was that the SA was a homoerotic alliance of men (*Männerbund*) conspiring against the state, a justification in terms of the still established and widely accepted discursive connection between sexual and political deviance.

The subtle interplay among discourses on race, gender, sex, and degeneration produced exclusions that stimulated the desire to be part of the so-called "Aryan body of the racialized nation" [*arischer Rassenkörper*]. It is important to note "that the denaturalization of one identity category is often achieved through a re-naturalization of another" (Somerville 2000, 175). Flexible homo-social desire among self-identified Aryan men was a form of denaturalizing the heterosexual norm, although it was instituted through the re-naturalization of women and Jews. This discourse was silent on female homosexuality, for it could not be reassessed in terms of its value to the state because the state identified itself exclusively with (homosexual or heterosexual) masculinity.

Outlook

Some of these early twentieth-century discursive strategies are still being used in contemporary Germany. In order to disparage a male politician, critics often attribute feminine characteristics to him. And, because of the effeminacy often associated with his sexual orientation, a homosexual man in a leading political position seems to many to imply a weakening of the state. This homophobic trope was visible in 2000 on the cover of the German satirical magazine *Titanic*, which portrayed Guido Westerwelle, who was later the Foreign Minister, against the background of a crocheted tablecloth, thus associating him with the needlework usually associated with old-fashioned, elderly women (see Figure 5.2).

The cover's headline questions even more directly his gender identity by asking: "Free Democratic Party on the Rise: Will the next Chancellor be a Woman?" The male politician is called a woman, which devalues him. The cover also lampoons Westerwelle's often agitated and passionate speeches, visually articulated by his raised fist, and his cry, in the barely visible speech bubble, "Let's fist for freedom!" Westerwelle's plea for freedom, an important plank in his party's platform, is transformed into a call for gay sex, obviously to associate him with perversion and decay and devalue his political

98 Claudia Bruns

Figure 5.2 Titanic. *Das endgültige Satiremagazin* No. 2, February 2009, p. 1

seriousness and perseverance. The identification of the two struggles shows how closely interconnected categories of gender, sexuality, and politics still are today and to what extent they rely on feminization, including the feminization of homosexuality, to undermine the other side in a political dispute.

We arrive at similar conclusions by examining the uses of homosexuality to criticize Russian politics. Thus, cartoons in the German media portray Vladimir Putin as a homosexual and also feminize him. Again, the cover of an issue of *Titanic* provides an example. It depicts Putin effeminately in tears over his re-election in March 2012 and asks, "How Gay is this Dictator?" Once again, then, feminization, homosexualization, and political critique go hand in hand. German demonstrators against anti-gay laws in Russia also use feminized images of Putin, depicting him as homosexual to express their criticism.

This nexus between discourses on homosexuality and those on national belonging remains a politically charged subject to this day. This became visible on the occasion of a public controversy that Judith Butler provoked in Berlin in June 2010, when she was to receive the Civil Courage Award [*Zivilcouragepreis*] of the CSD Berlin, Berlin's LGBT(QI) pride association.

During the ceremony, at the very moment the award was being handed to her, she refused it, charging members of the CSD Berlin of unjustly accusing Germans with immigration backgrounds, and others from non-white communities, of homophobia. Her action created a fierce debate on racist attitudes in the LGBT(QI) movement. Jasbir Puar calls the phenomenon criticized by Butler "homo-nationalism," by which she means that some members of the gay emancipation movement profit from racialized discourses or justify the degradation of non-whites by arguing that they are not emancipated and have not adjusted to the liberal Enlightenment principles of Western nation-building, which in contemporary Germany are attributed to LGBT(QI) communities. According to Puar, "the woman question" now often appears alongside "the homosexual question." In the colonial period, a nation's answer to the question "[H]ow do you treat your women?" was, from the perspective of the colonizers, a determining factor of its capacity for sovereignty. Today, this question has been rephrased as "[H]ow well do you treat your homosexuals?" (Puar 2007, 139).

Berlin's LGBT(QI) movement seems to locate the homophobic Other all too easily outside of the white national community. This attitude resembles the attitude incorporated in the dominant discourse in Germany that ascribes patriarchal attitudes and anti-feminist behavior toward women to the Muslim (immigrant) man, and it reveals that certain colonial discourses, which we are used to thinking of as historical, can be used by queer people today to invest in a racialized construction of the nation as a white possession. Moral outrage and the fight for those same liberal Enlightenment principles on the part of the queer community can function simultaneously in at least two different ways: they can integrate homosexuals into the norm of the white, middle-class, nuclear family, and they can be a medium for representing white selves (Riggs 2006, xii).

Thus, the subtle interplay among discourses on sex, gender, and race still produces exclusions that this time entrench the need to be a part of the "(white) body of the nation." Ignoring these intersections risks fuelling the cycle of racist exclusions (Somerville 2005, 175).

Notes

1 "Wie schwul ist Deutschland?", *Bild*, July 22, 2004, 1. See also "Wie homosexuell ist Deutschland?" *Welt am Sonntag*, July 11, 2004. www.welt.de/print-wams/article113175/Wie-homosexuell-ist-Deutschland.html [Accessed February 28, 2016].
2 Bernd Graff, "Rätsel des Alltags. Wie Schröder ist der Kanzler? Wie Bild ist die Zeitung?", *Süddeutsche Zeitung*, July 22, 2004. www.sueddeutsche.de/kultur/2.220/raetsel-des-alltags-wie-schroeder-ist-der-kanzler-wie-bild-ist-die-zeitung-1.415589 [Accessed February 28, 2016].
3 Lutz et al. (2010); Kerner (2009); Klinger, Knapp, and Sauer (2007); Walgenbach et al. (2007); Knapp (2005). For the Anglosaxon context, see Hardy-Fanta (2006); McCall (2005); Crenshaw (1991); Stepan (1990).
4 Die Gemeinschaft der Eigenen, "Flugschrift für Sittenverbesserung u. Lebenskunst," [Advertisement] *Der Eigene. Ein Buch für Kunst und männliche Kultur* 6 (1906), n.p. [Appendix].

5 Bruns (2005); Keilson-Lauritz (1997); Hewitt (1996); Oosterhuis (1983).
6 See the controversy between the racial hygienist Ernst Rüdin and Friedlaender: Rüdin (1904a, 1904b); Friedlaender (1904b).
7 Blüher was both a member and the controversial chronicler of the *Wandervogel* movement in Berlin. Later, he was in contact with the *Herrenklub* of the conservative revolution around Heinrich von Gleichen. See Bruns (2004); Hergemöller (2000); Plashues (1999–2001); Breuer (2001, 256–258).
8 The academic literature discusses Freud's attitude toward male homosexuality controversially. Manfred Herzer, for example, comes to the conclusion, that Freud, after a phase of indifference, pathologized male homosexuality (Herzer 2001, 161). In contrast, Henry Abelove stresses Freud's liberal position toward homosexuality (Abelove 1993). Following Freud's oedipal status of homosexuality, analysts theorized a gendered split between identification and desire (Domenici and Lesser 2016). However, the gender bias within Freud's analysis of male homosexuality is barely mentioned. For a differentiated analysis of Freud's position toward female homosexuality, see Lesser and Schoenberg (2013).
9 In the 1920s, as Blüher drifted to the radical right politically, his interest shifted from emancipation, sexology, and aesthetics to religion, and he focused not on the homo-social *Männerbund* but on the religious bond between the "Aryan Jesus" and his disciples. See Blüher (1921, 1924, 1930, 1931a, 1931b).

References

Abelove, Henry. 1993. "Freud, Male Homosexuality and the Americans." In *The Lesbian and Gay Studies Reader*, eds. Henry Abelove, Michèle Aina Barale and David M. Halperin, 381–396. London/New York: Routledge.

Blüher, Hans. 1912. *Die deutsche Wandervogelbewegung als erotisches Phänomen. Ein Beitrag zur Erkenntnis der sexuellen Inversion*, with a preface by Dr. Magnus Hirschfeld and an afterword by Hans Blüher. Berlin: Bernhard Weise Buchhandlung.

———. 1913a. "Studien über den perversen Charakter mit besonderer Berücksichtigung der Inversion." *Zentralblatt für Psychoanalyse und Psychotherapie* 4, 1–2: 10–27.

———. 1913b. *Die drei Grundformen der sexuellen Inversion (Homosexualität). Eine sexuologische Studie.* Leipzig: Max Spohr.

———. 1919. *Die Rolle der Erotik in der männlichen Gesellschaft*, vol. 2: *Eine Theorie der menschlichen Staatsbildung nach Wesen und Wert.* Jena: Diederichs.

———. 1920. *Werke und Tage.* Jena: Diederichs (expanded and revised version 1953).

———. 1921. *Die Aristie des Jesus von Nazareth. Philosophische Grundlegung der Lehre und der Erscheinung Christi.* Prien: Kampmann & Schnabel.

———. 1922. *Secessio judaica. Philosophische Grundlegung der historischen Sicht des Judentums und der antisemitischen Bewegung.* Berlin: Weisse Ritter.

———. 1924. *Die deutsche Renaissance. Von einem Deutschen.* Prien: Kampmann & Schnabel.

———. 1930. *Deutscher Katechismus des Christentums.* Küstrin: Carl Adler.

———. 1931a. *Der Standort des Christentums in der lebendigen Welt.* Hamburg/Berlin: Hanseatische Verlagsanstalt.

———. 1931b. *Die Erhebung Israels gegen die christlichen Güter.* Hamburg/Berlin: Hanseatische Verlagsanstalt.

Breuer, Stefan. 2001. *Ordnungen der Ungleichheit – die deutsche Rechte im Widerstreit ihrer Ideen, 1871–1945.* Darmstadt: Wiss. Buchgesellschaft.

Brunotte, Ulrike and Rainer Herrn eds. 2008. *Männlichkeiten und Moderne. Geschlecht in den Wissenskulturen um 1900.* Bielefeld: Transcript (Gender Codes 3).

Bruns, Claudia. 2011a. "Kontroversen zwischen Freud, Blüher und Hirschfeld. Zur Pathologisierung und Rassisierung des effeminierten Homosexuellen." In *Dämonen, Vamps und Hysterikerinnen. Geschlechter- und Rassenfigurationen in Wissen, Medien und Alltag um 1900*, eds. Ulrike Auga, Claudia Bruns, Dorothea Dornhof and Gabriele Jähnert, 161–184. Bielefeld: Transcript (Gender Codes 13).

———. 2011b. "Politics of Eros: The German 'Männerbund' – Discourse between Antifeminism and Anti-Semitism at the Beginning of the 20th Century." In *Masculinity, Senses, and Spirit in German, French and British Culture*, ed. Katherine Faull, 153–190. Lewisburg: Bucknell University Press.

Bruns, Claudia and Susanne zur Nieden. 2004. *Politik des Eros. Der Männerbund in Wissenschaft, Politik und Jugendkultur 1880–1934.* Köln u.a.: Böhlau.

———. 2005. "The Politics of Masculinity in the Homosexual Discourse (1880 to 1920)." *German History. The Journal of the German History Society. Special Issue: Sexuality in Modern German History* 23, 3: 306–320.

———. 2006. "'Und unsere germanische Art beruht bekanntlich zentnerschwer auf unserem Triebleben …' – Der arische Körper als Schauplatz von Deutungskämpfen bei Blüher, Heimsoth und Röhm." In *Verkörperung – Entkörperung. Körperbilder und Körperpraxen im Nationalsozialismus*, ed. Paula Diehl, 111–128. München: Fink.

Connell, R. [Raewyn] W. 1995. *Masculinities.* Cambridge: Polity.

Connell, R. [Raewyn] W. and James W. Messerschmitt. 2005. "Hegemonic Masculinity. Rethinking the Concept." *Gender & Society* 19, 6: 829–859.

Crenshaw, Kimberle W. 1991. "Mapping the Margins: Intersectionality, Identity Politics, and Violence against Women of Color." *Stanford Law Review* 43, 6: 1241–1299.

Domenici, Thomas and Ronnie C. Lesser eds. 2016. *Disorienting Sexuality. Psychoanalytic Reappraisals of Sexual Identities.* London/New York: Routledge.

Dose, Ralf. 2005. *Magnus Hirschfeld. Deutscher – Jude – Weltbürger.* Teetz: Hentrich & Hentrich 2005 (=Jüdische Miniaturen 15).

Dudink, Stefan, Karen Hagemann and John Tosh eds. 2004. *Masculinities in Politics and War. Gendering Modern History.* Manchester/New York: Manchester University Press.

Foucault, Michel. 1999. *In Verteidigung der Gesellschaft, Vorlesungen am Collège de France (1975–76).* Frankfurt am Main: Suhrkamp.

Freud, Sigmund. 1938. *The Basic Writings of Sigmund Freud.* Translated and edited by A. A. Brill. New York: Random House.

———. 2000a. "Drei Abhandlungen zur Sexualtheorie [1905]." In *Studienausgabe* vol. 5, eds. Alexander Mitscherlich, Angela Richards and James Strachey, 37–146. Frankfurt am Main: Fischer.

———. 2000b. "Eine Kindheitserinnerung des Leonardo da Vinci [1910]." In *Studienausgabe* vol. 10, eds. Alexander Mitscherlich, Angela Richards and James Strachey, 87–160. Frankfurt am Main: Fischer.

———. 2000c. "Totem und Tabu (Einige Übereinstimmungen im Seelenleben der Wilden und der Neurotiker) [1912/13]." In *Studienausgabe* vol. 9, eds. Alexander Mitscherlich, Angela Richards and James Strachey, 287–444. Frankfurt am Main: Fischer.

Friedlaender, Benedict. 1904a. *Die Renaissance des Eros Uranios.* Berlin: Renaissance.

———. 1904b. "Bemerkungen zu einem Artikel des Herrn Dr. Rüdin über die Rolle der Homosexuellen im Lebensprozeß der Rasse." *Archiv für Rassen- und Gesellschafts-Biologie* 1: 219–225.

Gerhard, Ute. 1990. *Unerhört. Eine Geschichte der deutschen Frauenbewegung.* Unter Mitarbeit von Ulla Wischermann. Hamburg: Rowohlt.

Geuter, Ulfried. 1994. *Homosexualität in der deutschen Jugendbewegung. Jungenfreundschaften und Sexualität im Diskurs von Jugendbewegung, Psychoanalyse und Jugendpsychologie am Beginn des 20. Jahrhunderts.* Frankfurt am Main: Suhrkamp.

Gilman, Sander.1991. *The Jew's Body.* New York: Routledge.

Hancock, Eleanor. 1998. "'Only the Real, the True, the Masculine Held Its Value.' Ernst Röhm, Masculinity and Homosexuality." *Journal of the History of Sexuality* 8, 4: 616–641.

Hardy-Fanta, Carol ed. 2006. *Intersectionality and Politics. Recent Research on Gender, Race, and Political Representation in the United States.* Binghamton: Haworth.

Hausen, Karin. 1977. "Die Polarisierung der 'Geschlechtscharaktere'. Eine Spiegelung der Dissoziation von Erwerbs- und Familienleben." In *Sozialgeschichte der Familie in der Neuzeit Europas*, ed. by Werner Conze, 363–393. Stuttgart: Klett Cotta.

Heilmann, Andreas. 2011. *Normalität auf Bewährung. Outings in der Politik und die Konstruktion homosexueller Männlichkeit.* Bielefeld: Transcript.

Hergemöller, Bernd-Ulrich. 2000. "Hans Blühers Männerwelten. Fragmente, Widersprüche, Perspektiven." *Invertito. Jahrbuch für die Geschichte der Homosexualitäten* 2: 58–84.

Herzer, Manfred. 2001. *Magnus Hirschfeld: Leben und Werk eines jüdischen, schwulen und sozialistischen Sexologen*, 2nd ed. Hamburg: MännerschwarmSkript-Verlag.

Hewitt, Andrew. 1996. *Political Inversions. Homosexuality, Fascism, and the Modernist Imaginary.* Stanford, CA: Stanford University Press.

Hödl, Klaus. 2007. "Performative Beiträge zum Diskurs über den 'effeminierten Juden.'" In *Feminisierung der Kultur? Krisen der Männlichkeit und weibliche Avantgarde*, eds. Annette Runte and Eva Werth, 137–156. Würzburg: Königshausen und Neumann.

Jellonnek, Burkhard. 1990. *Homosexuelle unter dem Hakenkreuz. Die Verfolgung von Homosexuellen im Dritten Reich.* Paderborn: Schöningh.

Keilson-Lauritz, Marita. 1997. *Die Geschichte der eigenen Geschichte. Literatur und Literaturkritik in den Anfängen der Schwulenbewegung am Beispiel des Jahrbuchs für sexuelle Zwischenstufen und der Zeitschrift "Der Eigene".* Berlin: Rosa Winkel (Homosexualität und Literatur 11).

Kerner, Ina. 2009. *Differenzen und Macht. Zur Anatomie von Rassismus und Sexismus.* Frankfurt am Main: Campus.

Klinger, Cornelia, Gudrun-Axeli Knapp and Birgit Sauer eds. 2007. *Achsen der Ungleichheit. Zum Verhältnis von Klasse, Geschlecht und Ethnizität.* Frankfurt am Main/New York: Campus.

Knapp, Gudrun-Axeli. 2005. "'Intersectionality' – ein neues Paradigma feministischer Theorie? Zur transatlantischen Reise von 'Race, Class, Gender.'" *Feministische Studien* 23, 1: 68–81.

Lesser Ronnie C. and Erica Schoenberg eds. 2013. *That Obscure Subject of Desire: Freud's Female Homosexual Revisited.* London/New York: Routledge.

Lutz, Helma, Maria Teresa Herrera Vivar and Linda Supik. eds. 2010. *Fokus Intersektionalität. Bewegungen und Verortungen eines vielschichtigen Konzeptes.* Wiesbaden: Springer VS.

Machtan, Lothar. 2001. *Hitlers Geheimnis. Das Doppelleben eines Diktators*. Berlin: Alexander Fest.
———. 2002. *The Hidden Hitler*. New York: Basic Books.
Mayer, Eduard. 1903. "Männliche Kultur. Ein Stück Zukunftsmusik." *Der Eigene. Ein Blatt für männliche Kultur, Kunst und Literatur*, 46–59.
McCall, Leslie. 2005. "The Complexity of Intersectionality." *Signs. Journal of Women in Culture and Society* 30, 3: 1771–1800.
Mehlmann, Sabine. 1998. "Das vergeschlechtlichte Individuum – Thesen zur historischen Genese des Konzepts von männlicher Geschlechtsidentität." In *Das Geschlecht der Moderne. Genealogie und Archäologie der Geschlechterdifferenz*, ed. Hannelore Bublitz, 95–118. Frankfurt am Main/New York: Campus.
Müller, Klaus. 1991.*"Aber in meinem Herzen sprach eine Stimme so laut." Homosexuelle Autobiographien und medizinische Pathographien im neunzehnten Jahrhundert*. Berlin: Rosa Winkel (Homosexualität und Literatur 4).
Neubauer, John. 1996. "Sigmund Freud und Hans Blüher in bisher unveröffentlichten Briefen." *Psyche. Zeitschrift für Psychoanalyse und ihre Anwendungen* 50, 2: 123–148.
Oosterhuis, Harry. 1983. "Homosocial Resistance to Hirschfeld's Homosexual Putsch. The Gemeinschaft der Eigenen 1899–1914." In *Among Men, Among Women. Sociological and Historical Recognition of Homosocial Arrangements*, ed. Mattias Duyves, 305–321. Amsterdam: Universität Amsterdam.
———. 2000. *Krafft-Ebing, Psychiatry and the Making of Sexual Identity*. Chicago, IL: Chicago University Press.
Planert, Ute. 1998. *Antifeminismus im Kaiserreich. Diskurs, soziale Formation und politische Mentalität*. Göttingen: Vandenhoeck & Ruprecht (Kritische Studien zur Geschichtswissenschaft 124).
———. 2000. "Der dreifache Körper des Volkes. Sexualität, Biopolitik und die Wissenschaften vom Leben." *Geschichte und Gesellschaft* 26, 4: 539–576.
Plant, Richard. 1986. *The Pink Triangle: The Nazi War Against Homosexuals*. New York: Henry Holt and Company.
Plashues, Jürgen. 1999–2001. "Hans Blüher – Ein Leben zwischen Schwarz und Weiß." *Jahrbuch des Archivs der Deutschen Jugendbewegung* 19: 146–185.
Puar, Jasbir K. 2007. *Terrorist Assemblages. Homonationalism in Queer Times*. Durham, NC: Duke University Press.
Puschner, Uwe. 2001. *Die völkische Bewegung im Wilhelminischen Kaiserreich. Sprache, Rasse, Religion*. Darmstadt: Wissenschaftliche Buchgesellschaft.
Riggs, Damien W. 2006. *Priscilla (White) Queen of the Desert: Queer Rights/Race Privilege*. New York: Peter Lang.
Rohde, Achim. 2005. "Der innere Orient. Orientalismus, Antisemitismus und Geschlecht." *Die Welt des Islams* 45, 3: 370–411.
Rüdin, Ernst. 1904a. "Zur Rolle der Homosexuellen im Lebensprozess der Rasse." *Archiv für Rassen- und Gesellschaftsbiologie* 1: 99–109.
———. 1904b. "Erwiderung auf vorstehenden Artikel Benedict Friedlaenders." *Archiv für Rassen- und Gesellschaftsbiologie* 1: 226–228.
Schmersahl, Katrin. 1998. *Medizin und Geschlecht. Zur Konstruktion der Kategorie Geschlecht im medizinischen Diskurs des 19. Jahrhunderts*. Opladen: Leske u. Budrich (Sozialwissenschaftliche Studien 36).
Schmidt, Georg. 1968. "Nein, nein! Das ist nicht unser Wandervogel!" In *Wandervogelführerzeitung* 3 (February 1913), reprinted in *Die Wandervogelzeit. Quellenschriften zur deutschen Jugendbewegung 1896–1919*. Quellenschriften,

ed. Werner Kindt, 247–248. Düsseldorf: Diederichs (Dokumentation der Jugendbewegung 2).

Sigusch, Volkmar. 2008. *Die Geschichte der Sexualwissenschaft.* Frankfurt am Main/ New York: Campus.

Somerville, Sibhan B. 2000. *Queering the Color Line. Race and the Invention of Homosexuality in American Culture.* Durham, NC/London: Duke University Press.

Stepan, Nancy Leys. 1990. "Race and Gender. The Role of Analogy in Science." In *Anatomy of Racism,* ed. David Theo Goldberg, 38–57. Minneapolis, MN/London: University of Minnesota Press.

Walgenbach, Katharina, Gabriele Dietze, Lann Hornscheidt and Kerstin Palm eds. 2007. *Gender als interdependente Kategorie. Neue Perspektiven auf Intersektionalität, Diversität und Heterogenität.* Opladen/Farmington Hills: Verlag Barbara Budrich.

Weingart, Peter, Jürgen Kroll and Kurt Bayertz. 1996. *Rasse, Blut und Gene. Geschichte der Eugenik und Rassenhygiene in Deutschland,* 2nd ed. Frankfurt am Main: Suhrkamp.

Widdig, Bernd. 1992. *Männerbünde und Massen. Zur Krise männlicher Identität in der Literatur der Moderne.* Opladen: Westdeutscher Verlag.

Wolff, Charlotte. 1986. *Magnus Hirschfeld. A Portrait of a Pioneer in Sexology.* London/New York: Quartet Books.

Zinn, Alexander. 1997. *Die soziale Konstruktion des homosexuellen Nationalsozialisten. Zu Genese und Etablierung eines Stereotyps.* Frankfurt am Main/New York: P. Lang.

zur Nieden, Susanne. 2004. "Die 'männerheldische heroische Freundesliebe' bleibt 'dem Judengeiste fremd.' Antisemitismus und Maskulinismus." In *Der Sexualreformer Magnus Hirschfeld (1868–1935). Ein Leben im Spannungsfeld von Wissenschaft, Politik und Geschichte,* eds. Elke Vera Kotowsky and Julius H. Schoeps, 329–342. Berlin: be.bra wissenschaft.

———ed. 2005a. *Homosexualität und Staatsräson. Männlichkeit, Homophobie und Politik in Deutschland 1900 bis 1945.* Frankfurt am Main/New York: Campus (Geschichte und Geschlechter 46).

———. 2005b. "Homophobie und Staatsräson." In *Homosexualität und Staatsräson. Männlichkeit, Homophobie und Politik in Deutschland 1900 bis 1945,* ed. Susanne zur Nieden, 17–51. Frankfurt am Main/New York: Campus (Geschichte und Geschlechter 46).

Part II
Middle East/North Africa

6 "An oriental vice"

Representations of sodomy in early Zionist discourse

Ofri Ilany

Much has been written about the emancipation and public acceptance of LGBT in contemporary Israel. This chapter investigates the formation of the Zionist discourse on homosexuality, and demonstrates how discourses on sexual alterity are prone to change along with historical, political, or socioeconomic circumstances (Thoreson 2014). Reading descriptions of sodomy and homosexuality in the Hebrew press of the British Mandate era (1920–1948), I argue that these accounts describe homosexuality and sodomy as an "oriental" vice and equate "homosexual perversion" with a transgression of the Zionist project and the Jewish nation.

Treatment of homosexuality in early-Zionist history has been scant, especially since relevant source material is spare and spread across a wide range of genres and media (Nordheimer Nur 2014). Writing the history of homosexuals in Mandatory Palestine is a fundamentally more complicated task than writing the history of other groups such as workers, the bourgeoisie or women, for two main reasons: first, though "homosexual" was an extant term in the medical and jurisprudential literature of the period, a significant part of the men and women engaged in homosexual practices did not identify as adhering to that group, either for ignorance of the term or for not identifying with it. Others in fact expressed reservations or feelings of shame vis-à-vis this very label.

Second, homosexual forms of interaction and organizing were by their very nature loose and hidden, leaving no real documentation. Associations, clubs and homosexual meeting sites were not documented by Zionist and other producers of knowledge and transmitters of memory. Based on extensive archival research by the author, well into the 1960s almost all descriptions of homosexuality in the Hebrew press and literature were negative and distorted. In the absolute majority of the texts discussed below, which deal with reports of "sodomy," the people engaged in the act are never quoted, appearing only as criminals or perverts.

The study is based primarily on a few dozen, previously unstudied, press articles which were published during the 1920s, 1930s and 1940s, which deal with indictments on sodomy charges, and with other cases of homosexuality. Most of them were published in the daily *Davar*, the official publication of the mainstream Zionist-Socialist Histadrut workers' union and the most popular newspaper in the Jewish settlement in Palestine (to which I will refer hereafter by its Hebrew name, the *Yishuv*). Alongside, I will examine a few texts on homosexuality published in the weekly *Iton Meyuchad* (literally, "special newspaper"). Founded in 1933, it was a right-leaning tabloid (or "boulevard paper," to use contemporary parlance). While limited in its audience, it closely covered the sensational criminal scandals of the day which were sometimes overlooked by *Davar*. Additionally, I will discuss other texts dealing with intimate relations between men, usually in pedagogical or hygienic contexts.

Based on these sources, I will focus here on the way sex between men is represented prior to the establishment of the state of Israel, attempting to understand how homosexual practices were perceived and what significances they were accorded: in this respect, the chapter deals more with the history of homophobia than the history of gay people. However propagandistic these texts surely are, they nonetheless supply rich information on the homosexual existence during the British Mandate. They uncover meeting places for men seeking contact with other men, relations between men of different groups and the actions of British law enforcement agencies regarding sodomy and cases of violence perpetrated against people of "abnormal" sexuality. Intimate relations between women were not considered illegal, and were not mentioned in the publications of the period. Therefore the chapter does not deal with lesbian relations.

Israeli LGBT historiography tends to describe the emergence of homosexuality as a social and juridical phenomenon representing the liberalization of Israeli society, the rise of a consciousness to civil liberties and Israel's opening up to the cultural influence of the United States and Europe. In this narrative, the period preceding the 1975 foundation of the Society for the Protection of Personal Rights (today's Israeli Gay, Lesbian, Bisexual and Transgender Association) is perceived as a kind of "prehistory" marked by a general denial of the existence of lesbians, gays and questions of sexual identity and orientation (Sumaka'i Fink 1999; Kama 2000). The one and only exception is Yehudah Sofer's (1992) interesting essay based on interviews he conducted in the early 1970s with men he'd met at public gardens in Israel. He offers rare evidence about intensive sexual relations between Jewish-Israelis and Palestinians (both Israeli residents and those living in the territories) after 1967. Furthermore he claims that most Israeli men during this period who have sex with other men do not consider themselves to be homosexuals.

The sources I survey here point to substantial discussion on homosexuality as a social, pedagogical and criminal question dating as far back as the 1930s. Indeed the fact that there were men having sexual relations with other men in the *Yishuv* was known and discussed in dozens of articles and publications. As I show in this chapter, during Zionism's first decades, sodomy was actually considered a form of "backwardness" linked to living among Arabs in the Middle East – and nothing like the "Western lifestyle" it has been described as since the 1980s (Walzer 2000). With the foundation of "out," "proud" gay and lesbian identity in the last three decades, the memory of earlier discourses on homosexuality and queerness has been effaced; but these narratives and imageries continued to reverberate through different social and cultural manifestations. Uncovering them may help elucidate the development of Zionist LGBT politics.

Previous research into sexual and gender dimensions in Zionist discourse characterized the movement's project of creating a "new Jewish man" as a transformative move meant to salvage the body of the exilic Jew from its passive, effeminate state: Sander Gilman (1991) demonstrated the prevalence of notions regarding Jews' "queerness" in both anti-Semitic and modern Jewish discourses; Daniel Boyarin (1997) has described the Zionist identification between Jewish exile and homosexuality as reproducing fin-de-siècle anti-Semitic conceptions (Mosse 1993; Tobin 2011). If we operate on the hypothesis that the main working category on gender during Zionism's first decades was the dichotomy old (feminine) Jew/new (masculine) Jew, it is easily understandable why the appearance of male homosexual behavior within the settler community of Palestine was interpreted as symptomatically persistent exilic characteristics, of a local "failure" in the rehabilitation of the Jewish body.

Ascribing an "oriental character" to Jews and depicting diasporic Jewish men as effeminate and leaning toward homosexuality have been components of nineteenth-century European antisemitism (Rohde 2005, 2014). When we survey explicit references to homosexuality and sodomy as they appeared in the popular Zionist media discourse fashioned in Palestine itself, we find that these concepts are usually presented in a different light: not as a lingering pathology of exilic existence, but as a threat embodied in European Jews' physical presence within the backward "orient," their bodies exposed to the dangerous temptations of an alien space. The Zionist discourse on non-normative sexuality is revealed as one with colonial traits and as having been fashioned within the context of settling the "orient" and of the national struggle with the land's inhabitants.

Sodomy as an oriental disease

"Why Did Schwartz Kill Mustafa?" asks the headline of the weekly *Iton Meyuchad* of August 21, 1938. Several days prior, police officer Mordechai Schwartz had been hanged for killing his tent-mate for unknown reasons. The subhead adds that "[h]e preferred death than carry the burden of shame" (Iton Meyuchad 1938).

A Hungarian-born Zionist youth, Schwartz had immigrated to Palestine in 1933, joining the British Mandate Police in 1937. He was stationed in the British High Commissioner's summer residence in Atlit, where he shared a tent with Officer Mustafa Khouri, a Palestinian policeman. On September 2, 1937, after several days of joint service, Schwartz shot and killed Khouri as he slept. He was arrested, convicted and eventually hanged in an Acre prison by the British authorities on August 16, 1938.

110   *Ofri Ilany*

The leaders of the *Yishuv* and different Zionist organizations protested Schwartz's sentencing, though the motive for his crime remained unclear. Some claimed it was motivated by revenge for the killings of Jews by Arabs, others argued that Schwartz carried out the murder in a haze. The waters were further muddied after the defendant sent a letter to major Zionist-Labor daily *Davar* from prison shortly before his execution, claiming he was "opposed to terror and bloodshed" and adding that he apologizes for betraying the values he'd been taught, stating the case was "a private mistake in a moment when I was seized by madness" (Davar 1938).

The Schwartz story was covered by most Hebrew papers, but *Iton Meyuchad* picked it up with special zeal. While *Davar* was satisfied with publishing Schwartz's prison letter, *Iton Meyuchad* did not shy away from covering the murder's motive as based on Schwartz's confession – which he made, according to the paper, an hour prior to his execution, in the presence of a Rabbi and a police officer.

The paper's writer wonders what reason could have "made Schwartz's young life intolerable," especially taking into consideration the fact that he was about to retire from the force and marry his fiancée. To clarify the issue, the writer references another case of a young Jewish officer who'd committed suicide several years prior. This second officer's name is not mentioned in the article, but it is stated that he ended his own life "because the Arab officer in charge of him raped and buggered him." The writer goes on to explain:

> It would seem that he couldn't bear the memory of the humiliation and outrage he was subjected to, and his disappointment that such an act can take place while he serves the police force of the land destined to be his people's national home ... Therefore he chose to commit his own body, wantonly subjected to abominable abuse, to the ground.
>
> (Iton Meyuchad 1938)

The writer goes on to expand on the prevalence of sodomy offences in Palestine, stating that crime statistics prove that "Arabs are prevalently predisposed to this abominable crime." The paper states that Schwartz felt intense shame for the circumstances surrounding his crime and vehemently opposed the defense mentioning sodomy in its case, "even threatening to commit suicide if what happened to him in that tent becomes public knowledge." The writer goes on to blame the British authorities, under whose watch innocent Jewish police officer Schwartz was exposed to the sexual obscenities practiced by the land's indigenous inhabitants:

> But from a Jewish policeman, who because of the equality enforced here on the sons of Europe and the sons of the Desert, became not merely witness but even the victim of such abuse, we cannot demand this sacrifice. And if after that suicide they had forgotten their lesson and sent officer Mordechai Schwartz to sleep every night in the tent with officer

Mustafa Khouri, against whom we have heard there were complaints of "sodomitic acts" during his service – the inevitable outcome was not hard to guess.

(Iton Meyuchad 1938)

While more mainstream papers (like *Davar*) shied away from dealing with the case's exact motives, this embarrassing and mysterious murder scandal brought *Iton Meyuchad* to bluntly formulate implicit Zionist conceptions regarding the link between sexuality, ethnicity and national struggle. According to its coverage, it was the mixed existence of "the sons of Europe" and "the sons of the Desert," foisted on the Jews with British might, which brought about the abominable abuse of a Jewish youth's pure body (Iton Meyuchad 1938). And in fact this understanding appears in less unique cases, that is, in its running reporting on sodomy cases.

British law against "unnatural offences" prohibited having "carnal knowledge of any person against the order of nature" and also convicted any person who "permits a male person to have carnal knowledge of him or her against the order of nature"; accordingly, many news items covering sodomy further on did not address the sex's consensuality (Han & O'Mahoney 2014, 272). Thus, for instance, in February 1937, *Davar* mentioned that "young Mr. Zivoni was sentenced to 18 months incarceration for sodomy" (Davar 1937a); in October of that year it reported that "Moshe Molcho attacked two teenagers on the beach," and was "sentenced to six months hard labor" (Davar 1937b); and in October 1939 we read that "Shlomo Molcho of Turkey was brought before Justice Rosenzweig for three grave accusations: sodomizing children, resisting officers during interrogation and attempted suicide" (Davar 1939).

Sometimes several cases were reported on in aggregate, suggesting a wave of arrests, for instance in a piece dated August 1931, reporting that "a 15-year-old Jaffa youth was sentenced yesterday to 12 lashes for sodomizing a child – for the same abomination a Yemenite was arrested on Sunday in Tel Aviv, and yesterday – a newspaper-selling adolescent" (Davar 1931). It should be noted that the law was enforced not only on those who preyed on children and youths, but also against those who "recklessly gave themselves in sodomy," as in a case of August 1941:

> A shocking case proving just how far our neglected youth has fallen was revealed yesterday in Magistrate Court Justice Azoulai's docket. A youth of about 13 was accused of recklessly giving himself in sodomy and contracting a disease. The justice sentenced him to incarceration in a young offenders' school for two years under the supervision of a doctor.
> (Davar 1941)

It is very apparent that in the great majority of sodomy reports, the perpetrators belong to groups which, from the viewpoint of the Ashkenazi-Zionist mainstream, lived on the margins of Yishuv society: more than half of the cases involve Arabs; others involve Turkish, Yemenite and neglected youths unaffiliated with any organized educational frameworks (Davar 1936). Cases of sodomy between Kibbutz members or members of the Histadrut Workers' Union – groups identified with the Zionist Labor Movement and with *Davar* itself – are rarely reported on.

Clearly the description of sodomy as endemic to the Orient was not invented by the Hebrew press: this perception of sodomy as a phenomenon linked to the Orient is known from European Orientalist discourse since the mid-eighteenth century. Sex between men was described as an expression of oriental men's excessive and unbridled sexuality. As Robert Aldrich notes in *Colonialism and Homosexuality* (2003, 63), an "outbreak" of sodomy was considered one of the dangers awaiting Europeans in the colonies, especially if they are surrounded by locals, subjected to hard conditions and/or are predisposed to "psychic degeneration." Given the above mentioned trope of diasporic Jewish men's effeminate oriental character in European antisemitism, a degree of overlap becomes visible between European colonialism and antisemitism. Early Zionist discourse mirrored both these currents and transformed them into a discourse legitimizing Zionist policy of non-interaction with Arab society.

Similar conceptions of "oriental sexuality" were also expressed in ethnographic, criminological and medical texts published in Hebrew in the 1930s, 1940s and 1950s. *The Enemies of Youth*, a book about sexually transmitted diseases, for instance, dwells on "homosexual prostitution" and "sexual relations among men," stating that "in the lands of the Orient this is common practice" (Seidman 1950, 127). Orientalist Yossef Waschitz (1947, 229) reported on "homosexual tendencies" in Samarian cities, foremost among them Nablus, while Dr. Tuvia Ashkenazi, considered a pioneer of Zionist Bedouin scholarship, wrote that "sexual awakening begins with the Bedouins at a younger age. Early lust spurs them to unnatural relations" (Ashkenazi 1957, 73).

German-born pedagogue and criminologist Carl Frankenstein of the Hebrew University dealt with the issue of homosexuality in greater depth. He also discussed Arab sexuality in his book *Youth Neglect* of 1947, identifying, like Waschitz, a sodomitic tendency in Nablus, where, he claims, "homosexual offences are fairly commonplace" (Frankenstein 1947, 140). But while the homosexuality of Arabs is mentioned casually as a known facet of "oriental" sexuality, "sexual offences" among Jewish youth require special explanation. Frankenstein links the phenomenon to environmental and genetic sources: neglect, on the one hand, and "a neurotic element" on the other. He goes on to claim, moreover, that the two elements are more prevalent with youths of an "oriental" background:

> Without dwelling on the problem, heretofore not sufficiently investigated, of the climate's effect on the sexual constitution, we can say with surety that sexual offences are more prevalent with oriental youths, in particular

neglected ones, than with European youths. There is no doubt that we must take account of the more intensive lasciviousness of oriental youths if we wish to ascertain the meaning of the heterosexual and homosexual acts that manifest in them.

(Frankenstein 1947, 140)

It is clearly apparent, then, that sodomy was identified by experts of different disciplines as an Arab-"oriental" phenomenon. While the British authorities prosecuted perpetrators of sodomy, apparently mostly with children and adolescents, the journalistic description uses the threat of sodomy as propaganda against socializing with Arabs and for ethnic separation.

Levantinization and degeneration

When it appears in the Jewish population, sodomy is described as symptomatic of the larger social danger of assimilating into the Orient or of turning into Arabs. The *Yishuv*'s leadership feared Jewish over-assimilation or "levantinization:" the adoption of "oriental" or Mediterranean characteristics. In this understanding – characteristic of colonial contexts – "contraction" of sodomy by Jews, and particularly by European Zionists, is described as an especially severe symptom of ideological laxity and the "harming effect" of the Arab environment.

Sodomy "outbreaks" are described as taking place in those "Levantine" spaces where the two communities comingle and assimilate – coffee houses, the beach and bath houses – but never in the organized framework of the Histadrut and the *Yishuv*. This characterization of the meeting-points between Jewish society and the Arab surroundings signifies sodomy as a national-political threat. Thus right-wing Revisionist leader Abba Ahimeir could describe the Jaffa neighborhood of Manshiyyah and the threat it poses to neighboring Tel Aviv:

> The Hebrew City has always been a source of attraction because of its lights and its bustle, day and night. Manshiyyah was a murderers' den and supplied much material to the private "underworld" as well as to the Mufti's underworld. It was hard to make distinctions about the Manashi *shabab* [youth] and draw a clear distinction between sodomite and pan-Arab patriot. At any rate the neighborhood was never characterized by any oriental romanticism of any kind. Even though its residents were Muslim, they weren't traditionally oriental but rather Levantine, in the worst sense of that term.
>
> (Ahimeir 1968, 1937)

During the first three decades of Zionist settlement, Jews and Arabs sustained fairly tight daily ties – for instance in coffee houses and hookah lounges in Jaffa and the Jewish settlements (Lev Tov 2009). But the leadership of the

Yishuv tirelessly worked to sever these ties and stem "Levantinization," namely normalization and assimilation into Arab culture, which would undermine Zionism's self-perception as a European national movement and as an extension of European civilization in the Orient (Azaryahu 2007, 61).

One of the most elaborate accounts of homosexual life in Mandatory Tel Aviv appears in an *Iton Meyuchad* article published January 1934 under the headline "In the Tel Aviv Underworld." The article aggregates juicy reports of German-born "cocainists" and "morphinists" lurking in Tel Aviv coffee houses, Rothschild Boulevard brothels and Jaffa hashish dens. Into all of this, the anonymous writer also weaves a description of "clubs for homosexualists" [מיטסילאוסקסומוהל םיבולק] set up in town, where he claims "'masculine' men meet 'feminine' men to have orgies." He describes dancing at the club, which he claims is "lascivious, sexually arousing to the dancers and disgusting to the onlooker," going on to explain the origins and prevalence of homosexuality:

> In the orient these types are more prevalent, and it is a well-known fact one does not have to search them out in our land. It suffices to take a little stroll down Jaffa's alleyways and its coffee houses. He whose eyes are open will notice these fancy boys making love publicly for all to see. And the couples are not satisfied with just Jaffa. They want good times, and therefore they go to Tel Aviv, in which city, or its periphery to be exact, they find residents of this sick inclination. And thus spontaneously a kind of [...] meeting club is set up, and right in the center of town, in one of its better-known coffee houses. There, in the depths of the shadows of a side room, these people congregate and party.
>
> (Iton Meyuchad 1934)

Iton Meyuchad's reports were never known for their credibility, as they often served semi-pornographic local scandals and imaginary fables (for instance, that non-Jewish German diplomat Franz von Papen was actually a Belz Hassid, that is, a member of a Hasidic community named after its place of origin in Ukraine, or that Tarzan's daughter was captured in the Judean Mountains). Therefore it is hard to ascertain if the club's description is believable or just the writer's fantasy. However, it affords a good view on how the sources and reasons of homosexuality were understood at the time. As opposed to other decadent phenomena – such as the abuse of cocaine and morphine, which the author links to German "bohemian types" – homosexual "types" are characterized in the account as an influence of Arab Jaffa on the Hebrew city of Tel Aviv. The "sick inclination" grows, according to this description, on the periphery of Hebrew society, where it is hidden from the center's view and open to foreign influence: "the alleyways of Jaffa," "in the depths of the shadows," in the "periphery" of the Hebrew city.

In fact as part of its scandal-seeking nature, *Iton Meyuhad* showed special interest in the homosexual subject. Another copy, July 1940, devotes an entire piece to "Homosexuals in Tel Aviv" (Iton Meyuhad 1940), made up mostly of "scientific clarification" in the form of a lengthy interview with sexologist Dr. Avraham Matmon. A native of Odessa, Matmon was one of a handful of sexologists then operating a clinic in Tel Aviv, and therefore was identified with the practice more than any other expert then working in the *Yishuv* (Kozma 2010). He was medically trained in Germany and apprenticed shortly after under Magnus Hirschfeld, the leading figure in the struggle for homosexual rights before World War II, at his *Institut für Sexualwissenschaft*. Perhaps under Hirschfeld's influence, he chose to call his clinic, located on Hashachar Street, *The Institute for Hygiene and Sexual Sciences*. He frequently gave lectures there, accompanied by a magic lantern, on "the hygiene of sexual intercourse."

Despite the article's shortness, Matmon manages to present a highly elaborated and scholarly theory of homosexuality in the Orient, predicated on several observations. First and foremost, he differentiates "pure homosexuality," which he defines as a "constitutional perversion of the sexual glands' natural way" appearing in "the intellectual echelons" as a function of "spiritual degeneration," and "buggery," prevalent mainly in the lower classes and especially in the orient:

> In the Orient this affliction, but especially buggery, is very prevalent. Instances of pure homosexuality are rare, in my opinion, in the Orient. Most cases are those of corruption and buggery-lasciviousness, especially in youths. In the cities of the far east (Indo-china, China and India), as well as in Egypt, you can see men sitting in the public space with their "boys," just as in Western lands you can see men sitting with their "girls."
> (Iton Meyuchad 1940)

Clearly Matmon's experience and the knowledge he'd gathered in Germany crystallized into a complex, if not totally coherent, understanding of the homosexual "type." Among the writers thus far cited, he is the only one to identify homosexuality with the European intellectual class. This description is likely a function of his acquaintance with Hirschfeld's Berlin circle. However Matmon was not promoting the *Institut für Sexualwissenschaft*'s tolerant, forward-leaning ideology but rather expressing distaste for homosexuals. Furthermore, he claims that the expanding phenomenon of buggery in Palestine is on the whole unconnected to the European "pure homosexuality" but to an occasional corruption taking place between "orientals:"

> Until several years ago this problem was not totally prevalent with Jews. I have seen anecdotal cases with Ashkenzis, but they were the sons of completely degenerative families (families of psychopaths) and were mainly cases of pure homosexualism. Most cases involved mentally infirm youths, the sons of drunkards, syphilis-stricken families and the like. In recent years the number of homosexuals here has grown, and most men afflicted, albeit educated, are spiritually and psychically degenerative

in the full sense of the word. I think that among the cases presenting here only a small fraction are pure homosexuals, and most are distinctly corrupt.

(Iton Meyuchad 1940)

Matmon's etiology in effect differentiates between two sources of the homosexual affliction. One is a hereditary degeneration presenting in certain Jewish families. It seems this characterization is highly influenced by the theory of "exilic degeneration" – an anti-Semitic trope first adopted by Max Nordau, which he went on to further in Zionist discourse, most notable in his influential *Muskeljudentum* (Nordau 1892, 1909).

In Zionist Sexologist circles, the distinct proponent of the "Jewish effeminacy" theory was Max Marcuse – one of the leading figures of Hirschfeld's Berlin sexual reform movement, who had immigrated to Palestine after the Nazis' rise to power (Kozma 2010, 235–237). In an essay he published in *Davar* in January 1938 regarding the sexual problems of first-grade students, he stresses the importance of maintaining "actual biological and biophysiological sex difference," stating that "many of adults' sexual neuroses and psychosexual deficiencies are grounded in alienation from or lack of a special sexual character, male or female" (Marcuse 1938). He claims this is of special importance for Jews:

> I believe this viewpoint merits special attention and appreciation here in *Eretz Yisrael*, as no few symptoms seem to suggest that we Jews tend to sexual Applanation, which could spread. We yet know not if this tendency to physical, and more importantly psychic, similarity of male and female sexual character is a racial manifestation or a pathological social phenomenon. At any rate [...] it is essential that we treat boys as boys, and girls as girls.
>
> (Marcuse 1938)

It is notable that such ideas were propagated mainly by German sexologists and psychologists who had immigrated to Palestine in the 1930s. They were heavily influenced by the racialized sexological theories then prevalent in the German-speaking world, which held this conception regarding the Jews' alleged androgynous sexuality. It remained within the confines of this rather small intellectual circle (Kozma 2010, 237).

In point of fact, even Matmon himself was not a proponent of this conception: he stresses the fact that homosexuality was not prevalent among the Jews. Furthermore, he implicitly ties the Jews' arrival in Palestine and the proliferation of cases of homosexuality among them. According to Matmon, it was indeed exposure to the Orient – and not the exile – that was the main corrupting influence on Jews' psyches and bodies. The centrality of this understanding is borne out by an idea prevalent well into the 1970s, according to which homosexuality did not exist traditionally in Jewish communities

(Livneh 1971). Generally speaking, Zionist writers saw the influence of the Orient as the only conceivable reason and justification for the appearance of "sodomy" among Jews.

Epilogue: how Jewish gays became white

In dominant Zionist discourse of the Mandate era, same sex practices between men were construed as more than a simple perversion: they were posited as a political danger, as the embodiment of all negative aspects inherent in a life under foreign rule, lacking political sovereignty. The struggle against buggery was part of the *Yishuv* leadership's intense effort to uphold a separation between Jews and Arabs and overcome several forms of mixing and assimilation that were happening along the margins of Yishuv society. Cases of sodomy were brought as warnings against the dire effects that assimilation to the Arabs may have, and sodomites were seen as extreme cases of political apostasy.

In the first years following the establishment of the state of Israel, the state's police continued arresting citizens for sodomy. A large number of such arrests was reported in 1949. On September 5, 1949, *Yediot Ahronoth* (1949a) reported on a "tidal wave of indecent acts" in different places around Tel Aviv. Police officers had broken into a public toilet on Gruzenberg Street overnight, finding "a 33-year-old resident of King George V Street sodomizing a 16-year-old." Simultaneously, police arrested four youths in different Tel Aviv public parks "who could not prove to the police [...] their reason for loitering in the park so late at night." Several weeks afterwards, the paper reported that several youths broke into an apartment on Mapu Street, disturbed the peace and turned the owner over to the police, claiming he'd invited several young men over and tried to sodomize them (*Yediot Ahronoth* 1949b).

In the following years, the number of arrests for suspected sodomy (and reports thereof) decreased significantly. With Haim Cohen's ascension to the role of Attorney General, he instructed police and the Attorney General's Office not to prosecute this offense unless acts were perpetrated in a public place or on a minor (Yonai 1998). It seems even the journalistic atmosphere changed, becoming less puritanical – apparently out of a desire to portray an ideal image of the young State society.

Additionally, interactions with Arabs in the urban centers apparently became less prevalent after 1948 – and those that did happen seemed less threatening after the establishment of the state, which ultimately closed the lid on what was perceived as a doomsday scenario of the mixed existence of Jews and Arabs under one political arrangement. However, the conception of homosexuality as a national threat survived in part into the following decades, for instance in the common argument, mobilized mainly by the Israeli Defense Forces, that homosexuals pose a security threat. Until 1993, the IDF questioned recruits to field and intelligence units for their sexual predisposition, and homosexuals were excluded from these units (Kaplan & Ben Ari 2000).

During the following decades, the context within which homosexuality was discussed in Israeli public life changed. The echoes of changing attitudes toward homosexuality in Britain and other Western countries made their way to Israel. In the 1970s, 1980s and 1990s homosexuality enjoyed a gradual and growing legitimacy, which was now described in terms of Israel's "integration into the West." Thus homosexuality, previously represented as an "oriental vice," began being identified with the influence of a liberalizing West – both by the LGBT community's spokespeople and by its detractors. Homosexuality was "whitened" and Americanized. In fact the word "gay" (which is used in Hebrew as a calque) does not connote those secretly meeting with Arabs in hooka-smoke-filled coffee houses, but rather with a cosmopolitan, middle-class man into fashion and design.

The new representation of this gay man gradually took up a specific function within secular Israel's current discursive regime, where legitimation of homosexuality is lauded as the prime demonstration of Israel's role as a frontier outpost of enlightened Western modernity in a dark, backward Middle East (Puar 2011). Israel is practicing "Pinkwashing," namely utilizing its relative "gay-friendliness" as an example of its commitment to Western democratic ideals, in order to redirect focus away from critiques of its repressive actions in the occupied territories. Thus, by the same token that the suppression of buggery was meant to signify that "we are not Levantines," tolerance of gays today is used as proof that "we are not Iran" – but in fact belong to the West, carrying the banner of Progress. In this way both the persecution of sodomites during the Mandate, and the "gay friendly" atmosphere of the liberal circles of our time, in fact serve the exact same project: that of distinction and separation from the Orient, justification for an ever-deepening regime of ethnic separation.

Actually, the only part of the formula that has changed is the treatment of homosexuality in Europe and the United States: while 60 years ago it was oppressed and forbidden (as "oriental"), today it has been assimilated into "the Western lifestyle." In the Israeli context, the essential condition for the legitimation of the label of homosexuality was its cleansing of an earlier affiliation to Arab-ness. No wonder, then, that romantic and sexual relationships between Arab and Jewish men are frowned upon by both discourse regimes: the old, hostile one – and the new, "liberal" one. It seems that Israeli society is still suspicious toward the transgressive potential of homosexual existence – and that wariness is well internalized by many homosexuals themselves, who are repeatedly demanded to prove that they are "different homosexuals" or "new gays."

References

Ahimeir, A. 1968. The Trial [*Hamishpat*]. In: *Selected Writing* [*Ktavim Nivharim*]. Tel Aviv: Ahimeir Publication Society.
Aldrich, R. 2003. *Colonialism and Homosexuality*. New York: Routledge.
Ashkenazi, T. 1957. *The Bedouins – Their Origins, Lives and Customs* [*Habedouim – motza'am, khayeihem uminhageihem*]. Jerusalem: Re'uven Mass.

Azaryahu, M. 2007. *Tel Aviv: Mythography of a City*. Syracuse, NY: Syracuse University Press.
Boyarin, D. 1997. *Unheroic Conduct: The Rise of Heterosexuality and the Invention of Jewish Man*. Berkeley, CA: University of California Press.
Davar. 1931. "Tel Aviv." *Davar*, August 11.
———. 1936. "Among the Neglected Children." *Davar*, July 21.
———. 1937a. "In the Courts." *Davar*, February 18.
———. 1937b. "Tel Aviv." *Davar*, October 16.
———. 1938. "A Letter to Davar from Schwartz before His Death." *Davar*, August 24.
———. 1939. "Tel Aviv." *Davar*, October 27.
———. 1941. "Jerusalem." *Davar*, August 6.
Frankenstein, C. 1947. *Youth Neglect: What is It, How it Came About and its Signs* [*Azuvat Hano'ar: Mahuta, hithavuta usimaneiha*]. Jerusalem: Szald Children and Youth Institute.
Gilman, S. 1991. *The Jew's Body*. London: Routledge.
Han, E. and O'Mahoney, J. 2014. "British Colonialism and the Criminalization of Homosexuality." *Cambridge Review of International Affairs* 24, 2: 268–288.
Iton Meyuchad. 1934. "In the Tel Aviv Underworld." *Iton Meyuchad*, January 31.
———. 1938. "Why Did Schwartz Kill Mustafa." *Iton Meyuchad*, August 21.
———. 1940. "Homosexuals in Tel Aviv." *Iton Meyuchad*, July 5.
Kama, A. 2000. "From Terra Incognita to Terra Firma: The Logbook of the Voyage of Gay Men's Community into the Israeli Public Sphere." *Journal of Homosexuality* 38, 4: 133–162.
Kaplan, D. and Ben Ari, E. 2000. "Brothers and Others in Arms Managing Gay Identity in Combat Units of the Israeli Army." *Journal of Contemporary Ethnography* 29, 4: 396–432.
Kozma, L. 2010. "Sexology in the *Yishuv*: The Rise and Decline of Sexual Consultation in Tel Aviv, 1930–39." *International Journal of Middle East Studies* 42, 2: 231–249.
Lev Tov, B. 2009. *Leisure and Popular Cultural Patterns of Eretz Israeli Jews in the Years 1882–1914 as a Reflection of Social Changes*. Ph.D. dissertation, Tel Aviv University.
Livneh, E. 1971. "Israel or Sodom? Public Allowance of Sexual Perversions – A Grave Matter [*Israel o sdom? Hatarah pumbit shel perversiot miniyot – inyan hamur*]." *Ha'aretz*, July 7.
Marcuse, M. 1938. "Sexual Problems in the First Grade [*Be'ayot sexualiot bishnat halimudim harishona*]." *Davar*, January 21.
Mosse, G. 1993. *Confronting the Nation: Jewish and Western Nationalism*. Lebanon, NH: Brandeis University Press.
Nordau, M. 1892. *Entartung*. Berlin: Duncker.
———. 1909. "Muskeljudentum." *Zionistische Schriften*, 379–381.
Nordheimer Nur, O. 2014. *Eros and Tragedy: Jewish Male Fantasies and the Masculine Revolution of Zionism*. Brighton, MA: Academic Studies Press.
Puar, J. 2011. "Citation and Censorship: The Politics of Talking About the Sexual Politics of Israel." *Feminist Legal Studies* 19, 2: 133–142.
Rohde, A. 2005. "Der innere Orient. Orientalismus, Antisemitismus und Geschlecht im Deutschland des 18. bis 20. Jahrhunderts." *Die Welt des Islams* 45, 3: 370–411.
———. 2014. "Asians in Europe. Reading German-Jewish History through a Post-Colonial Lens." In *Orientalism, Gender, and the Jews. Literary and Artistic Transformations of European National Discourses*, eds. U. Brunotte, A. Ludewig and A. Stähler, 17–32. Oldenburg: de Gruyter.

Seidman, M. 1950. *Enemies of Youth [Oyvey hano'ar]*. Tel Aviv: M. Neuman.
Sofer, J. 1992. "Testimonies from the Holy Land: Israeli and Palestinian Men Talk about Their Sexual Encounters." In *Sexuality and Erotism Among Males in Moslem Societies*, eds. A. Schmitt and J. Sofer, 105–120. Binghamton: Harrington Park Press.
Sumaka'i Fink, A. 1999. *Independence Park: The Lives of Gay Men in Israel*. Stanford, CA: Stanford University Press.
Thoreson, R. R. 2014. "Troubling the Waters of a 'Wave of Homophobia': Political Economies of Anti-Queer Animus in Sub-Saharan Africa." *Sexualities* 17, 1–2: 23–42.
Tobin, R. 2011. "Twins! Homosexuality and Masculinity in Nineteenth-Century Germany." In *Masculinity, Senses, Spirit*, ed. K. M. Faull, 131–152. Lewisburg: Bucknell University Press.
Walzer, L. 2000. *Between Sodom and Eden: A Gay Journey Through Today's Changing Israel*. New York: Columbia University Press.
Waschitz, Y. 1947. *The Arabs in Eretz Yisrael [Ha'aravim be'eretz yisra'el]*. Merhavia: Sifriyat Poalim/Lakol.
Yediot Ahronoth. 1949a. "Many Indecent Acts Were Performed in Tel Aviv Tonight." *Yediot Ahronoth*, September 5.
———. 1949b. "Youngsters Take Revenge on a Sodomy Perpetrator." *Yediot Ahronoth*, September 26.
Yonai, Y. 1998. "The Law Regarding Homosexuality – Between History and Sociology [Hebrew]." *Mishpat u-Mimshal* 4, 2: 531–586.

7 Arabic literary narratives on homosexuality

Jolanda Guardi

This chapter examines three contemporary Arabic literary texts, published in Egypt and Lebanon between 1983 and 2005, that present either female or male homosexual characters. The three works delineate the parameters of Arab literary discourse on homosexuality over the last few decades. Specifically, I discuss Alīfa Rifʿat's short story "My World of the Unknown" (1983), Musʿad Basta's novel *The Ostrich Egg* (1994), and Hodà Barakāt's novel *The Stone of Laughter* (2005). All are in print and available in the Arab world, and I refer to the Arabic editions (Barakāt 2005; Musʿad 2000) except for Alīfa Rifʿat's short story, which has only been published in Denys Johnson Davis's English translation.[1] Only *The Stone of Laughter* has been the subject of in-depth scholarly work (e.g. Winckler 2014); Rifʿat's work has been the subject of some academic articles while nothing has been published on Musʿad Basta's novel. In this chapter, I study the treatment of homosexuality in these literary narratives, an aspect of them that has either not yet been investigated or to which previous works, in my opinion, only allude without analyzing it in depth.[2]

I aim to show on the basis of analyses of these literary texts how a body that does not conform itself to the heteropatriarchal norm can function as a subversive political body in a system that defines gender and gender relations strictly. The works that I shall present exemplify the evolving treatment of homosexual characters in contemporary Arabic literature. In her book *Epistemology of the Closet*, Kosofsky Sedgwick (1990, 33–80) deconstructs through her analysis of literary texts the idea of a society based on binary oppositions. As she claims, this society is the result of codified socio-sexual models within a heterosexual matrix. Following the recipe of Kosofsky Sedgwick's critique, I shall reveal the binary constructions present in the three texts I have chosen in order to determine if they are manifestations of a malestream discourse that reproduces patriarchal heteronormative models. Overcoming binarism in the analysis of literary works helps us, first, to deconstruct the category of gender when discussing cultural specificity and to describe the dialectic between economic and political states and symbolic constructions of gender. Second, it underlines the effectiveness of literary analysis as a tool for sociological research because it can reveal certain discourses that are passed on through literature that mirror the relationships among "language, social institution, and power" (Weedon 1997, 45; 1987). Third, addressing social and cultural issues more generally while doing literary analysis can help overcome the social sciences' neglect of Arabic literature (Said 1978, 291).

Gender is an important dimension of any society's images of the self and others, images that are permeated by and reproduce existing power structures but which also may become sites that serve to subvert those structures. Against this background, I shall show that there is a new LGTBQ genre in contemporary Arabic literature and address the question of whether this genre moves from the margins to the core of the literary canon and modifies it. Joseph Massad (2007, 270) maintains, "Every Arabic novel, short story, or play (indeed every novel, short story, or play) is steeped in questions of desire." In contemporary Middle Eastern and North African countries, literary representations of desire and, more specifically, homosexuality are often perceived as allegories of ruling powers' brutality, class differences, or power differences among Arab countries. Activist scholars of such works stress the significance of homosexuality in Arabic literature (Habib 2007; Amer 2008a, 2008b), but in my contribution to this area of scholarship, I suggest that this kind of literary production may constitute a change in the Arabic literary canon. This hypothesis will need to be tested in more broadly based future research.

I believe that this reassessment is necessary because to "alienate conclusively, *definitionally*, from anyone on any theoretical ground the authority to describe and name their own sexual desire is a terribly consequential seizure" (Kosofsky Sedgwick 1990, 26), and this seizure was the first step toward homophobic oppression and violence in Western countries from the nineteenth century onwards. Applying literary analysis in a conceptual framework broadened by the contributions of Kofosky Sedgwick, Said, and Massad "will be most useful for our analysis in ways that laws, police reports, official histories, school textbooks, private letters, scholarly publications – the usual archive of the social and intellectual historian – are not" (Massad 2007, 271). What matters is being conscious of the "hermeneutical circle" and staying in it only

> when interpretation has understood that its first, constant, and last task is not to let fore-having, fore-sight, and fore-conception be given to it by chance ideas and popular conceptions, but to guarantee the scientific theme by developing these in terms of the things themselves.
>
> (Heidegger 1996, 143)

In this case, the hermeneutical circle allows the analysis of single text units or sections by inserting them into a broader context and, thus, situating the section or text in the narrative production frame of the author's work. As Deleuze and Guattari (1983, 50) remind us, the disjunction between heterosexuality and homosexuality (and other forms of sexuality) should bring to light their reciprocal inclusion and their transverse communication in the "decoded flow of desire."

Female homosexuality in "My World of the Unknown"

The existing scholarship on homosexuality in Arabic literature usually approaches the topic either in a philological-descriptive way, which locates texts and discourses in an "aseptic" environment (Allen, Kilpatrick, and De Moor 2001; Wright-Rowson 1997) or in a way that, although highly informative, is no more than a detailed description (Al-Samman 2008) that does not consider the relation between the homosexual character and the author's literary strategies. Literary text analysis has often denied the salience of patriarchal heteronormativity and often bound its criticism to a binary way of producing and receiving knowledge in what Massad (2007, 171) calls the "epistemological complicity of the critics."

In Alīfa Rifʿat's[3] "My World of the Unknown" (Rifaat 1983, 61–77), the protagonist, who is in search of a new house following her husband's change of job, is fascinated by an abandoned villa on the river which no one wants to rent because "there are all sorts of rumors about it – the people around here believe in ğinn and spirits" (Rifaat 1983, 64).[4] As she approaches the house, a woman named Anīsa tries physically to prevent her from entering. The husband calls the police, who arrest the woman upon their arrival. She does not resist but tells the protagonist, "'I leave her to you.' 'Who?' – I cried. 'Who Anīsa?'" Pointing […] at the foundation of the house, she answers, "Her" (Rifaat 1983, 67).

This episode is a prelude to the appearance of a snake, described as colorful and attractive, in the villa's garden. When the protagonist sees the snake on a tree branch, she is enchanted by it. At this moment, she falls into depression and no longer wants to see other people, preferring to stay in bed all day long. The cause of this change is clear to her: "Could it be that I was in love? But how could I love a snake? Or could she really be one of the daughters of the monarch of the ğinn?" (Rifaat 1983, 70). She wonders how she could possibly have a romantic relationship and sexual intercourse with what the translator explicitly presents as a female snake (and thereby implies that the author deliberately declined the Arabic word for "snake" in the feminine in the original Arabic text):

> There was no doubt but that the secret of my passion for *her*, my preoccupation with *her*, was due to the excitement that had aroused, through intense fear, desire within myself; an excitement that was sufficiently strong to drive the blood not only through my veins whenever the memory of her came to me, thrusting the blood in bursts that made my heart beat wildly, my limbs limp. And so, throwing myself down in a pleasurable state of torpor, my craving for *her* would be awakened and I would

wish for *her* coil-like touch, *her* graceful gliding motion. And yet I fell to wondering how union could come about, how craving be quenched, the delights of the body be realized, between a woman and a snake. And did *she*, I wondered, love me and want me as I love *her*?

(Rifaat 1983, 71)

We do not know the protagonist's name, but as a married woman she conforms to the patriarchal order. We know that she is in the middle or upper class (for her husband has been named the director of a firm). Written in the first person, the text presents the story of the protagonist and her feelings about what will be a homosexual experience. In fact, when the carnal contact with the female snake finally happens:

I began to be intoxicated by the soft musical whispering. I felt her cool and soft and smooth, her coldness producing a painful convulsion in my body and hurting me to the point of terror. I felt her as she slipped between the covers, then her two tiny fangs, like two pearls, began to caress my body; arriving at my thighs, the golden tongue, like an arak twig, inserted its pronged tip between them and began sipping and exhaling; sipping the poisons of my desire and exhaling the nectar of my ecstasy, till my whole body tingled and started to shake in sharp, painful, rapturous spasm – and all the while the tenderest of words were whispered to me as I confided to her all my longing.

(Rifaat 1983, 73)

The interaction with the snake, who takes on human features later in the story, develops into a romantic relationship sealed by a pact: the protagonist will never harm the snakes of the house because the she-ǧinn is their custodian. Rifʿat set the story of love and sex between a she-ǧinn and a human in the world of mythology, the *abqarī* world in which, following Muslim tradition, *ǧinn* – male and female – live. The non-normative relation can develop only in this world of fantasy, where it does not discard the patriarchal order. The protagonist's husband underlines this aspect: "One morning, he kills a black, ugly snake, almost two meters long" (Rifaat 1983, 76), which had entered the bedroom. Thereby, he breaks the pact between the woman and the she-ǧinn, and their relationship ends, to the woman's great despair. The family is forced to move from the house, and the story ends with the protagonist hoping to rekindle the relationship with the female snake in the future. Her return to reality is painful.

Scholars have offered different readings of this text. Some interpret it as a quest to give women a voice (Ahmed 1989, 41–55; Ogbeide 2012, 1–11; Ogbeide 2013, 27–32; Quawas 2014, 54–66). Nwachukwu-Abgada (1990, 109) reads the story as about female submission in accordance with Arab Muslim tradition. Olive (1996, 44–49) contends that it represents the protagonist's own female identity. Li (1999) offers a psychoanalytic reading of the snake, arguing that she symbolizes the subconscious of the protagonist, who is not satisfied with her marriage but cannot express her feelings. But these critics all engage in "notable omissions" (Mitra 2010, 313), as they do not consider the fact that the snake is female, morphs into a woman, and has sex with the protagonist. As for Gordon (2004, 77), Rifʿat's voice is revolutionary because her narratives "exist in spaces where Islam, and all its traditional weights, rest alongside female sexuality, pleasure, and pain – merging into a strong fundamental female identity." A careful reading of "My World of the Unknown" can take her point further, for on my understanding it is clearly the story of a same-sex relationship between two female characters.

One can read the snake as a feminine symbol and, in particular, as a symbol of the clitoris and female sexuality perceived as free and beautiful. The narrative includes descriptions that support this reading. The snake is a feminine symbol in different cultures, including ancient Egypt, where one finds the cobra goddess Wəḏjt (Erman & Grapow 1971, 269). She protects Lower Egypt but is *in harmony* with her goddess counterpart Nekhbet (who also symbolizes the feminine), who protects Upper Egypt. Wəḏjt is often depicted with some of Nekhbet's symbols (Hart 2005, 161). I argue that in presenting the relationship between the woman and the snake, Rifʿat recalls the cobra goddess of Egyptian mythology as a symbol of completeness. The protagonist, though enthralled by the snake, gives voice to her doubts, as she is not yet able to accept a homoerotic relationship: "But it is natural for you to be a man, I said in a precipitate outburst, seeing that you are so determined to have a love affair with me" (Rifaat 1983, 75). But the snake dissipates her doubts: "Perfect beauty is to be found only in woman, she said, so yield to me and I shall let you taste undreamed of happiness; I shall guide you to worlds possessed of such beauty as you have never imagined" (Rifaat 1983, 75).

This, I claim, is the reason why the husband kills the snake; he considers the homoerotic relationship dangerous to himself because it does not conform to the patriarchal order and a binary vision of gender.

Another interesting aspect of the story is the emotional nuances in the relationship between the protagonist and the *ğinn*-snake-woman. Contrary to other literary works that include lesbian relationships (Guardi 2014a), this encounter is not a reaction to an unsatisfactory marriage nor to the boredom of bourgeois middle-class life but, rather, leads to true love, as the text more than once underscores. In their relationship, the woman finds fulfillment, and both complement one another, just as the two Egyptian goddesses do.

At the request of Denys Johnson-Davies, a well-known translator of Arabic, Rifʿat (1983) published the short story, in 1983, in English. He maintains that he translated it from Arabic, although the original text has never been published. The collection in which the story was published contains 15 short stories centered on the lack of interest in sexual intercourse between husband and wife. In "Badriyya's Husband" (Rifaat 1983, 29–38), the protagonist, Badriyya, discovers that her husband is homosexual. Everybody knows of his orientation except for his wife, who becomes aware of it through a neighbor. Badriyya's feelings are badly hurt when she learns of her husband's homosexual relationships, but Rif'at does not depict homosexuality, in and of itself, negatively. On the contrary, when the husband returns home from a meeting with his secret male lover, he entertains his ill stepmother. As a result, she changes her opinion of her stepson. Rif'at thus also acknowledges the agency of his female characters, as the stepmother changes her opinion against society's pressure. But she does not fully overcome the woman/man binarism.[5]

Male homosexuality in Ra'ūf Mus'ad's *The Ostrich Egg*

The Egyptian (born in Sudan) Ra'ūf Mus'ad's novel *Baiḍat an-na'āma* (*The Ostrich Egg*) (1994)[6] presents a shift in perspective similar to the one present in "My World of the Unknown." Mus'ad has treated homosexuality more than once in his several novels.[7] Like Rif'at's, his work hasn't received the attention of Western scholars. The protagonist of *Baiḍat an-na'āma*, which the author explicitly states is autobiographical (Mus'ad 2000, 7), permeates the story with his narrations of the homoerotic relationships that he has observed since his childhood. The encounters that he has witnessed, which are thoroughly physical, though not necessarily sexual, are never stigmatized. The author's interest is one's discovery of one's own body (Maltagliati 2008, 114), and the experiences that the narrator describes are not violent, contrary to what is stated, for example, in the preface to the novel's Italian translation (Mus'ad Basta 1998, 14).

Mus'ad analyzes homosexual relations against the background of his experiences in prison, where he was sent for political reasons. The subject surfaces in *Baiḍat an-na'āma* when the author/narrator meets his friend, the writer Sonallah Ibrahim, and tells him of his intention to write a book "about the idea of body for its different possible goals" (Mus'ad 2000, 98).[8] In prison, he explains, one is deprived of everything in order to destroy one's sense of identity, which the "jail subculture" has already subdued (Brunetti-Sapia 2007, 108). Prisoners adapt to their environment by going through the "jailing" process (Clemmer 1941, 442). And only the body, Mus'ad adds, is left:

> The political prisoner attempts – and I underline "political prisoner" – to use his own body to preserve his offended humanity, to affirm his will to love and to be loved, to give something to someone else, while in jail the free will principle is totally denied, and this offers him [the prisoner] a very personal opportunity to express the will to protect his own person and his soul through the body.
>
> (Mus'ad 2000, 99)

In Mus'ad's novel, then, there is no condemnation or instrumentalization of the homosexual relationship, although the author distinguishes, more than once, the homosexual relationships among political detainees, which Mus'ad presents as the result of a conscious choice to express one's desire for love, from sexual intercourse between criminals (e.g. Mus'ad 2000, 203). Nevertheless, the novel discusses the possibility of re-discovering one's body in a place where it is impossible to express one's feelings in words. This re-discovery is more than intercourse merely to satisfy sexual urges:

> Meaningless things become important, care for the other's everyday life grows, as a common oasis in the middle of that sand sea. A gradual revelation begins, and it begins with the body: fingers touch, hands, one cares for the other's body. If they are lucky, they don't get discovered by curious eyes, on the contrary, they can be so lucky to live in the same cell, they can approach their mats and then sleep one near the other so that in the end one of them makes the step that had been so long postponed.
>
> It's a mistake to think this is the same relationship as between two common criminals. No comparison is possible. Body is not "action" rather "outfit," not "secretion" rather "revelation" not "active" or "passive" rather "one and one" mutually to help each other survive detention.
>
> When they are out, each one returns to his previous life, or he goes towards a new one, to the family, to his wife or to marry and procreate. If they occasionally meet, they speak about the present and the future. They both know, instinctively, that that body's revelation happened under very curious conditions, and that would they try to recreate it these conditions would not be the same.
>
> There is only one such relationship, as far as I know, that goes on until now, safe and solid, but it is ... the exception confirming the rule.
>
> (Mus'ad 2000, 203–204)

Nevertheless, prison is a protected space in relation to the outside, where it is possible to build relationships that one has no desire to remember once freed. Thus, the protagonist recounts his meeting with a former fellow inmate named Nasr, with whom he had a chance relationship outside of prison:

> [In prison] relationships were, for the most part, due to a lack of privacy, to the impossibility of being alone, of being apart ... Nasr told me he "loved" a mate who had been transferred to al-Fayyum jail. He spoke of his mate's love in a normal way, with no problems or feeling a lack of "virility". He said that he felt like that for the first time. ... [W]e did not talk about jail nor about the past.
>
> (Mus'ad 2000, 93–94)

In *The Ostrich Egg*, the homosexual relationship is a love relationship, though a restricted one, as it can be lived only in prison, that is, in a confined space whose exceptional circumstances allow everything. Under the normal conditions of everyday life on the outside, one does not speak about these relationships. One can only allude to them melancholically, knowing that one experienced something important which, however, was possible only in a specific moment of one's life. Thus, the "intellectual" homosexual behaves like an ostrich. He experiences same-sex love but later distances himself physically and mentally from the experience, just as the ostrich moves far away from where it buries its egg in order to prevent predators from discovering it.

Musʿad's discourse on homosexuality occurs against the background of Nasser's Egypt, when he was imprisoned for his Marxist affiliations. For political prisoners, sexual practices deviating from the heteropatriarchal norm were a political stand and a form of resistance to the Egyptian nationalism of the 1960s and 1970s, which propagated an ideal of heroic, heterosexual masculinity. Rejecting this norm opened a fissure in the hetero-patriarchal canon. But, in order for homosexuality to constitute a subversive agency, it is necessary, according to Musʿad, clearly to distinguish this kind of relationship, strongly affective and satisfying a deeply felt emotional need, from homosexual practices merely aimed at satisfying physical needs, which Musʿad describes as widespread among common criminals. Thus, the non-normative body becomes a revolutionary body that contributes to the critique of power without, however, completely distancing itself from the heterosexual norm that it re-affirms once free (Guardi & Vanzan 2012, 70–72).

In the passage quoted above, Musʿad mentions his friend Sonallah Ibrāhīm, whom he knew in prison and who is well known for his opposition to Nasser's regime. In a conversation (in the novel), the character Ibrāhīm warns the narrator not to write a book about the use of the body in prison because it might be censored and the secret police might use it to criticize democrats who were already subject to persecution and arrest (Musʿad 2000, 89). In his own novel *The Committee*, Ibrahim (2001; Arabic version 1981) also uses homosexuality but in a very different way. The protagonist is called by an unidentified committee that is investigating him in depth to verify his loyalty to the regime, and his supposed homosexuality is the subject of the committee's strong dispraise.

Rifʿat's and Musʿad's works constitute an alternative reading of the prevailing canon in contemporary Arabic literature although neither fully overcomes the heteropatriarchal norm. In their work, the homosexual relationship, usually dispraised, becomes a symbol of completeness, in Rifʿat, and an expression of affection and revolutionary power, in Musʿad. Nonetheless, both works lie on the margins of the literary field. Yet, they still affect the mainstream literary canon because Rifʿat sets her lesbian relationship in the world of myth, and Musʿad marks a difference between the homosexual relationships of "intellectuals" and those of "criminals."

Beyond homosexuality: Hodà Barakāt's *Stone of Laughter*

The Lebanese writer Hodà Barakāt (1990) takes a different approach in *Ḥāǧar aḍ-ḍaḥk* (*The Stone of Laughter*).[9] In my opinion, Barakāt proposes

Arabic literary narratives on homosexuality 129

that self-identifying as either male or female causes one to lose part of one's self. The novel is set during the Lebanese Civil War. There are different strategies to survive war; but in *Ḥāǧar aḍ-ḍaḥk* survival is far removed from both sexual binarism and the prison of a fixed gender.

In *Ḥāǧar aḍ-ḍaḥk*, one is free to choose one's gender or androgynously combine masculine and feminine characteristics and impulses (Heilbrun 1964). To choose to be androgynous is to refuse to have a fixed gender identity in a society in which such identities have important sexual and religious implications and in which men are warriors and women are confined to the private sphere. Androgyny, then, is an adequate instrument for avoiding a sexualized death culture because it allows one to overcome the barrier between masculine and feminine.

In Barakāt's (1990) novel, the human body possesses a potentially revolutionary power. Ḥalīl, the hero, who is male by birth, increasingly identifies as female as the story unfolds. He does not accept his society's ideal of masculinity:

> Ḥalīl's companions could really be divided into two groups. The first group, which looks like him, is made up of youths a lot younger than he, who have broken down the door of conventional masculinity and entered manhood by the wide door of history. Day by day they busy themselves shaping the destiny of an area of patent importance on the world map, concerned with people's public and private lives, even with water, with bread, with dreams, with emigration. The second group, which does not look like him, is made up of men of his own age who have got a grip on the important things in life, and who, holding the tools of understanding, awareness, and close attention to theory have laid down plans to fasten their hold on the upper echelons ... in politics, in leadership, in the press ...
>
> But the doors of both kinds of manhood were closed to Ḥalīl and so he remained, alone in his narrow passing place, in a stagnant, feminine state of submission to a purely vegetable life, just within reach of two very attractive versions of masculinity, the force that makes the volcano of life explode.
>
> (Barakāt 2005, 17–18; Barakāt 2006, 12)[10]

As his feelings of alienation brought on by the civil war increase, emotions that he identifies with his feminine side grow stronger, which is hard for him to accept when he makes it explicit to himself:

> Ḥalīl knew that a fear of blood to the point of faintness, having short legs, a slight build, straight chestnut hair and large eyes, all these do not make a man a hermaphrodite, or effeminate, or make him any less masculine, or ... queer ... [H]e knew that the temporary breakdown that he was suffering was only a psychological crisis that the mad world

outside had imposed upon him ... [H]e knew that there were certainly more female hormones in him than there should naturally be, for they protected him from committing the crime of the act, so it was only a passing crisis, it would come to an end ... [H]e definitely desired women but, at this moment in time, he did not feel particularly susceptible to any particular woman.

(Barakāt 2005, 86; Barakāt 2006, 75)

His subsequent retreat into himself and the female hormones that he believes are dominant in his body symbolize his resistance to the military masculinity that finds its paramount manifestation in war and death (Accad 1990; Cooke 1996).

Barakāt's language in this section is poetic and gender-ambivalent as he describes a fluid moment when androgyny is positive. Ḫalīl has become much more feminine than masculine. Barakāt describes him here as a mother, a wife, and a sister. He spends much of his time cleaning, cooking, knitting, and passively waiting for events to take their course, all of which are typically considered to be feminine activities:

He used to take the little metal tray and sit next to the radio for hours, picking over lentils or rice for the soup he had at dawn, his only meal. Or, he would sit next to the radio unraveling old woolen sweaters then wrapping the crinkled threads around a thick book to smooth them out, in the hope that he might knit them up again as soon as he went shopping and bought the right needles. Women, who tame external time, in their wisdom know that knitting, stitch after stitch, row upon row, is what guarantees that the thread of the days is drawn out as grains of worry are drawn out from troubled souls.

(Barakāt 2005, 78; Barakāt 2006, 65)

Toward the end of the section, there is a rupture in the narrative, and in Ḫalīl's attitude toward his identity, as he meets his cousin Yūsuf. At the beginning of the novel, when Ḫalīl was still fluctuating between two universes, the feminine and the male, he enjoyed the attentions of his cousin Zahra, so much so that he almost persuaded himself that he could have a relationship with a woman. But:

All this paled into ridiculous nonsense the moment Ḫalīl saw Yūsuf. The moment he saw him. Yūsuf was younger than Zahra. He did not stay around the house much for he was passionately in love with the city, he used to go out to it all the time even if, most of the time, he did not get beyond the corner where Flippers was at the end of the street. Yūsuf, headless with his new experiences and busy with children of his own age, was breaking Ḫalīl's heart ... shattering it like thick, glass dishes flung to the ground... There was something in Ḫalīl's stomach dead set, as if

physically, against Yūsuf's seeing that thing – which, were the Prophet Yūsuf to see it, would make him drop dead.
(Barakāt 2005, 93; Barakāt 2006, 80–81)[11]

Halīl had previously expressed his resistance to war and death through his self-identification as female. But later in the story, he is more gender-ambivalent, alternately embracing feminine and masculine aspects of his personality, a dynamic that his romantic relationship with Yūsuf brings to the surface. Yūsuf does not share Halīl's gender uncertainty and volunteers for the militia. Halīl waits for him to return, "clutching the egg of my dreams like an old hen ... waiting until he knows, until he gets bored and comes back" (Barakāt 2005, 122; Barakāt 2006, 105).

Yūsuf dies, and Halīl completes a change that began when he saw Yūsuf laughing as he was leaving home to fight. In fact, Yūsuf began to laugh a lot when he joined the militia, and Halīl had loved seeing him "bursting"[12] into loud laughter. The meaning of the novel's title, *The Stone of Laughter*, is not made clear until the last page, when the narrator states, "You've changed so much since I described you in the first pages! You've come to know more than I do. Alchemy. The stone of laughter" (Barakāt 2005, 235; Barakāt 2006, 209). The narrator compares laughter to the philosopher's stone, which was believed to transform base metal into gold. Laughter here symbolizes strength and virility, and Halīl sees it as the magical expedient to help him demonstrate his strength and resolve his identity crisis.[13] The novel explicitly uses laughter as a symbol of violent masculinity:

> But the war that goes on in cities hates laughter ... detests laughter. The two explosions yesterday did not both happen in the street. In fact, there was more than one ... yesterday there were two, and the two exploded in two cinemas. One in the "Beirut" cinema in Mazra'a and the other in the "Hamra" cinema on Hamra Street. The cinemas were showing comic films. What a coincidence. No, it was no coincidence ... [W]ar is a serious matter. People die in the streets while there are those who go and pay money and give up their spare time to laugh. It is forbidden to laugh like that. It is forbidden for whichever group of friends to agree, in a particular place, to laugh. Laugh on your own, sob with laughter, burst with your companion. It is a solitary activity which relieves people only to recharge their batteries. But for laughter to become a social activity, that is against the law of a warring community. They want to laugh until they burst? Then let them burst!!!
> (Barakāt 2005, 125–126; Barakāt 2006, 108)

Thus, only members of the militia – males – may laugh in public. The philosopher's stone of laughter gradually makes Halīl an integrated person, a soldier who laughs in public. But the transformation also dehumanizes him. He is loving before the transformation, but his new self-identification as masculine entails a rejection of his femininity, and his survival now depends on his ability to hate. With this device, Barakāt incorporates a discourse on sexuality while discussing the Lebanese Civil War because "sexuality is centrally involved in motivations of war, and if women's issues were dealt with from the beginning, wars might be avoided, and revolutionary struggles and movements for liberation would take a very different path" (Accad 1990, 27).

Ironically, this transformation occurs precisely when Ḥalīl becomes the object of another man's love, a virile man who declares himself overtly to Halīl:

> I don't want you to get me wrong. To hell with money. Forget about it completely ... He took a sip from his glass. I was supposed to go abroad a month ago but you paralyzed me and I couldn't move.
> (Barakāt 2005, 216; Barakāt 2006, 190)

The experience of becoming the object of someone else's love induces Halīl to change his gender and identify himself as a man. He subsequently joins the militia, adopts its male chauvinist language, and even rapes a young woman. Paradoxically, as Barakāt puts it in the novel, "for you to love yourself means to hate others" (Barakāt 2005, 227; Barakāt 2006, 199). And, Ḥalīl can express hate against everybody, against nobody, and against himself. Hate becomes the expression of his new integrity, his authenticity, and even his freedom. As Julia Kristeva maintains, "But there, at the borders between himself and others, hatred does not threaten him. He lies in wait, reassured each time to discover that it never misses an appointment" (Kristeva 1991, 13). Subjugated to the love of a powerful man, Ḥalīl becomes a slave because of "the violence of his desire." Nonetheless:

> the slave who hates his master, even were he bound hand and foot to that master, is a free slave. A free slave because he hates, because he fences in his hatred day after day. Stronger. Stronger. Dug in as deep as it can go. Season after season ... [T]he slave who hates his master loves himself and is free. Freer than the master. Higher than his master and the master cannot reach him. The master's freedom is like a foul old maid.
> (Barakāt 2005, 230–231; Barakāt 2006, 202)

Barakāt's language changes at the end of the novel. Previously, the narrator and Halīl were not clearly distinguishable from one another, a fact testified to by Barakāt's use of the first person plural without a specific gender inflection. By the end of the novel, the narrator abruptly shifts to the first person singular, which signifies a departure:

> Ḥalīl's henchman opened the back door of the car.
> God be with you, sir, say the Bridegroom.

The henchman got in and turned over the engine.
I went up to the rear window … Ḥalīl had a mustache and a pair of sunglasses. Where are you going, I asked, and he did not hear me.
It's me, I told him, and he did not turn around.
The car moved off and, from the back window, Ḥalīl seemed broad-shouldered in his brown leather jacket …
The car moved off and began to draw away. Ḥalīl was leaving the street as if he were rising upwards.
(Barakāt 2005, 234–235; Barakāt 2006, 209)

When Ḥalīl abandons his androgyny for a definite sexual identity, the separation of hero from narrator is complete. As a result, the narrator, of whose sex/gender we have been unaware throughout the novel, now explicitly takes on the female gender and expresses her love for Ḥalīl at the moment he is killed: "Ḥalīl is gone, he has become a man who laughs. And I remain a woman who writes. 'Ḥalīl, my darling hero. My darling hero …'" (Barakāt 2005, 235: Barakāt 2006, 209).

In an interview (Whitaker 2004), Barakāt stated that she uses her writing to reflect upon her own gender ambiguity, suggesting a degree of identification with both the narrator and the protagonist: "Maybe to write is just when I can be both at the same time."

Queering the literary canon

In this study, I have moved from describing the homosexual relationship as a functional element in authors' literary strategies to interpreting the sexual act as a symbol to interrogating expressions of the protagonists' sexual and gender orientations. It is notable that the symbolic use of homosexual practices in literary works has never encountered censorship. The critics have ignored works that contain explicit discussions of gender ambiguity and homosexual relationships. However, the shift from a purely symbolic employment of homosexual practices to an enactment of articulated relationships has moved the subject to the center of the literary discourse, which, in turn, indicates changes in attitude toward homosexuality among the potential readers of such works in Arab countries.

The study of this shift requires an interdisciplinary approach that moves beyond the purely philological tradition. When authors write about non-normative sexual orientations, they subvert established discourses on Arab Muslim identity that are enshrined in official state discourse and propagated by religious authorities. The path toward a literary genre formed on the basis of what I have discussed in the present chapter, moreover, reveals the correlation between sexual repression and political oppression. By interrogating representations of homosexuality in Arabic literature, as in this chapter, scholars reveal oppressive structures portrayed in that literature and help rearticulate the literary discourse. As Butler (1993, 4) states:

the persistence of disidentification is equally crucial to the rearticulation of democratic contestation. Indeed, it may be precisely through practices which underscore disidentification with those regulatory norms by which sexual difference is materialized that both feminist and queer politics are mobilized. Such collective disidentifications can facilitate a reconceptualization of which bodies matter, and which bodies are yet to emerge as critical matters of concern.

As the literary works discussed in this chapter address crucial aspects of contemporary Arab societies, they delineate the shifting determinants of the perceivable and function as seismographs of social change in the region. Therefore, moving the discourse on homosexuality and non-normative gender from the margins to the center of the literary field, as well as Arabic studies, supports the agenda of queering the state. Although the anti-queer discourse dominates in Arab countries, this literature takes a step forward in the treatment of the subject, and, so, it contributes to opening a discussion on a taboo subject and to shaping an Arab intellectual consciousness. Therefore, the study of the homosexual character in Arabic literature should first go backward in order to trace the character's evolution as part of acknowledging its distinctive role in building the literary canon. As Lisa Duggan says, "The time has come to think about queering the state" (Duggan 1994, 1) and, I would add, the academy.

Notes

1 The short story is published in English translation as part of a collection because the author could not publish it in Arabic (Rifaat 1983, vii–viii). I could not find any reference to an Arabic edition. But, according to Massad (2007), its existence has lately become an object of speculation.
2 This chapter is part of a broader research project on the subject that I have pursued over the last few years. See Guardi (2014a, 2014b).
3 Alīfa Rifʿat (1930–1996) began to write when very young, but she published her work only much later because of the opposition of her family and her husband to what they considered unsuitable for a woman. She resumed writing only after her husband's death. Among her works are *Ḥawāʾ taʿūd lī-Ādam* (*Eve Returns to Adam*, 1975, short stories), *Man yakūn ar-raǧul* (*Who is the Man?* 1981, short stories), *Ṣalāt al-ḥubb* (*Love Prayer*, 1983, short stories), *Fī layl aš-šitāʾ aṭ-ṭawīl* (*A Night in the Long Winter*, 1985, short stories), and *Ǧawharat farʿūn* (*The Pharaoh's Jewel*, 1978, novel). For further information on her life, see Salti (1991).
4 *Ǧinn* are spirits who live in nature and influence human life in good and bad ways.
5 Al-Ali (1994, 39) correctly affirms that the narrators in "My World of the Unknown" and "Badriyya's Husband" are feminine and that both stories are told through women's experiences.
6 The novel has been translated into Italian, Spanish, French, Dutch, and Swedish. No English translation is available. In quoting, I refer to the following Arabic edition: Musʿad (2000).
7 See, for instance, his novel *Īṯākā* (Musʿad 2000) which tells of the Queen Boat affair of May 2001, when 52 men were arrested in a club on the river Nile on charges related to their alleged homosexuality. For a complete analysis, see Pratt (2007, 129–144). A complete bibliography is available on his site (Musʿad 2016).

8 All translations from Arabic are mine.
9 *Hağar aḍ-ḍaḥk* was published in 1990 by Riyāḍ ar-ra'īs, Lundun. I refer to the 2005 edition, published by Dār an-nahār, Bayrūt. The English quotations are taken from the English translation *The Stone of Laughter*, transl. by Sophie Bennet, Interlink Books, Northampton, 2006. I changed the translation where I found it necessary.
10 I changed "Khalil" in the English text to "Ḥalīl" in all of the quoted passages.
11 In the original Arabic text, Barakāt plays with the name Yūsuf (Joseph), naming the Prophet *Yūsuf al-qadīm* (Yūsuf the ancient) and Ḥalīl's cousin *Yūsuf al-lāhī* (Yūsuf the minor). There is no trace of this in the English translation; therefore I have changed it accordingly.
12 The Arabic uses the verb "infağara," which is also used for bombs. The parallel between laughing and bombs' bursting continues from here throughout the novel.
13 Author's conversation with Hodà Barakāt, May 5, 2010.

References

Accad, E. 1990. *Sexuality and War. Literary Masks of the Middle East*. New York and London: New York University Press.
Ahmed, L. 1989. "Arab Culture and Writing Women's Bodies." *Gender Issues* 9, 1: 41–55.
Al-Ali, N. S. 1994. *Gender Writing/Writing Gender. The Representation of Women in a Selection of Modern Egyptian Literature*. Cairo: The American University in Cairo Press.
Allen, R., Kilpatrick, H. and De Moor, E. eds. 2001. *Love and Sexuality in Modern Arabic Literature*. London: Saqi Books.
Al-Samman, H. 2008. "Out of the Closet: Representation of Homosexuals and Lesbians in Modern Arabic Literature." *Journal of Arabic Literature* 39, 2: 270–310.
Amer, S. 2008a. "Cross-Dressing and Female Same-Sex Marriage in Medieval French and Arabic Literature." In *Islamicate Sexualities. Translations across Temporal Geographies of Desire*, eds. K. Babayan and A. Najmabadi, 72–113. Cambridge, MA: Harvard University Press.
———. 2008b. *Crossing Borders. Love between Women in Medieval French and Arabic Literature*. Philadelphia, PA: University of Pennsylvania Press.
Barakāt, H. 1990. *Hağar aḍ-ḍaḥk*. Lundun: Riyāḍ ar-ra'īs.
———. 2005. *Hağar aḍ-ḍaḥk*. Bayrūt: Dār an-nahār.
———. 2006. *The Stone of Laughter*. Northampton: Interlink Books.
Brunetti, C. and Sapia, C. eds. 2007. *Pedagogia Penitenziaria*. Napoli: Edizioni Scientifiche Italiane.
Butler, J. 1993. *Bodies that Matter. On the Discursive Limit of "Sex."* London: Routledge.
Clemmer, D. 1941. "The Prison Community." *Social Forces* 19, 3: 442–443.
Cooke, M. 1996. *Women and the War Story*. Berkeley, CA, Los Angeles, CA, London: University of California Press.
Deleuze, G. and Guattari, F. 1983. *Anti-Oedipus: Schizophremia and Capitalism*. Minneapolis, MN: University of Minnesota Press.
Duggan, L. 1994. "Queering the State." *Social Text* 39(Summer): 1–14.
Erman, J. P. A. and Grapow, H. 1971. *Wörterbuch der ägyptischen Sprache im Auftrage der deutschen Akademie*. Berlin: Akademie-Verlag.

Gordon, N. 2004. "To Write What Cannot be Written: Female Circumcision in African and Middle Eastern Literature." *Changing English: Studies in Culture and Education* 11, 1: 73–87.

Guardi, J. 2014a. "Female Homosexuality in Contemporary Arabic Literature." *DEP Deportate Esuli Profughe* 25: 17–30.

———. 2014b. "The 'Urmann' is a Woman. A Re-Reading of Yūsuf Idrīs' Abū arriǧāl." *Kervan. International Journal of Afro-Asiatic Studies* 18: 47–58.

Guardi, J. and Vanzan, A. 2012. *Che genere di islam. Omosessuali, queer e transessuali tra shari'a e nuove interpretazioni.* Roma: ediesse.

Habib, S. 2007. *Female Homosexuality in the Middle East.* New York and London: Routledge.

Hart, G. 2005. *The Routledge Dictionary of Egyptian Gods and Goddesses.* London & New York: Routledge.

Heidegger, M. 1996. *Being and Time.* New York: SUNY Press.

Heilbrun, C. G. 1964. *Towards a Recognition of Androgyny.* New York and London: W.W. Norton & Company.

Ibrahim, S. 1981. *Al-Lagna.* Cairo: Matbu'at al-Qahirah, 1982.

———. 2001. *The Committee.* Syracuse, NY: Syracuse University Press.

Kosofsky Sedgwick, E. 1990. *Epistemology of the Closet.* Berkeley, CA: University of California Press.

Kristeva, J. 1991. *Strangers to Ourselves.* New York: Columbia University Press.

Li, L. 1999. "'My World of the Unknown': A Catharsis for the Sexual Awakening of an Egyptian Woman Writer." *Community Review* 17(September): 71–75.

Maltagliati, C. 2008. *Le rappresentazioni della sessualità nella letteratura araba.* MA Thesis. Università degli Studii di Milano.

Massad, J. A. 2007. *Desiring Arabs.* Chicago, IL: The University of Chicago Press.

Mitra, I. 2010. "There Is No Sin In Our Love: Homoerotic Desire in the Stories of Two Muslim Women Writers." *Tulsa Studies in Women's Literature* 29, 2: 311–329.

Musʿad, R. 1994. *Ostrich Egg.* London: Riad el-Rais Books.

———. 2000. *Baiḍat an-naʿāma.* Al-qāhira: Maktabat Madbūlī.

———. 2016. *Bibliography* [Online]. Available at: www.raoufmousaad.com/bibliography/ (Accessed October 19, 2016).

Musʿad Basta, R. 1998. *L'uovo di struzzo.* Roma: Jouvence.

Nwachukwu-Agbada, J. O. J. 1990. "The Lifted Veil: Protest in Alifa Rifaat's Short Stories." *The International Fiction Review* 17, 2: 108–110.

Ogbeide, O. V. 2012. "Deconstructing Phallocentric Cultural Ascendancy: Alifa Rifaat's subtle Sexist Agenda in Distant View of a Minaret." *Advances in Arts & Social Sciences* 1, 1: 1–11.

———. 2013. "Behind the Hidden Face of Eve: Alifa Rifaat's Distant View of a Minaret as a Metaphor." *Greener Journal of Agricultural Science* 3, 1: 27–32.

Olive, B. A. 1996. "Writing Women's Bodies: A Study of Alifa Rifaat's Short Fiction." *The International Fiction Review* 23: 44–49.

Pratt, N. 2007. "The Queen Boat Case in Egypt: Sexuality, National Security and State Sovereignty." *Review of International Studies* 33, 1: 129–144.

Quawas, R. 2014. "Pinched Lives and Stolen Dreams in Arab Feminist Short Stories." *Journal of International Women's Studies* 15, 1: 54–66.

Rifaat, A. 1983. *Distant View from a Minaret and Other Stories.* Translated from Arabic by D. Johnson-Davies. London: Heinemann.

Said, E. W. 1978. *Orientalism.* New York: Vintage.

Salti, R. 1991. "Feminism and Religion in Alifa Rifaat's Short Stories." *The International Fiction Review* 18, 2: 108–112.
Weedon, C. 1987. *Feminist Practice and Post-Structuralist Theory*. Oxford: Basil Blackwell.
———. 1997. *Postwar Women's Writing in German: Feminist Critical Approaches*. Providence, RI/Oxford: Berghahn Books.
Whitaker, B. 2004. An Interview with Hoda Barakāt. Available at: http://al-bab.com/liiterature-section/modern-arab-writers [Accessed October 19, 2016].
———. 2014. *Grenzgänge. Androgynie-Wahnsinn-Utopie im Romanwerk von Hūdas Barakāt*. Wiesbaden: Reichert Verlag.
Wright, J. W. Jr. and Rowson, E. K. 1997. *Homoeroticism in Classical Arabic Literature*. New York: Columbia University Press.

8 Gay in North African literature?

Max Kramer

In the contemporary Western world, *sexual object-choice* is one of the principal parameters defining the self and prominently includes same-sex sexuality. The notion moves the focus away from casual same-sex practices and relationships; instead, it emphasizes the exclusiveness of such practices and relationships and contributes to a person's social self-identification through this sexual object-choice, which becomes the basis of their *sexual orientation*. Through this ontological shift, the set of males who had sex with males in an earlier era, a rather helpless collection of isolated individuals, has morphed into the postmodern community of gays with a certain amount of biopolitical power over their lives.

In 2001, the Netherlands permitted people of the same sex to marry and granted same-sex relationships equal legal status. A substantial number of countries have followed suit. So far, however, no Muslim-majority nation has legalized same-sex marriage, although there have been attempts to do so in some of the many Muslim-majority countries where same-sex intercourse is legal. Yet, the new situation in the West has been accompanied by the burgeoning of an unfamiliar kind of literature coming from the southern shore of the Mediterranean. The latest generation of young male Maghribi writers of fiction has reacted to the previously unknown concepts of homosexuality and gayness now circulating by producing short, subversive, autobiographical novels about same-sex sexuality in countries the laws of which punish same-sex sexual practices. The representation of lesbian, intersex, or trans characters, on the other hand, faces radically different challenges within the heteronormative and patriarchal gender order of the Maghrib, which is why my own contribution will focus on men who have sex with men.

Following the example of many of their predecessors, these authors, who speak Arabic or Tamazight dialects at home, write in French, which provides them access to Western readers. The former colonizers' language thus distances their fictional accounts from the linguistic reality of North African locales, but the use of Standard Arabic or Standard Tamazight would entail similar problems, and writing in the dialects is not common. Crucially, however, this new generation portrays same-sex interactions in its fiction from the first-person perspective. This trend started with Rachid O. from Morocco whose first book, *The Dazzled Child* (*L'Enfant ébloui*), published in 1995, caused a sensation. Rachid O. has since published other works in the same vein: *Several Lives* (*Plusieurs vies*) in 1996, *Hot Chocolate* (*Chocolat chaud*) in 1998, *What Remains* (*Ce qui reste*) in 2003, and *Illiterates* (*Analphabètes*) in 2013. Other young authors from the Maghrib include Eyet-Chékib Djaziri from Tunisia, who published a book in 1997 entitled *A Fish on a Swing* (*Un poisson sur la balançoire*) with a sequel a year later entitled *A Promise of Pain and Blood* (*Une promesse de douleur et de sang*), and the Moroccan Karim Nasseri, who published *Chronicles of a Hammam Child* (*Chroniques d'un enfant du hammam*) in 1998, *Wedding and Funeral* (*Noces et funérailles*) in 2001, *Soulaimane's Secret* (*Le Secret de Soulaimane*) in 2006, and *The Sailor from Magador* (*Le Marin de Magador*) in 2008. The latest addition to this list is the prolific writer Abdellah Taïa, who, like Rachid O. and Nasseri, is from Morocco and has published a series of homosexual *Bildungsromane*, among them *My Morocco* (*Mon Maroc*) in 2000, *The Red of the Fez* (*Le Rouge du tarbouche*) in 2004, *Salvation Army* (*L'Armée du salut*) in 2006, *An Arab Melancholia* (*Une mélancolie arabe*) in 2008, *The King's Day* (*Le Jour du roi*) in 2010, *Infidels* (*Infidèles*) in 2012, and *A Country for Dying* (*Un pays pour mourir*) in 2016.

In their fiction, these representatives of francophone Maghribi literature tackle head-on and unabashedly the theme of same-sex relationships. In a review of Rachid O.'s *The Dazzled Child*, Hédi Abdel-Jaouad stated that, though other authors had already treated the theme of homosexuality, "this [was] the first time, to [his] knowledge, that an author addresse[d] this question directly and from a personal perspective without provocation, outlandishness, or prudish reserve" (Abdel-Jaouad 1996). Thus, these authors' work challenges the local attitude toward same-sex sexuality not so much through revealing what is ordinarily carefully hidden in the closet but by writing "I," by involving the first-person narrators themselves in the same-sex acts that they describe. A first-person narrator need not indicate the author's perspective, of course, but with a subject like this, the likelihood that readers actually do identify him with it is high. Also, it is not that such acts are unheard of in the present-day Maghrib, quite the contrary, but these practices are usually condemned whenever they surface.

Yet, instead of defending the Western notion of sex *qua* social identity in a Muslim-majority society, the subjectivity that these novels showcase runs counter to what gay activists may have hoped for. In short, rarely has same-sex sexuality in the Maghrib been cast in the identitarian terms to which Western readers are accustomed, and the minority-group thinking – valorizing minority status, relativizing historical paradigms – that Western gay liberation employs is, when not criticized, mostly absent from the work of these writers. The Sartrean question "For whom does one write?" is therefore not easily answered for these authors. Their subject, same-sex sexuality, which is taboo (even when not illegal) in contemporary Muslim culture, appeals to Western audiences, who are increasingly interested in how queers live around the globe. The exoticism of its locales adds to the allure of this new literature.

At the same time, through their motifs these narratives set themselves apart from mainstream Western gay lore and complicate the middle-class, Western notion of *gayness*. Rachid O., Abdellah Taïa, and Eyet-Chékib Djaziri, for instance, describe mostly status-differentiated relationships. These are established relationships between sexual partners who are clearly on opposite sides of a strong gender binary, with one partner portrayed as *active*, bisexual, and hegemonically masculine and the other as *passive* and effeminate. In addition, in several of his novels Rachid O. stages same-sex sexuality from the angle of a pederastic, that is, age-differentiated, relationship, which, thrown into the bargain, is written from the perspective of the younger partner, a minor who may be the victim of sexual abuse. And in Eyet-Chékib Djaziri's novel *A Fish on a Swing*, a teenage boy recounts his sexual experiences, which are marked by violent and otherwise harmful behavior directed toward him. As I will show, these themes have very little in common with the Western notion of *gay* with its principles of egalitarianism and sameness at its core and its basis in the hetero/homo opposition.

These novelists also face a problem of language and literariness. Their narratives involve practices to which, it seems, their compatriots could relate, if, that is, they were to read them. However, many such potential allies or enemies either do not have access to their books, which with some exceptions are not much in circulation in North Africa; do not read French; or even struggle with Standard Arabic, the primary language of communication being the Maghribi Arabic vernaculars. The authors themselves, apart from Djaziri, whose mother tongue is French, face a similar dilemma in that they write in a second language, which offers them fewer rhetorical possibilities than it would a native speaker. Khalid Zekri speaks of "spontaneous writing" and "basic sentence constructions" (Zekri 2006, 194).[1] Nonetheless, these books, though written in French, are, to paraphrase Kateb Yacine, Arab works and deeply rooted in their authors' local traditions even when they criticize them.

Of course, this does not rule out that their use of an acquired language handed down by former colonizers, with their native languages as substrata, offers special *literary* possibilities. Réda Bensmaïa is right to bemoan the fact that in the past Maghribi novels were "almost invariably reduced to anthropological or cultural case studies" and that "[t]heir literariness was rarely taken seriously" (Bensmaïa 2003, 6). According to Zekri (2006, 192), it is their paratextual apparatus, above all, that sustains the literariness of these works as it institutionalizes them. For instance, Zekri reminds us how all texts "show their generic label in their paratexts," which state "novel," "story," or "intimate tale" and which include at times a "preface," which is another way of conferring upon themselves the status of "self-writing" (ibid., 193). To this it might be objected that "an important part of the pact is missing: Rachid O.'s complete signature" (Hayes 1997, 501). There is no room here to respond in full to these objections, but the differences between these authors on the periphery and mainstream contemporary authors writing in French, such as Anouar Benmalek, Siham Benchekroun, Boualem Sansal, Yasmina Khadra, and Kamel Daoud, may stem from, among other things, the former's deeper roots in oral storytelling as compared with the latter's more literate, sophisticated *écriture*.

Still, the "subversive quality" of Rachid O.'s or Taïa's "literary accounts does not necessarily reside in their poeticity" but "rather ties in with their thematic function, which as it happens gives them an originality within the Moroccan field of literature" (Zekri 2006, 190). Therefore, I, too, want to concentrate on the *ethnographic* insights into Muslim social spaces that these novels offer. They show that the hybrid Berber-Arab-Muslim-French Mediterranean culture of the Maghrib still largely ignores the understanding of the hetero-homo axis that defines Western thinking and, indeed, separates not sexes but sexual orientations. When, however, the Western binarism of homo- versus heterosexuality does get introduced, it is usually through the narrator-character's encounter with a Western tourist in North Africa or his travels to Switzerland or France.

To comprehend the economy of same-sex sexuality in North Africa and, more generally, in Muslim-majority countries, it is important to remember how much the middle-class, Western economy of same-sex sexuality is the result of a long historical process. For, when comparing different theoretical approaches to the understanding of same-sex sexuality, there is always the danger of naturalizing the unique Western view of the phenomenon and conceptualizing it as normative, globally. Since the end of the nineteenth century, *sexual orientation* has slowly become an ontological category, and, beginning with this category, the gay-liberation movement has promoted the LGBTQI *community* in the manner of ethnic, national, and religious communities. As has been shown by Foucault, the current state of affairs reveals a considerable movement away from pre-nineteenth-century concepts of same-sex sexuality, which were primarily about same-sex *practices* – think of eighteenth-century sodomites, for instance, or ancient Greek pederasts – and which did not necessarily presuppose that individuals define themselves by their sexuality. Despite more recent efforts at intersectionality, the West still largely conceives of being gay as an exclusive social identity, which is distinct from and incompatible with other sexual identities, notably being heterosexual. This conception brings with it a new form of segregation, namely, by sexual orientation, which replaces the former segregation by sex. For gays, such an identity excludes by definition heterosexual marriage and reproduction within it. Western societies have made sexual object-choice a key criterion of subjectivity, which in the LGBTQI cases, through the experience of a homosexual rite of passage (*viz.*, coming out of the closet) and the subsequent consolidation of a *visible* gay social identity, leads to a new body politic.

We know from Edward Said that Western writers who turned their imaginations toward the *Orient* (and sometimes even went there) constructed its population as a fixed *Other*. Partly, this *Other* was sexualized, which is an aspect Said did not explore in depth in *Orientalism*. He limited himself to saying that "the Orient was a place where one could look for sexual experience unobtainable in Europe" (Said 1979, 190). Such escapist descriptions tended to exoticize local traditions beyond recognition and created the impression of unbridled and polymorphously perverse sensual indulgence, and they were permanently to define the Oriental world. Said's book became one of the foundational texts of Postcolonial Studies. One question that remains unanswered today, then, is how one of the regions that he discussed, the Maghrib, which for centuries Westerners orientalized as an Eden of sexual practices censured at home, came to be considered repressive today. In her review of Rachid O.'s *Illiterates*, Claire Devarrieux construes the novel as a challenge to the local economy of same-sex sexuality and, thereby, the sociocultural norms of the Maghrib: "He takes to heart the denunciation of homophobia in Moroccan society" (Devarrieux 2013). In the same way, David Parris argues that these "authors claim a sexuality that has become banal in Europe ... but that is still banned for religious reasons in the Arab world" (Parris 2009, 656). Zekri adds, "in contrast to the American context, which recognizes the existence of a homosexual community, the Moroccan context feigns to ignore it entirely" (Zekri 2006, 187). This sort of criticism is representative of a school of thought that looks at Maghribi literature through the prism of Eurocentric values and standards. While it is true that the contemporary Maghribi literature with which I am here concerned deconstructs a local phobia against self-identifying homosexuals, Devarrieux's, Parris's, and Zekri's angle of assessment overlooks the fact that this literature portrays other sexual aspects of the Maghrib. These include a *laissez-faire* attitude toward cross-generational same-sex sexuality and a criticism of the Western economy of same-sex sexuality. The former includes adolescent and prepubescent boys. The latter requires men who engage in sex with other men to conform to the hetero/homo binary, pressing them to confine their emotional interactions to the boundaries of the *gay village* or gay-friendly social and cultural spaces while adopting a gay habitus. The Empire's writing back – even with its depiction of the Western situation, which is flawed because it is monolithic – is either not noticed or flouted in these assessments. The correlative of this restricted or manipulative sort of reading is that Maghribi texts come across as confirming the Western gay way of life, which, in turn, pinkwashes their content. According to one teleological argument for this attitude, gay identity would ultimately be embraced by a large number of same-sex practitioners in this part of the world and be experienced as a form of liberation, with the avant-garde of young Maghribi authors contributing to this predicted watershed. However, that is very uncertain. Besides, the disturbing aspects of these novels for Western readers are not the components that come across as countercultural within the context of North Africa – namely the hetero/homo binary and the gay habitus – but, rather, the fact that they call into question social norms that come from the West and, so, problematize what it means to be of the male gender and have sex with other males in a globalized world.[2]

The prevalent gender binary

In the last two decades, aided by tourism, satellite television, and global media (e.g. online dating services, virtual social networks, instant messaging, and Internet telephony), Western gay culture has unsettled the notions of gender and sexuality that have prevailed in other geographic spaces, one of which is the Maghrib, and that distinguished themselves in the past from other spaces by non-identitarian models of same-sex sexuality. The essentialist drift inherent in the circulation of a hegemonic naturalized gay identity disrupts pre-existing local identities. In the case of North Africa, young male Maghribis re-enacting Western modernization conceive of themselves as *gay* or *homosexual* by referring to the Western episteme and renouncing or adapting their own cultural heritage. At the same time, Western but also local LGBTQI rights organizations have increasingly agitated for the emancipation and civil freedom of sexual minorities outside the West. Thus, contemporary writers from North Africa are primarily under the influence of two modes of same-sex sexuality between which the characters in their fiction hesitate, namely, the gender binarism with which they are culturally familiar and the new hetero/homo binarism that they encounter in travelling to Europe or through contact with Western tourists in their countries.

One of the major features of the gender binary is the active/passive (top/bottom) distinction, which is paralleled by the bisexual/effeminate distinction and the gender division of male/female. The active/passive binary is nothing new and can already be seen in Maghribi authors of the previous generation, such as Driss Chraïbi. In *The Simple Past*, published in French in 1954, Chraïbi has the narrator reject Si Kettani's sexual advances on the grounds that "[he doesn't] like old men" (Chraibi 1990, 50), like Si Kettani, who will not play the passive role in relationships. This indicates that he engages in same-sex practices provided that he is the active partner. This type of narrative tropes homosexuality as sexual *passivity* and, thus, femininity and, by implication, makes the active partner heterosexual.

The difference between the post-independence generation and contemporary North African writers is that, by and large, occurrences of same-sex sexuality in the formers' novels are not avowals of their authors' homosexual proclivities. Rather, they serve to denounce the hypocrisy of Maghribi society, where men pretend to be pious or otherwise respectable while engaging in sexual relations that are criminal or morally reprehensible in their social context, namely, same-sex sexuality, rape, pedophilia, and so on. The generation of Maghribi writers of the 1950s and 1960s, another example of whom is Rachid Boudjedra, though not known for being homosexuals themselves, frequently portrayed characters engaging in same-sex practices. They did do so in two ways. First, they used heterodiegetic narrators and wrote from the safe distance of zero focalization. Second, they clearly distanced their narrators from the sexual act by portraying it as something that happens against their will or as something they engage in only for money or some sort of advantage.

Unlike autobiographical avowals of homosexuality, these older narratives were intended to provide additional force to their authors' argument against the homogenizing utopias of postcolonial nations in which homosexuality had no place, no more than in their former colonizers' politics. Jarrod Hayes argues that such narratives "attempt ... without rejecting identity altogether, to articulate a national identity that is heterogeneous in relation to language, ethnicities, sexualities, and religions, and that questions any totalizing binary opposition to the former colonizer" (Hayes 2000, 16). In this larger picture, the candid representation of homosexual practices was but one of various overdetermining elements in the criticism of the then-current national discourse and, as such, was different from contemporary queer literature from the Maghrib in which descriptions of queer sexuality take center stage.

Crucially, the narrator in each of the contemporary books I have mentioned is autodiegetic, that is, he is the protagonist of the story he tells and, thus, directly involves himself in an exegesis that deals with a taboo subject in North African culture. Given that readers often identify an autodiegetic narrator with the author, the risk that these authors take is much higher than if they had chosen to tell their stories through narrators not involved in the homosexual acts that they report.

What has not changed much since the previous generation, though, is the gender binary in Maghribi same-sex sexuality. The terms "active" and "passive" are frequently employed in the contemporary novels I have mentioned, and those novels leave little room for egalitarian, gender-neutral, or *versatile* notions of erotic desire and sexual practice. At some point in Rachid O.'s *The Dazzled Child*, for instance, the 10-year-old narrator-character Rachid falls in love with Khalil, a 13-year-old boy, who says to Rachid, "you are sweet, like a girl" or "like a little girl" (O. 1995, 48). Rachid summarizes Khalil's attitude toward having sex with him, "For me, we were making love. For him, he was making love to me" (ibid., 49), which is to say that the male role is entirely conferred on the active partner in the sexual relationship. Similarly, in his relationship with Mounir later in the story, the young Rachid is characterized as Mounir's "little buddy (*copain*)" and as "his girlfriend (*copine*)" (ibid., 60), which again plays on confusing the gender binarism. That is to say, the apparently receptive partner in the relationship is characterized as female, or at least effeminate, while the active partner is portrayed as virile or as a "ladies' man" (ibid., 69). Consequently, the active male does not belong to the ostracized group of homosexuals. Rachid even refers to himself as a "little feminine faggot" (ibid., 70).

In Abdellah Taïa's novel *The Red of the Fez*, the narrator tells the story of Amr, an effeminate Egyptian boy. The son of a rich family from Cairo, his parents continually reproach him for being an *effeminate* homosexual: "you're not like the others," "you prefer to play the woman, that's right ... a man's woman." Taïa repeats this scenario in *An Arab Melancholia*, in which the 12-year-old narrator Abdellah is called "Leïla" by other adolescent boys, who also call him "effeminate," "*zamel*,"[3] and a "*passive* faggot" (Taïa

2012, 14).[4] Eventually, this group of adolescents rapes Abdellah; Chouaïb, the leader of the gang, says, "I'm not going to rape you all by myself ... We're all going to rape you ... We're all going to make a real girl out of you" (ibid., 25). All through the ordeal, Abdellah tries to defend himself verbally by insisting that "a boy is a boy and a girl is a girl" (ibid., 21) and that "[j]ust because [he] love[s] men and always [will] [doesn't] mean that [he is] going to let [Chouaïb] think of [him] as the opposite sex" (ibid.). The scene culminates in Abdellah shrieking, "My name's not Leïla ... I'm not Leïla ... I'm Abdellah ... Abdellah Taïa..." (ibid., 24). His ordeal ends only when the *muezzin* starts the Al-Asr call to prayer, and his soft and solemn voice halts the God-fearing adolescents in their tracks. Another call shortly follows; this time the leader's mother needs him to buy beignets, which finally puts an end to the attack. Abdellah's notion that "a boy is a boy and a girl is a girl" is a clear sign of Western gay identity, signaling that Abdellah is gay but not to be confused with the opposite gender. Rather, Abdellah is a boy who loves boys, which goes against the local matrix. The disconcerting facts are that Abdellah feels an attraction for Chouaïb, despite the rape, and that he eventually accepts his effeminacy, his status as a woman: "I wished I were born a woman. A real woman" (ibid., 29).[5] No sooner has the Western paradigm been noted than it disappears again in favor of the local understanding.

Eyet-Chékib Djaziri, who is from Tunisia, sets his strongly autobiographical novel *A Fish on a Swing* in Bourguiba's Tunisia of the 1960s and 1970s. His main character, Sofiène, who acts out his homosexuality from the ages of 12 to 17, tells us that "it is true that the mentality over here is so constituted that he who plays the active role does not lose any of his manliness and can brag about his exploits" (Djaziri 1997, 70). Sofiène goes on to say that the active partner might even "be applauded" and "encouraged," while "the man who is the passive partner will be called a faggot and be despised" (ibid.). One instance where this gender binary comes to the fore is the comparison of the narrator's, Sofiène's, father to the father of Sofiène's boyfriend Khélil. When Sofiène's father catches Sofiène and Khélil naked together in the bedroom, he beats his son severely, accompanying each strike with the rhetorical question, "Who was playing the woman?" (ibid., 65). This fit of rage on the part of the passive boy's father contrasts with the reaction of the active boy's father when he subsequently catches the two in a compromising embrace. Though he clearly sees what is going on, and even exchanges glances with Sofiène, Khélil's father says nothing and makes no fuss over his son's sexual involvement. As Sofiène explains Khélil's father's behavior, "I sensed that he was not going to make a fuss. He could be sure of the role that his son held in our couple. Thereby he shared with my father the certainty that the female role was not held by Khélil" (ibid., 69). The partner perceived as receptive in a male homosexual relationship is compared with a woman, since his role is interpreted as the refusal of hegemonic masculinity in a phallocratic system and, by extension, as that of an invert, a view that betrays less homophobia than misogyny. Later on, however, Sofiène's father asks his son to forgive him and reproaches himself for having been absent during his childhood. This leads Djaziri, the ethnographer, in the person of his character Sofiène, to another conclusion: "The older I got, the more this hostility toward me took shape. What was I reproached with? My difference? Why was I envied? For my loves? They might as well have reproached me for being dark-haired!" (ibid., 190).

According to these novels, the notion that the receptive partner, willingly or out of resignation, assumes the role of the female still forms the basis of most male same-sex relationships in North Africa.

The pederasty theme

An even more important issue than the prevalent gender binary is pederasty or pedophilia. Karim Nasseri and Rachid O. both portray sexual acts between adults and teenagers or prepubescent children. This theme is also not new in Maghribi literature. A case in point is Boudjedra's novel *The Repudiation*, from 1969, in which the narrator, who has the same first name as the author, frequently alludes to his brother's homosexuality as well as to his own situational same-sex experiences in recounting the events of his childhood. The latter include giving in to the Quranic schoolteacher's sexual advances in exchange for being allowed to sleep in class and he and his pals letting longshoremen "fondle [their] behinds" (Boudjedra 1995, 53) in order to be able to swim in the harbor. As Boudjedra describes it:

> In winter I enjoy snoozing a great deal and the schoolteacher can do nothing about it since I am blackmailing him: last year he made some indecent propositions which I accepted so he would leave me alone and let me dream in peace of my stepmother's opulent body. Everyone accepts the propositions of the Koranic schoolteacher. He caresses your thighs furtively and something hard burns your tail-bone ... The parents, usually aware of such practices, close their eyes to them so as not to have to accuse a man carrying the word of God in his breast.
>
> (Ibid., 79–80)

In 1969, Boudjedra most likely would not have included such a description of a schoolteacher's pedophilia in the narrative to denounce child abuse *per se* but, rather, as part of his criticism of Islam and its representatives.

Such denunciations of the hypocrisy of Islamic clerics are also found in contemporary literature. In Karim Nasseri's novel, *Chronicles of a Hammam Child*, for instance, the *faqih* repeatedly sexually abuses the children of the local Quranic school, among them the three-year-old narrator:

> From the first day, I had my dose like all pupils. The faqih spent a quarter of an hour kissing me and introducing his big tongue stinking of hashish into my small mouth. Then he took my right hand and made it enter the

pocket of his jellaba. I felt disgusted when my small hand met his hard and smooth sausage.

(Nasseri 1998, 46)

Much of Nasseri's story constitutes a denunciation of the *faqih* for the statutory rape he repeatedly commits. In his second novel, *Wedding and Funeral*, Nasseri offers a different picture of a transgenerational relationship, this time between the 11-year-old narrator Idriss and his history teacher Ali. Sensing that Idriss is suffering, Ali talks with him, which leads to Idriss's crying about his tortured family life. Ali responds by kissing Idriss's hands. The episode blossoms into a pedophilic relationship in which the teacher leads the consenting and thankful 11 year old to the discovery of love and "the passion of sex" (Nasseri 2001, 103). Summarizing the relationship, Idriss says, "I found in him the tender father, the soft and caressing lover" (ibid.). Ali also explains to Idriss that the *faqih* was a "vulgar rapist of innocent *ephebes*" (ibid.).[6]

The same sort of ambiguity toward pedophilia can be observed in Rachid O.'s *The Dazzled Child*, which, like *Wedding and Funeral*, unabashedly depicts same-sex sexuality from the first-person perspective. Rachid O.'s 13-year-old narrator Rachid describes a love affair with his schoolmaster. The other students realize what is going on. Rachid's classmate Mounir observes, "[t]his teacher is hitting on you, it's obvious, he's too nice to you" (O. 1995, 61). Subsequently, the teacher's whole family catches on. Visiting the teacher at home under the pretext of helping him grade papers, Rachid recounts:

I was very much on time. He was waiting for me in front of the house ... He was waiting for me in his pajamas ... I entered the house, I met everybody. All those people looking at me, his mother, his brother, his younger brother, it was all frightening to me because I knew what I could expect. And for them it was a kid who was coming to take Arabic classes. And the way his 16-year-old brother was looking at me ... each time he looked at me it wasn't in a mean way but it was clear that he had understood everything. We entered his bedroom. It took five minutes ... While looking at a photo, I remember, he jumped on me, he couldn't resist any longer. I couldn't resist any longer. We went for a kiss, which was, I don't know, a fire, something really beautiful. After, he locked the door so that we could continue without being disturbed. I felt ashamed because they could hear how the lock snapped shut. I was imagining their looks behind the door. Luckily, when we left, nobody was there anymore.

(Ibid., 64–65)

In this scene, Rachid O. does not portray a pederast and his victim. Quite the contrary, the character Rachid enjoys the encounter and describes their kiss as "beautiful." Nor does Rachid O. denounce an abuse of power on the part of the teacher; rather, the scene expresses Rachid's wholehearted love for him: "I started being crazy about him" (ibid., 65). What is astonishing is that the teacher's family seems to condone his behavior; at least no one intervenes during the encounter. What is more, the sexual relationship between Rachid and his teacher does not surprise his classmate Mounir either. Thus, the author represents an age- and status-differentiated sexual relationship between males, an adult and a pubescent minor, as tolerated by both adults and minors, or at least not explicitly criticized. As Gianfranco Rebucini reminds us, "homoerotic practices, while being subaltern to heterosexual reproductive practices, subsist in the same social construction of masculinity and on the same basis as other sexual practices" because "they are integrated in the general construction of a certain hegemonic masculinity" (Rebucini 2011, 8). Later, and tellingly, when the teacher ends the relationship Rachid is devastated, and his family, intuiting Rachid's heartache, tries to soothe him. Rachid's father tells him "you don't have to hide ... like eight years ago, when you pretended to be ill only to be free to cry about your teacher" (O. 1995, 87).

Rachid O.'s novels abound with similar stories. In *Several Lives*, 10-year-old Rachid's father encourages him to spend time with the man whom Rachid has been led to believe is his uncle and with whom he is going to have his first sexual experience: "Without telling me, my father felt that I was old enough too, so he drove me toward my uncle" (O. 1996, 11). As it turns out, though, the so-called uncle is the father's former lover, who, according to Jarrod Hayes, being "'free and without a family,' also resists the pressure of a normative sexuality that would require him to marry and reproduce" (Hayes 1997, 516). The relationship between the pre-adolescent boy and the grown man includes various sexual encounters during one of which the putative uncle has an orgasm while Rachid snuggles with him (O. 1996, 19). They also enjoy an erotically charged kiss ("baiser"), which Rachid carefully distinguishes from an ordinary kiss ("bisous"). When the supposed uncle dies, Rachid's father grieves by sleeping for more than 24 hours. "So much did he love his friend" (ibid., 35), Rachid tells us by way of a conclusion. What is disturbing about Rachid O.'s depictions is that, as Bruno Perreau (2011, 158) states, "[n]ever is the relationship presented in psychological terms (a sexual predator and his victim)." Earlier on, Perreau argues that "his narrative is never based upon institutionalized European sexual categories: these relationships are neither adolescent experiments, nor are they termed pedophilic" (ibid., 157). In another novel, *What Remains*, in which Rachid O. analyzes his first two books, he summarizes the problem, "I related years of sexuality with French-speaking pedophiles described through the voice of a boy who was not a victim" (O. 2003, 112).

Gay culture: a Maghribi perspective

In *Several Lives*, the character Rachid contrasts his happy childhood and his multiple same-sex experiences with the experience of Luc, one of the European men he meets in Rabat, who tells him the story of getting caught by his family while having sex with an underage boy: "I was severely upbraided for it and almost excluded from my family" (O. 1996, 40). Luc likes "very young boys" (ibid.) and for this reason is shunned by his relatives. The exception is his brother, but even he keeps Luc away from his children when he can. Luc, who grew up in Morocco, is now an art teacher in Paris, but he returns to Morocco because there he can "find what he is looking for with the boys he likes" (ibid., 41). Rachid and Luc form a platonic friendship while traveling, among other places, to Tangiers and to Jean Genet's grave in Larache. In no way does Rachid judge Luc's penchants; instead, he shows how aware he is that he would be prosecuted for them in Europe:

> I think also of all the men whom I met after him and to whom I bragged by talking about this story and by stating only at the very end: "It was with my own teacher." I was like a storyteller. And inevitably all these men to whom I gave myself over, all of them Frenchmen, told me: "It's crazy; it's very beautiful; by all means you have to write about it, [but] in our country it's impossible."
>
> (O. 2003, 109–110)

Morocco is, however, not only an attractive holiday spot for travelers with pedophilic or pederastic tendencies but also for effeminate Western gays some of whom Rachid and Luc encounter in Tangiers. Luc states that "[he] never see[s] this type of old fairy in Paris" and that "this couldn't happen in the Paris metro, in public places," but he finds that "it is totally accepted in Morocco" (O. 1996, 47).

This perplexing view of same-sex sexuality, pederasty, and pedophilia that we find in fictional accounts of Morocco can also be found in accounts of Western countries such as Switzerland and France. Both of the characters, Rachid and Abdellah, travel to Europe where they visit men they had met in Morocco. However, this new environment that is marked by the exclusivity of homosexuality and its subcultural segregation, often intimidates the novels' characters, and they struggle to find happiness. Georg Klauda avers that "[t]he transformation of erotic relations among men from a system of friendship to that of homosexuality changes one's own lifeworld in a threatening way" (Klauda 2008, 22). A case in point is Rachid's reaction when he discovers the Western paradigm of an egalitarian gay relationship. Vincent, Rachid's lover in *Several Lives* and a man in his forties, whom he visits in Schaffhausen, Switzerland, tells him that he "hate[s] pederasts" and finds that the "word '*pédé*'[7] that [Rachid] uses [is] vulgar" and "that it applie[s] only to pederasts." Vincent feels more "gay than *pédé*, and all his friends agree with him that he is that" (O. 1996, 77). Vincent also thinks that it is "crazy" (ibid.) that Rachid had a sexual relationship with his teacher when he was younger. The relationship between Vincent and Rachid, who are also differentiated by age, eventually sours because of their diverging views of it: Rachid craves an age-differentiated relationship while Vincent prefers them to have an egalitarian *rapport*, despite the distance separating their ages. Westerners' and

Maghribis' diverging views extend to their attitudes toward children. In *The Dazzled Child*, the character Rachid comments that in France his father, who is infatuated with children without being erotically attracted to them, "would be taken for a pedophile, he likes children so much" (O. 1995, 42).

Abdellah's relationships with Westerners – in *Salvation Army*, Jean, a Swiss man from Geneva, and in *An Arab Melancholia*, Javier, a Parisian – also end when he visits them in their homes. The stories insinuate that either these men took the young and racially marked Abdellah for a prostitute or he was only a sex object for them while they vacationed in Morocco. According to Jean, "Abdellah [is] after all just a little whore, like there are so many in Morocco" (Taïa 2006, 153), and, for Javier, "[t]hat [is] all [he] meant to him," "hooking up and fucking" (Taïa 2012, 49). Instead of these unhappy relationships with Europeans, in *An Arab Melancholia* Abdellah has a relationship with Slimane, an Algerian, that is, a fellow North African. Despite the fact that they live in Paris and are roughly the same age – Abdellah is 27 years old, Slimane is 36 – Abdellah assumes the role associated with Arab women:

> For you, I became a submissive Arab woman. Every day I had to stop whatever I was doing before you came home, sometime around 5, and have everything for your comfort and convenience. The tagine made, the mint tea ready. The laundry done ... And I swear to you, I swear that I like doing all these things.
>
> (Ibid., 129)

Thus, the most fulfilling relationship that Abdellah has had in the West is one that upholds a strict gender opposition.

Other forays into Western societies and their cultural economies of sexuality are equally frustrating for the main characters in this North African literature. Rachid, the narrator-protagonist of *Several Lives*, finally makes it to Paris, which he has always wanted to visit, only to discover that same-sex seduction and the sensualized gaze are not parts of everyday life there:

> I was staring at everybody, sometimes it was mutual, sometimes I felt that people thought I was a fool. Where I come from, we all look at each other, one is interested in the other, and it's the play of the glance.
>
> (O. 1996, 112)

Before arriving in Paris, he had gone to Mulhouse, a city with approximately 280,000 inhabitants in its metropolitan area, where he tried in vain to find a "bar where there would be *men* and *boys*" (ibid., 104).[8] He was instead given directions to an immigrant center full of "Arabs" (ibid., 105). However, Rachid had been warned by his French friend and host in Mulhouse that in such a small city there are no "bars to his liking, where there would be *boys*, that there [is] nothing like that in Mulhouse, that he ha[s] to wait for Paris" (ibid.).[9] Much to his astonishment, Rachid finds out that gay bars are not as common in the West as he had thought they were and that the *gay village* is rare. The character Abdellah Taïa makes a similar ethnographic discovery in Switzerland. He goes to a public urinal in Geneva "dominated by something that was missing elsewhere" in the city, namely, an "exuberant and poetic sexuality" shared by "over ten men of all ages" (Taïa 2006, 130–131). All in all, most of the characters in this North African literature find it hard to deal with the widespread human coldness and compartmentalization of sexuality in the West, where male–male cruising and romance is confined to certain locales and largely channeled through the discourse of minority.

Are gay rights transnational?

As these examples show, the Western paradigm of same-sex sexuality has circulated some in North African societies. The characters in these Maghribi novels have frequent and formative encounters with Westerners who confront them with new notions of male–male sexuality. The narrators are aware of some of the icons of Western gay culture, such as Jean Genet and Pier Paolo Pasolini. Yet, the multifaceted, distinctive patterns of Maghribi same-sex sexuality – the gender binary, homosexuality as a substitution sexuality, pederasty and even pedophilia, a high degree of sensuality among men of all sexual orientations, the readier availability of men for same-sex erotic encounters, and the more abundant acting out of bisexual desires – have by no means been replaced.

The enforcement of laws protecting children is considerably less far-reaching in North Africa than it is in the West. Western critics rightfully denounce this lack of child protection as do some of the authors considered in this chapter. So, it is no surprise that the "Gay International" (Massad 2002, 361) and the West in general cast a mostly critical eye on the social and sexual paradigms in Muslim-majority societies and more often than not caricature them as Western society's worst nightmares. It goes without saying that the representatives of the international gay community cannot be suspected of acting in collusion; still, Joseph Massad is not inappropriately polemical in summarizing the overall negative attitude of Western researchers and political and social activists toward the same-sex situation in the Muslim world. Their criticism rightfully also concentrates on the fact that in most Muslim-majority societies homosexuality is illegal and sometimes punishable by death; that gay rights are often not protected by law; that there is no recognition of same-sex unions or *marriage for all* in the French egalitarian way; and that, generally speaking, there is much intolerance, both legal and cultural, of gay people and gay culture. George Mosse has shown how at the beginning of the twentieth century, European "[n]ationalism" as a "movement" "evolved parallel to modern masculinity" (Mosse 1996, 7) in its militarized, aggressive, virile form. Conversely, according to Jasbir Puar, the contemporary "national and transnational political agendas of U.S. imperialism" (Puar 2007, 9) and those of the West more generally are tied in with the "recognition of homosexual subjects, both legally and representationally" (ibid.). In other words, "*the new homonormativity*,"[10] to use Lisa Duggan's terminology (2003, 50), reflects "a politics that does not contest dominant heteronormative assumptions and institutions, but upholds and sustains them, while promising the possibility of a demobilized gay constituency and a privatized, depoliticized gay culture anchored in domesticity and consumption" (ibid.). This politics is circulated in the Global South, intentionally or not, even though researchers and activists engage in solidarity activism without supporting homonationalist imperialism. Put another way, some Western tourists, guide-book writers, scholars, and journalists who focus on LGBTQI rights (e.g. *marriage for all*, adoption, and assisted reproduction) tend to be complicit in a right-wing, imperialist, gay-friendly agenda in putatively homophobic Muslim-majority countries. Their voices dismiss these countries' biopolitical management of sexuality as premodern and anti-democratic. In opposing this tendency, it is crucial to call attention to a more culturally sensitive approach that must denounce any form of abuse but also understands that worldwide same-sex practitioners cannot necessarily be secured through just one framework of rights. A respect for self-determination also suggests that the Western middle-class epistemology of coming out, public visibility, and social identity, which is often coopted by normative homo-nationalism, is perhaps not an effective way to de-stigmatize same-sex sexuality in Muslim locales or to make sense of forms of same-sex sexuality that do not primarily exist under the rubric of identity. At the same time, though, Massad's condemnation of the "Gay International" has a "preservationist nativist" (Hasso 2011, 656) quality that is also counterproductive. It is obvious, then, that LGBTQI rights, which are often cast as global human rights, clash with the rights of specific local cultures, in this case the Muslim-Arab culture. This clash arises from a universalistic and evolutionistic view of same-sex sexuality that both privileges the homogeneous global gay community and devalues the many local approaches to same-sex sexuality. In describing this phenomenon, Stephen O. Murray and Will Roscoe rightfully speak of a belief in a "history of homosexuality as a progressive, even teleological, evolution from pre-modern repression, silence, and invisibility to modern visibility and social freedom" (Murray & Roscoe 1997, 5).

Conclusion

In this chapter, I have sought to flesh out various exemplars of the current biopolitics of same-sex sexuality in hybrid and diverse North Africa. I have analyzed each exemplar through the lens of the witness statements of the current generation of young Maghribi authors. Of course, literary criticism cannot make the same assumptions that anthropology does, but, insofar as all of the authors I have considered write in forms of fictionalized autobiography, or what Serge Doubrovsky has termed "autofiction," I believe that these novels/diaries/testimonies/intimate tales shed light on the sexual practices in today's Maghrib. From a Western point of view, the characters' families may come across as dysfunctional and abusive, but Bruno Perreau reminds us in his analysis of cross-generational sexuality in Rachid O.'s writing that "religion is seen as a bridge between people [and] that pederasty is considered as such too–rather than being conceived as a fixed and exclusive category" (Perreau 2011, 163). Teenage sexuality and, so, same-sex sexuality in North Africa are transitional phases. This is borne out by the attitude of a character in Djaziri's *A Promise of Pain and Blood* who says, "We're not children anymore, Sofiène. We need to forget this stage in our lives. We mustn't touch each other anymore" (Djaziri 1998, 57). Similarly, Khélil, Sofiène's closest lover in *A Fish on a Swing*, tells Sofiène, "Today you're fifteen years old, and I thought that it was about time for you to stop children's play, to build yourself a reputation and to stop tongues wagging. Only a girl could help you" (Djaziri 1997, 25–26).

Thus, various present-day North African novelists have it in common that they portray male same-sex sexuality as a passing adolescent phase to which society turns a blind eye because it considers it to be situational sexual behavior that partly results from sex segregation in Muslim-majority societies. There is ample space for such closeted same-sex practices but little for identitarian claims, much less for long-term exclusive same-sex relationships, and virtually none for a communitarian gay social identity that replaces the traditional family unit. Thus, Western concepts of same-sex sexuality cannot be applied in North Africa, much less applied anthropologically. This does not mean that the work of these authors does not transgress the socio-sexual order of traditional Islamic orthodoxy and does not denounce same-sex child abuse. Rather, their work shows the homosocial framework within which same-sex sexuality can be spoken of and that the "will not to know" – I borrow this phrase from Stephen Murray – on the part of society can be broken in the contemporary Maghrib. The fact that these narrations are autodiegetic and closely identify protagonist, narrator, and author makes them all the more transgressive, for it closely relates these fictional accounts to real life in North Africa. However, it is also worth mentioning that some of these novelists now live in France, which, given the obvious links between fact and fiction in their work, does not bode well for the teenage homosexuals and their lovers portrayed in their stories. Still, these authors expose the fluidity, hybridity, and ambivalence of same-sex sexuality in the Maghrib and thereby execute a narrative shift in postcolonial collective thinking.

Notes

1 Unless otherwise indicated, all translations are my own.
2 This hypothesis corresponds to Hester's (2014) argument regarding the structural and context-dependent character of sexual transgression.
3 This is an offensive term for the *passive* homosexual.
4 Author's emphases.

5 The French original does not use the word "born" but remains vague: "J'aurais aimé être une femme" (Taïa 2008, 30). My translation: "I would have loved to be a woman."
6 The events of Nasseri's second novel relate to those of the first.
7 "Pédé" is colloquial or slang French for *gay* and as such is an ingroup/outgroup word. The term is potentially offensive while "homosexuel" and "gay" are the more neutral, non-judgmental terms.
8 Author's emphases.
9 Author's emphases.
10 Author's emphases.

References

Abdel-Jaouad, Hédi. 1996. "Review of *L'Enfant ébloui* by Rachid O." *World Literature Today* 70, 2: 457.
Bensmaïa, Réda. 2003. *Experimental Nations or the Invention of the Maghreb*, trans. Alyson Waters. Princeton, NJ: Princeton University Press.
Boudjedra, Rachid. 1995. *The Repudiation*, trans. Golda Lambrova. Colorado Springs, CO: Three Continents Press.
Chraibi, Driss. 1990. *The Simple Past*, trans. Hugh A. Harter. Washington, DC: Three Continents Press.
Devarrieux, Claire. 2013. "Les enchantements de Rachid O. Histoires marocaines de familles, d'honneur et d'"Analphabètes,'" *Libération*, February 20. Available at: http://next.liberation.fr/livres/2013/02/20/les-enchantements-de-rachid-o_883256 [Accessed October 25, 2016].
Djaziri, Eyet-Chékib. 1997. *Un poisson sur la balançoire*. Paris: GayKitschCamp.
———. 1998. *Une promesse de douleur et de sang*. Paris: GayKitschCamp.
Duggan, Lisa. 2003. *The Twilight of Equality? Neoliberalism, Cultural Politics, and the Attack on Democracy*. Boston, MA: Beacon Press.
Hasso, Frances S. 2011. Review of *Desiring Arabs* by Joseph A. Massad. *Journal of the History of Sexuality* 20, 3: 652–656.
Hayes, Jarrod. 1997. "Rachid O. and the Return of the Homopast: The Autobiographical as Allegory in Childhood Narratives by Maghrebian Men." *The Journal of Twentieth-Century/Contemporary French Studies* 1, 2: 497–526.
———. 2000. *Queer Nations: Marginal Sexualities in the Maghreb*. Chicago, IL: University of Chicago Press.
Hester, Helen. 2014. *Beyond Explicit. Pornography and the Displacement of Sex*. New York: SUNY Press.
Klauda, Georg. 2008. *Die Vertreibung aus dem Serail: Europa und die Heteronormalisierung der Islamischen Welt*. Hamburg: Männerschwarm.
Massad, Joseph. 2002. "Re-Orienting Desire: The Gay International and the Arab World." *Public Culture* 14, 2: 361–385.
Mosse, George L. 1996. *The Image of Man: The Creation of Modern Masculinity*. New York: Oxford University Press.
Murray Stephen O. and Will Roscoe eds. 1997. *Islamic Homosexualities*. New York: New York University Press.
Nasseri, Karim. 1998. *Chroniques d'un enfant du hammam*. Paris: Denoël.
———. 2001. *Noces et funérailles*. Paris: Denoël.
Parris, David. 2009. "Amours 'inter-dites': allers (et retours) Maroc-France." *International Journal of Francophone Studies* 12, 4: 655–670.

Rachid, O. 1995. *L'Enfant ébloui*. Paris: Gallimard.
———. 1996. *Plusieurs vies*. Paris: Gallimard.
———. 2003. *Ce qui reste*. Paris: Gallimard.
Perreau, Bruno. 2011. "Rachid O.'s Inner Exile: Gay Heterotopia and Postcolonial Textuality." In *Masculinities in Twentieth and Twenty-First Century French and Francophone Literature*, ed. Edith Biegler Vendervoort, 155–172. Cambridge: Cambridge Scholar Publishing.
Puar, Jasbir K. 2007. *Terrorist Assemblages: Homonationalism in Queer Times*. Durham, NC: Duke University Press.
Rebucini, Gianfranco. 2011. "Lieux de l'homoérotisme et de l'homosexualité masculine à Marrakech: Organisation et réorganisation des espaces dédiés." *L'Espace Politique* [En ligne] 13, 1, mis en ligne le 03 mai 2011, consulté le 25 octobre 2016. URL: http://espacepolitique.revues.org/index1830.html.
Said, Edward. 1979. *Orientalism*. New York: Vintage Books.
Taïa, Abdellah. 2006. *L'Armée du salut*. Paris: Seuil.
———. 2008. *Une mélancolie arabe*. Paris: Seuil.
———. 2012. *An Arab Melancholia*, trans. Frank Stock. Los Angeles, CA: Semiotext(e).
Zekri, Khalid. 2006. *Fictions du réel: Modernité romanesque et écriture du réel au Maroc, 1990–2006*. Paris: L'Harmattan.

9 The struggle of LGBT people for recognition in Turkey

An analysis of legal discourses

Pinar Ilkkaracan

Introduction

This chapter addresses the struggle of LGBT activists and organizations for legal recognition, in particular the right of association, in Turkey. It aims to shed light on recent legal debates and trends through an analysis of certain landmark legal cases that were processed between 2006 and 2009, concerning the recognition of LGBT organizations as legal associations. This was a period of many cases against LGBT organizations seeking to establish themselves as legal NGOs. Since the court decision on Lambda Istanbul in 2009, which I discuss later on in this chapter, there were no other similar cases. The analysis shows that the clauses on general morality in the Turkish Constitution and Civil Code constituted the bases of arguments against the right of LGBT groups to register as organizations. But it also shows that state prosecutors and judges were aware of Turkey's changing norms and the EU's conventions and generally ruled in favor of recognizing LGBT associations. As I shall show, the meaning of the term "general morality" as it occurs in Turkish law differs significantly from that of the term "public morality," which occurs in the European Union's conventions. The Turkish term blurs the distinction between the private and the public, which leaves its application open to the interpretations of prosecutors and judges that vary based on their subjective values and prejudices. Despite the obstacle that the general-morality clauses in the Turkish Constitution and Turkish law raise against the right of LGBT people to associate freely, in all of the court cases that I shall analyze in this chapter, state prosecutors and judges have, in the light of their progressive interpretations of those clauses, recognized that right. These landmark cases have paved the way for other LGBT associations in Turkey. My data include the decisions of courts and public prosecutors, press statements and publications of Turkish LGBT organizations, and media reports.

In 2015, Turkish authorities banned, for the first time, Istanbul's annual LGBT Pride Parade, which has been held every year, with increasing support and popularity, since 2003. Indeed, the Istanbul Pride march was so popular by 2013 that more than 100,000 people from all walks of life participated in support of LGBT rights, human rights, and liberal democracy. One should note that Turkey is, or was before 2015, the only Muslim-majority country in the Middle East and North Africa to hold pride parades, making it, with its message of overcoming homophobia, sexism, and misogyny, a beacon of hope for the whole region. In 2015, the parade was held despite the ban, and police used tear gas, rubber bullets, and water cannons against the marchers. The situation further deteriorated in 2016. Merely a week before the parade was to be held, a Turkish Islamist group calling itself the *Anatolia Muslim Youth* posted on its Facebook page: "We don't want them to walk naked on the sacred soil of our country in the blessed month of Ramadan." The group claimed that it had a responsibility to stop "such perversion." (Haberturk 2016). The Islamist daily newspaper *Yeni Akit*, which frequently runs homophobic articles, including one earlier that week about the gay nightclub massacre in Orlando (USA), gave the group its full support (Yeni Akit 2016).

Religious fundamentalists were not alone in openly targeting the LGBT event. At a press conference, the *Alperen Hearths*, a far-right youth organization with links to the ultra-nationalist Great Union Party, declared, "We are not responsible for what will happen beyond this point. Degenerates will not be allowed to carry out their fantasies in this country" (*Hurriyet* 2016). Shortly after these threats were issued, the governor of Istanbul banned the parade, citing security risks, instead of opposing the agitators and ensuring conditions for a peaceful parade. Thus, the Istanbul Pride Committee had to cancel the 14th Pride Parade, but thousands of people gathered at Taksim Square, nevertheless, in defiance of the ban. The Pride Comittee issued a press statement on the day the parade would have been held, June 26, amidst the tear gas and rubber bullets:

> In our marches, we stand up in this dark time that is our share in world history, with our love and desire … We show that a different world, sexuality, body, and life is possible. Those who banned our march used "society's sensitivities" as an excuse. But what's being guarded is not society's but the government's sensitivities. Society is none other than us … Banning our march is an unsuccessful attempt to silence our voices.
> (LGBTI News Turkey 2016)

It seems that the governing conservative Justice and Development Party had wanted to demonstrate its authority to LGBT people and their liberal supporters. Its implicit support of the above-mentioned extremist groups opposing the parade was in line with the increasingly autocratic style of governance it began in 2013.

An ambiguous victory

On April 30, 2009, after a trial lasting almost three years, Istanbul's Civil Court of the First Instance decided that Lambda Istanbul, a major LGBT organization in Istanbul, had the right to register as a non-governmental organization. This verdict came as a result of the decision of the Supreme Court of Cassation, overturning the civil court's initial decision to deny the members the right of free association on the grounds that permitting the organization would be against general morality (*genel ahlak*) and be incompatible with the state's duty to protect the family. It is important to note that the English translation of the Turkish legal term "genel ahlak" is "general morality," not "public morality," which is the term common in international laws and covenants. I shall discuss the difference between these terms below.

The case was the last in the organization's arduous, three-year-long struggle, which started in July 2006 when the Istanbul Governor's Office demanded that the group be disbanded. It pointed to the fact that the words "lesbian," "gay," "bisexual," "transvestite," and "transsexual," all of which occurred in the group's name, Lambda Istanbul LGBTI Solidarity Association, and the organization's objectives, violated Article 56 of the Turkish Civil Code and Article 33 of the Turkish Constitution. Both clauses stipulate that the freedom of association can be restricted to preserve general morality, for instance, in order to protect the peace and well-being of the family, which is declared a duty of the State also in Article 41 of the Constitution. However, Lambda Istanbul's members could celebrate their victory only half-heartedly. For, though the Supreme Court of Cassation had approved the organization's registration, the court had stated in its decision that "the association can be closed in the future if it engages in activities that motivate, encourage or proliferate homosexual behavior." (Supreme Court of the Turkish Republic, Court of Cassation 2008). Lambda Istanbul protested against this part of the decision in its press statement, saying that it constituted a constant threat against them:

> We accept that we encourage! We encourage the right to the freedom of association. We encourage not hiding oneself. We encourage everybody to live as she/he is. If these actions constitute a crime, and if the law is still threatening us, we ourselves openly state that we encourage freedom!
>
> (Lambda Istanbul 2008)

What's in a name? Public versus general morality

"Public morals" and "public morality" are terms that appear in many constitutional charters and several international covenants protecting human rights, including the European Convention for the Protection of Human Rights and Fundamental Freedoms (ECHR). However, the ECHR also lists the protection of public morality as a legitimate reason to restrict some of the rights that it itself grants, for instance, individuals' and families' right to privacy; the freedoms of thought, conscience, and religion; the freedom of expression; and the freedom of assembly and association. As Perrone (2014) notes, it is important to understand the meaning of "public morality" and determine its scope and boundaries in order to prevent arbitrary restrictions of these rights.

The translation of "public morality" into Turkish is "kamu ahlakı." However, the term used in Turkish law, "genel ahlak," which translates into English as "general morality," is more problematic than "kamu ahlakı," as it refers roughly to the morality accepted by the majority of people in a society. Thus, "general morality," in contrast to "public morality," blurs the legal distinction between the private and the public, leaving the scope and boundaries of general morality a matter of interpretation and, so, subject to jurists' subjective values and prejudices.

The difference in meaning between "general morality" and "public morality" has been the subject of many legal and philosophical debates between conservatives and liberals in the West. Arguments for restricting freedoms based on general morality usually cite the religious values of the majority and have been used to justify restrictions of sexual freedoms in particular. For example, in Great Britain in 1957, the Wolfenden Committee issued its *Report of the Committee on Homosexual Offenses and Prostitution*, which concluded that there must be a private realm, where the perceived morality or immorality of one's behavior is not the law's business (Hart 1963). Judge Devlin of the British High Court criticized this conclusion, arguing that general morality requires the prohibition of homosexuality (Richter 2001). However, the distinctions between public and general morality and the exact meaning of these terms have not yet become subjects of legal debate in Turkey.

The struggle of LGBT organizations for legal recognition

In May 2009, only a month after the Istanbul court's decision allowing Lambda Istanbul to register as an association, the application of an LGBT organization in Izmir, the Black Pink Triangle, to register as a non-governmental organization was rejected by the Governor's Office of Izmir. Once again, it was argued that the group's aims violated general morality and endangered the well-being of the family.[1] In fact, between 2005 and 2009, all of the LGBT groups in Turkey, including KAOS GL and the Pink Life Association in Ankara, the Rainbow Association in Bursa, Lambda Istanbul in Istanbul, and the Black Pink Triangle in Izmir that had applied to register officially as non-governmental organizations, had faced threats of being outlawed. However, only Lambda Istanbul had to endure a three-year court case to gain the right to register. This shows that some public prosecutors, judges, and governors have contradictory interpretations of the general-morality and family-protection clauses and contradictory views regarding their applicability to restrict LGBT people's rights to free expression and association. These contradictory views reflect and contribute to the public controversies in Turkey over the rights of LGBT people.

Although LGBT people began agitating for their rights at the beginning of the 1990s, the issue of LGBT rights had been marginalized in Turkey until recently. The leaders of the LGBT movement in Turkey characterize the refusal to recognize LGBT people as "the last denial of the Turkish Republic" (Erol 2008). However, the growing number of LGBT organizations throughout the country and their increasingly strident calls for recognition have changed the situation considerably. Yet, the conservative Justice and Development Party, which came to power in 2002, maintains its opposition to LGBT rights. Given President Erdogan's increasing authoritarianism, particularly since 2011, this is unlikely to change in the near future.

Nonetheless, the political struggle of LGBT people for recognition and their rights will continue to be a subject of public and political debate in Turkey, for LGBT people and organizations have increased their visibility and activism considerably over the last two decades and have gained the support of opposition parties, *viz.*, the Republican People's Party and the People's Democratic Party, and many other groups. For example, two of the country's largest labor unions, the Confederation of Progressive Trade Unions (DISK) and the Public Employees Trade Union (KESK), inserted a clause on the right to sexual orientation into a draft constitution for the Turkish state that they had prepared and proposed to the government (DISK 2009).

Recognition of LGBT people, democratic citizenship, and liberal democracy

In recent decades, demands for democratization, liberty, and equality have led to calls for the legal recognition of politically excluded or marginalized groups. Among the candidates for such inclusion are ethnic and religious minorities, indigenous people, women, gays and lesbians, and immigrants and refugees. Such calls share the claim that democracy can only be strengthened by granting equal rights to marginalized groups, who have been excluded and oppressed by states despite their formal promises of democratic equality for all citizens (Phillips 1995).

The "politics of recognition," a term coined by Charles Taylor (2004), has become the subject of heated debates in political theory. Fraser (1997) argues that we must distinguish analytically between struggles for recognition and those for a more just distribution of resources, though they intersect and influence one another. According to Fraser, the injustice that homosexuals suffer, though it includes economic injustice, is quintessentially a matter of the lack of recognition for a despised sexual minority because of the construction of authoritative norms that privilege heterosexuality, culturally devalue homosexuality, and spawn homophobia as a result.

However, transgender sex workers in Turkey falsify Fraser's analysis.[2] Transvestite and transsexual people experience a wide range of human rights violations in Turkey, not only state violence, that is, harassment and abuse by the police, but also widespread social discrimination, for example, exclusion from the labor market. Gays and lesbians live with the fear that they will be fired if their employers learn of their sexual orientation; so, they often disguise their identities and/or sexual preferences. However, cross-dressers and transgender persons, who are unable or unwilling to change their outer appearance, are especially subjected to hiring discrimination, and, thus, sex work is often their only available source of income (Öz 2009). This in turn leads to their depiction in the media as sex workers and the public's identification of them as such. As sex work is widely considered to be against the values of society, this economic marginalization of queer people contributes further to their cultural devaluation. Thus, transsexuals and transvestites in Turkey suffer a vicious cycle of public marginalization and economic discrimination, each fueling the other, that is almost impossible to break.

Tully (2001) argues that recognition politics is an aspect of democratic politics, and therefore, identity politics should be considered a legitimate political strategy to attain public acknowledgment. Thus, he characterizes calls for recognition as part of the broader politics of deliberation (Tully 1999). Drawing on Tully, Maclure (2003) further suggests that the struggle of various groups for their rights is an expression of both their disapproval of, and dissent from, the policies of a present government as well as "particular moments in the on-going quest for self-determination" (Maclure 2003, 18).

Another tool that movements employ to achieve recognition and secure their rights is the concept of democratic citizenship. Women's movements and feminist academics all over the world have been at the forefront of the criticism of traditional discourses on citizenship, whose emphasis on the relationship between social class and citizenship they criticized as gender-blind (Phillips 1991; Pateman 1988; Joseph 2000). O'Donnell (1993) treats citizenship as a key concept for institutionalizing representative democracy and asserts that "in formal (versus representative) democracies, the component of democratic legality and, hence, of citizenship, fades away at the frontiers of various regions and class, gender and ethnic relations" (O'Donnell 1993, 1361). Increasingly, LGBT movements around the world formulate their demands in terms of their rights as citizens. A common aim of such demands is to challenge ideas of citizenship that make assumptions about sexuality, in particular, hegemonic heterosexuality. Similarly, research on the intersection of democratic citizenship and sexuality has demonstrated that citizens are normatively constructed as (hetero)sexual subjects, and analyzed the resultant inequalities that excluded citizens face because of the institutionalization of heterosexuality (Cooper 1993; Richardson 2000; Armas 2007). As Dietz (1987) maintains, the concept of democratic citizenship includes more than negative liberties. It incorporates a relationship among civic peers, the guiding principles of which are mutual respect, the positive liberties of democracy, and self-government.

As I further discuss below, the LGBT movement in Turkey has been very active, especially in the legal sphere, in its demands regarding democratic citizenship. Yet, the wide-ranging socio-political discrimination LGBT people in Turkey face, compared to their counterparts in other Western countries, constitutes a significant barrier to their formulating their demands for their rights and liberties in positive rather than negative terms. Although various rights included in the citizenship rights of LGBT people (for instance, the rights to marry, receive marriage benefits, and adopt or foster children) are at the top of the LGBT agenda in many Western countries, the LGBT movement in Turkey has not yet demanded such rights. Rather, it has constructed its discourse around its demands concerning legal and social mechanisms related to freedom from violence and discrimination. Arguably, the political opportunities open to a group are influenced by the perceived features of the broader political environment, which also affect the group's expectations for the success or failure of collective action. These features include the accessibility of government, the stability of existing political alignments, the sympathy of local elites, and the possibility of building stable alliances with other groups. The resources available to the group may also partly determine the scope of its political agenda (Tarrow 1998; McAdam, Tarrow, and Tilly 2001).

The legal context of human-rights violations against LGBT people in Turkey

An exhaustive analysis of the legal status of the rights of LGBT people and violations of their human and civil rights in Turkey is beyond the scope of this chapter.[3] My aim here is, rather, to sketch briefly the legal situation of LGBT people in Turkey as of 2016, in particular with respect to the lack of anti-discrimination provisions in Turkish law and the often arbitrary application of laws to discriminate against LGBT people and groups.

Though homosexuality is not illegal in Turkey, the state does not recognize same-sex marriages or civil unions, and gay and lesbian couples are not eligible for domestic-partnership benefits.[4] In 1982, the Supreme Court ruled that lesbian mothers cannot have custody of their children. This decision set a precedent for later decisions regarding the custody rights of lesbian women.

Since the Campaign for the Reform of the Turkish Penal Code between 2002 and 2004, the LGBT movement in Turkey has advocated for various anti-discrimination provisions being entered into the Turkish Constitution and Turkish law. As of 2016, there are no laws prohibiting discrimination or hate violence against LGBT people in Turkey. Although European Commission Directive 2000/78/EC explicitly demands as part of Turkey's accession process that it enact legislation prohibiting labor discrimination on the basis of sexual orientation, such legislation has not yet been realized (Council Directive 2000/78/EC). The new labor law enacted in 2003 includes provisions in Article 5 prohibiting discrimination on the basis of race, religion, and disability but not sexual orientation, which the directive also requires.[5] The European Commission has criticized this lack in its progress reports on Turkey since 2002, including the report in 2015 (European Commission 2015).

In March 2014, the Turkish Parliament adopted as part of a "democratization package" a law that included amendments to Article 122 of the Penal Code, penalizing hate crimes (Law No. 6529). The new law defines hate crimes based on race, nationality, skin color, gender, disability, and political and religious views and makes them punishable with imprisonment from one to three years. However, despite years of activism for the inclusion of sexual orientation in hate-crime legislation there are no such provisions because of the opposition of the government. A resolution of the European Parliament in April 2016 calls on Turkey "to undertake serious efforts to protect the rights of the LGBTI community." It expresses strong concern at the lack of protection provided to LGBTI people against acts of violence; stresses its disappointment at the failure to include protection against hate crimes on the grounds of sexual orientation and gender identity in the Hate Crimes Bill; and it regrets that hate crime against LGBTI people often remains unpunished, or that offenders' sentences are reduced on account of the victim's alleged "unjust provocation" (European Parliament 2016, paragraph 24a).

Various laws are used to discriminate against LGBT people. Article 225 of the Turkish Criminal Code, on "public exhibitionism," is often misused by security forces to harass, abuse, detain, and arrest transgender people (Altıparmak & Öz 2007; Human Rights Watch 2008). Legislative changes in recent years have given the police additional authority to arrest people. For example, the Misdemeanor Law (*Kabahatler Kanunu*), which the AKP government passed and which went into force in March 2005, "aims to protect public order, general morality, general health, the environment, and the economic order" (Law No. 5326, Article 1). The law empowers the police to arrest or fine transgender and transvestite people on suspicion of engaging in sex work, with fines starting at 105 Turkish lira as of 2016 (Zabita 2016). Furthermore, the Law on the Powers and Duties of the Police (*Polis Vazife ve Selahiyet Yasası*) was amended in June 2007 to allow police, for the first time, to stop individuals at their discretion and ask for identification in order to "prevent a crime or a misdemeanor (*kabahat*)." This discretionary power substantially increases the scope of police activity, without judicial scrutiny, because the law does not define "general morality," "public order," or "misdemeanor" in terms that appropriately limit police authority. The amendment thus authorizes police to act in ways that limit (or violate) human rights. Almost all LGBT groups in Turkey have harshly criticized the use of these laws against transgender people but without success, given the government's staunch opposition to LGBT people, until 2016.

Legislative provisions referring to general morality, which are often used to violate the human and other rights of LGBT people (Altıparmak & Öz 2007), require special attention. The violation of the right of LGBT people to associate freely, which I described above, exemplifies the use of general morality to restrict LGBT rights in Turkey. Below, I examine the legal controversy over the issue through various petitions, decisions of public prosecutors, and court findings on the freedom of association as it pertains to LGBT organizations.

Results: landmark cases concerning the legal recognition of LGBT organizations in Turkey

Lesbian, gay, bisexual, and transgender activism has been publicly visible in Turkey since the 1990s. Lambda Istanbul, the first LGBT organization in Turkey, was founded in 1993 in response to a ban imposed by the Governor's Office of Istanbul on a series of public events intended to bring gay and lesbian issues to public attention for the first time in Turkey. A year later, in September 1994, another LGBT group, KAOS GL, was founded in Ankara to fight discrimination against gays and lesbians. Both organizations have been very active since their founding, though they were not registered as associations until 2009 and 2005, respectively.

KAOS GL was the first LGBT organization to file for registration as an association, which it did in 2005. The new Law on Associations of 2004 was intended to strengthen the legal framework for non-governmental organizations, and it played a significant role in the group's decision. The law remains valid in 2016 (Law No. 5253). The long-awaited democratization that the law brought came as a result of years of criticism and activism by NGOs in Turkey as well as pressure from the European Union and the European Court of Human Rights (ECHR). However, though the Law on Associations puts no explicit restrictions on the formation of LGBT organizations, the authorities in several provinces have found ways to interpret the law so as to restrain what they perceive as immorality. Thus, LGBT organizations soon discovered that democratization had limits in their case.

KAOS GL sent its application for official registration to the Ministry of the Interior in July 2005. The Ministry forwarded the application to the Governor's office, asking for its opinion. Ankara's deputy governor, Selahattin Ekremoğlu, responded by initiating proceedings to outlaw the organization, claiming that its name (KAOS Gay and Lesbian Cultural Research and Solidarity Association) and aims violated Article 56 of the Turkish Civil Code on general morality. However, the Office of the Attorney General in Ankara was quick, in turn, to deny the Governor's petition, upholding the right of KAOS GL to form a legal association. In turning the petition down, Kürşat Kayral, a state prosecutor in Ankara's Attorney General's Office, noted that homosexuality is no longer considered an illness, according to the DSM IV (the Diagnostic and Statistical Manual of Mental Disorders of the American Psychiatric Association), and that "gay" and "lesbian" are common words used in both everyday and academic discussion. He then remarked on the subjectivity and relativity of morality. He referred to the first debate on sexual orientation in the Turkish parliament, which the Women's Platform for the Reform of the Turkish Penal Code from a Gender Perspective had just initiated, demanding that discrimination based on sexual orientation be criminalized. Kayral stated:

> In examining the notion of morality ... while noting that the concept of morality includes a notion of subjectivity and varies from society to

society; and at a time in which discrimination against sexual orientation is debated within the context of the reform of the Turkish Penal Code, being a homosexual cannot be identified with immorality and the reality should be based on a notion of morality based on freedom of human will, as all experts of ethics concur.

(Office of the Attorney General 2005)

He maintained that the new law on associations should be implemented in accord with the principle that "the state should adopt not an oppressing, but a facilitating manner towards associations," in accordance with international human rights conventions, the European Human Rights Convention (EHRC), the decisions of the European Court on Human Rights (ECHR), and norms prescribed by international bodies of which Turkey is a member (ibid.). The Governor's Office of Ankara complied with the decision, and KAOS GL was allowed to register officially as an organization.

However, in 2006, only one year later, the same governor's office rejected the application of another LGBT organization, the Pink Life LGBT Association, again filing a petition for its dissolution. While the petition was similar to its previous one, the legal reasoning was more sophisticated. The Governor's Office claimed that the group's name and its aims were not only in breach of Article 56 of the Turkish Civil Code but also of Article 41 of the Constitution, which states that "Family is the foundation of Turkish society (...) The state takes necessary precautions (...) to protect the peace and welfare of the family." Moreover, the Governor argued, probably in response to the State Prosecutor's reference, in denying the previous petition, to what the European Human Rights Convention (EHRC) says on the freedom of association, that the case was an instance of the sort in which the state can limit the freedom of association in accord with Article 33/3 of the Turkish Constitution and Article 11/2 of the EHRC, which cite general morality and morals, respectively, as legitimate grounds to restrict that freedom.[6]

In his response, State Prosecutor Kayral was accordingly more nuanced in refusing the petition. Expanding on his previous reasoning, Kayral also maintained that being homosexual, bisexual, lesbian, gay, transvestite, or transsexual are just ways of being human and that any interpretation of "general morality" incompatible with this fact would inappropriately limit the freedom of the individual. In addition to his previous references supporting the responsibility of the Turkish state to uphold the freedom of association, he added a reference to the International Covenant on Civil and Political Rights (Office of the Attorney General 2006).

Nonetheless, Kayral included in his decision a small but significant restriction on the right of LGBT people to the freedom of expression. While asserting that the freedom of expression regarding sexual orientation should normally take precedence over the protection of general morality, he allowed that an exception could be made "in case this self-expression/self-disclosure should extend its limits, becoming an aim to encourage a certain sexual orientation" (ibid.). The Supreme Court of Cassation was later to echo Kayral's argument in its decision in Lambda's case, as I discussed above.

The Governor's petitions and the Public Prosecutor's denial of them became the blueprint for the legal actions of other authorities. It has become a rule of thumb that whenever an LGBT organization tries to register as an association, the responsible governor's office petitions for its dissolution. The Governor's Offices of Bursa, Istanbul, and Izmir have filed such petitions against The Rainbow Association, Lambda Istanbul, and the Black Pink Triangle, respectively. The argument common to all of these petitions is that the association's full name, which includes the words "gay," "lesbian," "bisexual," "transvestite," and/or "transsexual," and its aim are in breach of the articles of the Turkish Civil Code and Constitution pertaining to the protection of general morality and the family.[7] Each also refers to the articles of the Turkish Constitution and the EHRC that say that general morality and morals, respectively, are appropriate grounds for restricting the freedom of association in the case of LGBT organizations. In the case of Lambda Istanbul, the Governor's Office also claimed that the group's name contravenes the Law on Associations because "lambda" is not a Turkish word and, so, the group must use its Turkish translation (Governor's Office 2006). The group chose to name itself "Lambda" in 1993 because the 11th letter of the Greek alphabet became an international symbol of the LGBT community in the 1970s. But it has no Turkish translation. Thus, this case is a good example of the arbitrariness of the means with which local authorities pressure LGBT organizations.

The Attorney General's Offices of Bursa and Istanbul also rejected the petitions of the Governor's Offices of those provinces to outlaw the relevant LGBT associations on the basis of arguments similar to those of the Public Prosecutor of Ankara, Kürşat Kayral.[8] In Istanbul, Public Prosecutor Muzaffer Yalçın, whose decision reads almost exactly the same as Kayral's, added that no Turkish law makes homosexuality a crime.

The Governor's Offices of Bursa and Izmir complied with the decisions of their Public Prosecutors and allowed the registration of the relevant associations. In Istanbul, however, the Governor's Office insisted on its claim against Lambda and took its case to criminal court, which, despite the opposing view of the legal expert appointed by the court to evaluate the petition, accepted it, thus overturning the Public Prosecutor's decision. In its decision, the court argued once again, that freedoms can be restricted on the grounds of general morality, public order, the protection of children and the family, and the protection of the Turkish language. It also stated that, though values vary from country to country, one cannot conclude that "what exists in another country would be definitely right for our own country and the opposite of this could also be true" (Istanbul 5th Criminal Court 2007). This statement, which rejects international principles in favor of what a judge believes to be right for Turkey, is not only open to legal criticism; it also implies that the courts have the authority to determine Turkey's values. Moreover, the decision referred extensively to provisions of international conventions pertaining to what they refer to as "public morality" and "morals" as grounds for restricting the freedom of association, though the decision uses "general morality," instead of "public morality" and "morals," which is an incorrect translation with significant implications.

Lambda appealed the decision to the Supreme Court of Cassation, which determined that it has a right to exist and register itself as a legal association. An analysis of the arguments of the civil court and the Supreme Court regarding general morality reveals that, though courts' interpretations of the relevant laws vary, interpretations of "general morality" remained the most significant obstacle for LGBT organizations in Turkey. The Supreme Court rejected the decision of the civil court, which in its closure of Lambda on the grounds of protecting general morality went so far as to cite the existence of a "strongly patriarchal family structure" in Turkish society, "the sacredness of the family," and "religious rules" as justifications for its decision (ibid.). However, the Supreme Court's decision also mentions general morality as grounds for restricting the freedom of association of LGBT people in case they were to "motivate, encourage or spread lesbian, gay, bisexual, transvestite or transsexuality" (Supreme Court of the Turkish Republic, Court of Cassation 2008). This provision, which Kayral, the public prosecutor in Ankara, also made, suggests that some officials think of sexual orientation as like a contagious disease that threatens public order, rather than as an individual right.

In its decision, the Supreme Court also held that "sexual identity or orientation is not something that people choose of their own will, but a situation that people are *unwillingly* faced with through birth or upbringing" (my emphasis), which implies that the Supreme Court views LGBT gender identity and sexual orientation as disorders (ibid.). Though views on the genetic or psychological causes of sexual orientation differ, international experts tend to agree that LGBT orientations are not disorders. And Kayral concurred in his decision. The Supreme Court's decision included an elaborate statement on the objectives of LGBT organizing, which makes a step forward toward liberal, pluralistic democracy in Turkey:

> It is understood that the association, in its aim to strengthen solidarity among lesbian, gay, bisexual, transvestite or transsexual individuals, will contribute to the evidence that they are constituents of the society and to the creation of an environment of freedom in the society through facilitation of their right to freedom of expression, prevention of social prejudices against them and the prevention of their marginalization and social discrimination.
>
> (Ibid.)

Discussion

Through intense and effective advocacy since the 1990s, LGBT groups in Turkey have succeeded in putting the rights of LGBT people on the Turkish agenda. Despite initial difficulties, the LGBT movement has grown throughout Turkey and received the support of the liberal public, opposition parties, and trade unions, among others.

The Campaign for the Reform of the Turkish Penal Code (2002–2004) first brought feminist and LGBT activists in Turkey together over the issue of sexual orientation; that coalition demanded that a law penalizing discrimination on the basis of sexual orientation be added to the penal code. Though the government did not accede to their demand at the time, this first attempt of LGBT people to lobby parliament made the issue of sexual orientation a subject of parliamentary debate for the first time (Ilkkaracan 2010). Parliament's Justice Committee agreed to meet the demand and proposed such a law, but Cemil Çicek, the Minister of Justice, ultimately removed the committee's proposal from the draft law in May 2004. He argued that since Article 10 of the Constitution already prohibited discrimination on the basis of sex, and since sex was sufficiently similar to sexual orientation, there was no need to add any such law to the penal code. The only objection to the Minister's withdrawal of the revision came from a member of parliament of the oppositional Kemalist CHP faction, who explained to the assembly the difference between sex and sexual orientation. However, the Minister insisted on their similarity, and his rejection of the revision was sustained without further discussion by a majority vote (Ilkkaracan 2007).

Despite the failure of the campaign to criminalize discrimination on the basis of sexual orientation, LGBT organizations view it as a successful step in raising public awareness of sexual orientation. Indeed, the fact that the Public Prosecutors of Ankara and Istanbul referred to the campaign in their decisions defending the freedom of association for LGBT people is evidence of the impact of advocacy and consciousness-raising on LGBT rights.

Tracing the legal developments concerning LGBT people and associations over the last decade shows that, though their struggle has made some political and legal headway, those gains are very limited. The hard-won registration of various LGBT organizations as legal associations, and the increased visibility of LGBT people and popularity of their movement, constitute, arguably, significant steps toward the recognition of LGBT people as legitimate members of Turkish society. LGBT rights will continue to be on the public and political agendas in Turkey, as they have been since 2013, despite President Erdogan's increasingly authoritarian regime. Given the accelerated trend in Turkish politics toward authoritarianism and in view of the intensified persecution of political opposition to Erdogan since the failed *coup d'état* in summer 2016, the future of LGBT rights and, thus, of the democratization process in Turkey, will depend to a significant degree on the interventions of the EU and the international community.

Notes

1 Izmir is the third largest city in Turkey after Istanbul and Ankara.
2 See also the critique of Fraser's approach by Judith Butler (1997) and Fraser's response (1997b) to Butler.
3 For more information on the subject, see Altiparmak and Oz (2007), Pink Life et al. (2014), Yilmaz and Gocmen (2015).
4 In comparison, 24 European countries have legalized same-sex marriages, civil unions, or other forms of recognition for same-sex couples in the 2000s.
5 The EC Directive states that the principle of equal treatment in the area of employment covers disability, religion or belief, sexual orientation, and age.
6 According to Article 33/3 of the Turkish Constitution, the protection of national security, public safety, general morality, public health, the freedoms of others, and the prevention of crime constitute grounds to limit the freedom to association. Article 11/2 of the ECHR states that no restrictions shall be placed on the exercise of the freedom of peaceful assembly or the freedom of association with others except those that are prescribed by law and/or are necessary in a democratic society in the interests of national security, public safety, the prevention of crime or disorder, the protection of health or morals, or the protection of the rights and freedoms of others.
7 These are Article 56 of the Turkish Civil Code and Article 41 of the Turkish Constitution.
8 Bursa Office of the Attorney General (2006); Istanbul Office of the Attorney General (2006).

References

Altıparmak, Ö. and Öz, Y. 2007. Türk Hukuk Mevzuatında LGBTT Bireylere Yönelik Ayrımcılık Yaratan Düzenlemeler [Unpublished report].
Armas, H. 2007. "Whose Sexuality Counts? Poverty, Participation and Sexual Rights." *IDS Working Paper 294*. Brighton, University of Sussex, Institute of Development Studies.
Bursa Office of the Attorney General. 2006. Decision no: 2006/26401, October 6. Bursa.
Butler, Judith. 1997. "Merely Cultural." *Social Text* 52/3, Vol. 15, 3/4: 265–277.
Commission of the European Communities. 2008. "Turkey 2008 Progress Report." SEC (2008) 2699. November 5. Brussels. Available at: http://ec.europa.eu/enlargement/pdf/press_corner/key-documents/reports_nov_2008/turkey_progress_report_en.pdf [Accessed November 2, 2016].
Cooper, D. 1993. "An Engaged State: Sexuality, Governance and the Potential for Change." In *Activating Theory: Lesbian, Gay and Bisexual Politics*, eds. J. Bristow and A. R. Wilson, 190–218. London: Lawrence and Wishart.
Council Directive 2000/78/EC. November 27, 2000. Establishing a General Framework for Equal Treatment in Employment and Occupation. Available at: http://eur-lex.europa.eu/LexUriServ/LexUriServ.do?uri=CELEX:32000L0078:en:HTML [Accessed October 30, 2016].
Dietz, M. G. 1987. "Context Is All: Feminism and Theories of Citizenship." *Daedalus* 116, 4: 1–24.
DISK. 2009. *Özgürlükçü – Eşitlikçi, Demokratik ve Sosyal Bir Anayasa İçin Temel İlkeler Raporu*. Istanbul: DISK Yayınları. Available at: www.slideshare.net/BizsizAnayasaOlmaz/di-sk-anayasa-raporu [Accessed November 2, 2016].

Erol, A. 2008. "Cumhuriyetin Son İnkarı: Eşcinsel Realitesi." *Birgün*, November 17.
European Commission. 2015. *Staff Working Document: Turkey 2015 Report*. Available at: http://ec.europa.eu/enlargement/pdf/key_documents/2015/20151110_report_turkey.pdf [Accessed October 30, 2016].
European Parliament. 2016. *Report on Turkey: European Parliament resolution of 14 April 2016 on the 2015 report on Turkey (2015/2898(RSP)*. Available at: www.europarl.europa.eu/sides/getDoc.do?pubRef=-//EP//TEXT+TA+P8-TA-2016-0133+0+DOC+XML+V0//EN [Accessed October 30, 2016].
Fraser, N. 1997a. *Justice Interruptus*. New York: Routledge.
———. 1997b. "Heterosexism, Misrecognition, and Capitalism: A Response to Judith Butler." *Social Text* 52/53, Vol. 15, 3/4: 279–289.
Governor's Office. 2006. Letter to the Board of Lambda Istanbul by the Istanbul Governor's Office, Directorate of Provincial Associations. June 9. No: B.05.4VLK4340800-07/34–130/005.
Haberturk. 2016. "Müslüman Anadolu Gençliği'nden LGBTİ'nin Onur Yürüyüşü'ne Karşı Tehlikeli Çağrı." June 14 [online]. Available at: www.haberturk.com/gundem/haber/1253669-musluman-anadolu-gencligi-mag-lgbtinin-onur-yuruyusune-karsi-cagri [Accessed on July 30, 2016].
Hart, H. L. 1963. *Law, Liberty, and Morality*. Stanford, CA: Stanford University Press.
Human Rights Watch. 2008. *We Need a Law for Liberation: Gender, Sexuality, and Human Rights in a Changing Turkey*. New York: Human Rights Watch.
Hurriyet. 2016. "Alperen Ocakları: LGBT yürüyüşünü yaptırmayacağız." *Hurriyet* [online] June 15. Available at: www.hurriyet.com.tr/alperen-ocaklari-lgbt-yuruyusunu-yaptirmayacagiz-40117653 [Accessed July 30, 2016].
Ilkkaracan, P. 2007. "How Adultery Almost Derailed Turkey's Aspiration to Join the European Union." In *Sex Politics – Reports from the Front Lines*, eds. S. Correa, R. Parker and R. Petchesky, 247–275. New York: Sexuality Policy Watch.
———. 2010. "Re/forming Laws to Secure Women's Rights in Turkey: The Campaign on the Penal Code." In *Citizen Action and National Policy Reform*, eds. J. Gaventa and R. McGee, 195–216. London: Zed Books.
Istanbul 5th Criminal Court. 2007. Decision no: 2007/556, May 30. Istanbul.
Istanbul Office of the Attorney General. 2007. Decision no: 2007/991. February 8. Istanbul.
Joseph, S. ed. 2000. *Gender and Citizenship in the Middle East*. Syracuse, NY: Syracuse University Press.
Lambda Istanbul. 2008. Lambda Istanbul Press Statement [Press Release]. April 30. Available at: www.lambdaistanbul.org/php/main.php?menuID=5&altMenuID=5&icerikID=7138 [Accessed May 29, 2009].
Law No. 5253. November 4, 2004. Dernekler Kanunu [Law of Associations].
Law No. 5326. March 13, 2005. Kabahatler Kanunu [Misdemeanor Law].
Law No. 6529. March 2, 2014. Amendment to Various Laws In Order To Enhance Fundamental Rights and Liberties. Kabahatler Kanunu.
LGBTI News Turkey. 2016. 14th Istanbul LGBTI + Pride Week Committee Press Statement on June 26, 2016 [Press release]. Available at: https://lgbtinewsturkey.com/2016/06/26/14th-istanbul-lgbti-pride-week-committee-press-statement-on-26-june-2016/ [Accessed July 31, 2016].
Maclure, J. 2003. "The Politics of Recognition at an Impasse? Identity Politics and Democratic Citizenship." *Canadian Journal of Political Science* 36, 1: 3–21.

McAdam, D., Tarrow, S. and Tilly, C. 2001. *Dynamics of Contention*. Cambridge, MA: Cambridge University Press.
O'Donnell, G. 1993. "On the State, Democratization and Some Conceptual Problems: A Latin American View with Glances at Some Post-communist Countries." *World Development* 21, 8: 1355–1369.
Office of the Attorney General. 2005. *Decision no: 2005/1491, 10 October. Ankara*.
———. 2006. *Decision no: 2006/1456, 14 October. Ankara*.
Öz, Y. 2009. "Ahlâksızların Mekansal Dışlanması." In *Cins Cins Mekan*, ed. A. Alkan, 284–302. Istanbul: Varlık Yayınları.
Pateman, C. 1988. *The Sexual Contract*. Palo Alto, CA: Stanford University Press.
Perrone, Roberto, 2014. "Public Morals and the ECHR." University of Leicester School of Law Research Paper No. 14-02. Available at: https://papers.ssrn.com/sol3/papers.cfm?abstract_id=2382086 [Accessed October 30, 2016].
Phillips, A. 1991. Citizenship and Feminist Theory. In *Citizenship*, ed. G. Andrews, 76–88. London: Lawrence and Wishart.
———. 1995. *The Politics of Presence*. Oxford: Oxford University Press.
Pink Life LGBTT Solidarity Association, KAOS GL Asoociation, IGLHRC and LGBTI News Turkey. 2014. "Human Rights Violations of LGBT Individuals in Turkey. Shadow Report submitted to the United Nations Universal Periodic Review." Ankara. Available at: http://ilga.org/wp-content/uploads/2016/02/Shadow-report-16.pdf [Accessed February 15, 2017].
Richardson, D. 2000. "Claiming Citizenship? Sexuality, Citizenship and Lesbian/Feminist Theory." *Sexualities* 3, 2: 255–272.
Richter, D. J. 2001. "Social Integrity and Private 'Immorality' The HartDevlin Debate Reconsidered." *Essays in Philosophy* 2, 2: Article 3. Available at: http://commons.pacificu.edu/eip/vol2/iss2/ [Accessed November 1, 2016].
Supreme Court of the Turkish Republic, Court of Cassation. 2008. *Decision no: 2008/4109 – 2008/5196. 25 November. Ankara*.
Tarrow, S. 1998. *Power in Movement: Social Movements and Contentious Politics*. Cambridge, MA: Cambridge University Press.
Taylor, C. 2004. "The Politics of Recognition." In *Contemporary Political Theory: A Reader*, ed. C. Farrelly, 269–281. London: Sage.
Tully, J. 1999. "The Agonic Freedom of Citizens." *Economy and Society* 28, 2: 161–182.
———. 2001. "Introduction." In *Multinational Democracies*, eds. A.G. Gagnon and J. Tully, 1–34. Cambridge, MA: Cambridge University Press.
Yeni Akit. 2016. "Müslüman Anadolu Gençliği Sapkınlığa Dur Diyecek." *Yeni Akit* [online] June 15. Available at: www.yeniakit.com.tr/haber/musluman-anadolu-gencligi-sapkinliga-dur-diyecek-185025.html [Accessed July 30, 2016].
Yilmaz, Volkan and Gocmen, İpek. 2015. "Summary Results of the Social and Economic Problems of Lesbian, Gay, Bisexual and Transsexual (LGBT) Individuals in Turkey Research." *Center for Policy and Research on Turkey* 4, 6: 97–105. Available at: http://researchturkey.org/?p=9142 [Accessed March 7, 2017].
Zabita. 2016. "Various Fines to be Imposed within the Framework of the Misdemeanor Law, 2016." *Zabitapersoneli* [online]. Available at: http://zabitapersoneli.com/mevzuatlar/2016%20KABAHATLER%20KANUNU.pdf [Accessed October 25, 2016].

10 Gays, cross-dressers, and Emos

Non-normative masculinities in militarized Iraq[1]

Achim Rohde

Much has been written about gender-based violence against Iraqi women under the 35-year dictatorship of Saddam Hussein and since the fall of the regime in 2003.[2] While the mass recruitment of men as soldiers and fighters often temporarily expanded spaces for women's participation in the Iraqi public sphere (Efrati 1999, 28, 30–32; Rohde 2010, 86–91), militarism and militarist discourse before and since 2003 have reinforced gender polarity and heroic forms of masculinity, marginalizing and degrading the non-combat social positionalities of the majority of men and women (Rohde 2010, 124–143; 2011, 100–104, 109–110; Fischer-Tahir 2012, 93–94; Abdulameer 2014). Nevertheless, organized violence against queer positionalities, or men and women perceived to violate sexual and gender norms, occurred only after 2003. This chapter explores ruptures and continuities in organized violence against sex/gender non-conformity in recent Iraqi history.

For the late Ba`thist period in Iraq, I analyze scholarly and journalistic sources, including items published in Iraqi newspapers and transcripts of a conversation between Saddam Hussein and tribal leaders in 1991–1992. For the years after 2003, I systematically analyzed four Iraqi (Arabic) daily newspapers (*Al-Zaman, Al-Sabah, Al-Mada, Al-Manara*) and a weekly journal (*Al-Esbu`iyya*) from late 2008, 2009 and spring 2012. I draw on other sources as well, including news videos, human rights reports, scholarship, and other journalistic sources. Given the dangers and restrictions of research in Iraq, the available sources allow some preliminary analysis that can inform systematic future studies on gender and sexual diversity in Iraqi society.

Non-normative masculinities in Late Ba`thist Iraq

There is little research about the Iraqi Ba`thist regime's handling of non-normative sexualities and masculinities. Regime propaganda during the Iran–Iraq war (1980–1988) propagated a crude heroic and heterosexual military masculinity (Saghieh 2006, 242; Rohde 2010, 124–143). Hitherto classified sources from the innermost circle of the Hussein regime became accessible after the 2003 US invasion of Iraq, which military personnel captured and transferred to the National Defense University in Washington DC (Woods,

Palkki, and Scott 2011). Among the sources was a recorded conversation dated from 1991 or 1992 between Hussein and tribal elders from what was then called Saddam City (Sadr City today), a notoriously rebellious Baghdadi slum inhabited by some 2.5 million impoverished Shi`i Iraqis, most of whom had migrated from rural areas in southern Iraq over the previous decades. The area had been the scene of insurgent activities and demonstrations during the 1991 popular uprising. Many soldiers who had deserted the Iraqi army after being crushed by Western firepower in early 1991 reportedly blended into this densely populated area in various forms of dress and survived as burglars and beggars.

In a regime bid to reassert control, Hussein approached local tribal leaders in Saddam City to enlist them to police the neighborhood since state and party institutions had proven unsuccessful in this respect. In the conversation, Hussein termed opponents of his regime "rabble-rousers" (*ghugha'iyyin*), a term that started to appear in internal records of the Ba`th Party from 1991 and used to refer to insurgents. Faust contends this is a sign that operates as a "euphemism for Shi`ites" because the majority of insurgents came from predominantly Shi`i provinces (2015, 133, 242n64). No sectarian connotation is apparent in this account. Rather, Hussein decries non-normative masculinities as a scandal against Islam and the Iraqi nation:

> The rabble-rousers do not know these notions [of tribal loyalty to the dictator]. Those who dye their hair in green and red do not know these meanings, and it is a shame for you to let them live. You should slaughter them with your own hands. Those people who dye their hair and wear red lipstick like women, I say you must slaughter them and hold me responsible for it. … Whoever dyes his hair and wears makeup like women is effeminate. In my knowledge, the first fatwa of our master Ali [Ibn Abi Talib, the prophet's nephew and son-in-law, and the founder of Shi`i Islam] was related to one case that happened to Muslims the first time someone deviated. When … they asked [Ali] about the solution, "What should we do with this man?" He replied, "We should climb to the highest point, throw him upside down and let him fall down head first". This was a big fatwa. … I am seeking your help with the issue of those who dye their hair and wear women's clothes. This is shameful for Iraqis and against Islam. If a Syrian, Egyptian or Moroccan saw those people, he would laugh and say "What is that? Is that a man or a woman?" Iraqis are not like that, Iraqis are real men.
> (Woods, Palkki and Scott 2011, 207–210)

The former dictator refers to men and boys who engage in non-normative bodily practices such as dying their hair and wearing makeup, and the fatwa he refers to explicitly addresses homosexual acts. The commonly used term for effeminate men (*mukhanathiyyin*) is a synonym for male homosexuals in Iraq (Luongo 2010, 105). While I cannot verify whether the anti-regime activities that triggered this conversation included significant numbers of cross-dressing boys and men, Hussein's emphasis on this issue suggests that he thought so; moreover, the fatwa he refers to is often cited by Islamist ideologues in order to legitimate violence against gays (Zollner 2010). While it may seem odd for a secular dictator to quote this fatwa, it was likely an opportunistic mobilization appeal to a Shi'i audience that Hussein understood to be Islamist and conservative. The rebuff from one of the tribal elders to Hussein's appeal, which Hussein repeated three times, is equally remarkable: "Master, there is a more important issue than that, it is hurting citizens' feelings" (Woods, Palkki, and Scott 2011, 210). The sheikhs apparently refused to engage Hussein on his homophobic terms, indicating that cross-dressers were not scandalous to them. And they were courageous enough to point out their perceptions that the cause of social unrest in the neighborhood was the rising crime rate attributed to deserters from the Iraqi army.

Homosexual men and male-to-female transgender persons were visible and widely known to be part of Baghdad society at the time. Ali al-Hilli, an activist in the organization Iraqi LGBTQI who left Iraq in 2000, remembers that the regime "allowed a measure of liberation" between the end of the Iran-Iraq war in 1988 and the Iraqi invasion of Kuwait in August 1990. There was increased visibility of male homosexual scenes in more affluent parts of Baghdad: "There were so many guys, from Kuwait, from Saudi Arabia, guys in the streets with makeup" (Buckley 2007). The conversation between Hussein and the tribal leaders indicates that such communities also existed in poor neighborhoods. Dhia al-Saray (2009) mentions that in the late Ba'thist period, female hormones were freely available in Iraqi pharmacies. In a 2007 interview, al-Hilli mentions an old friend named Haidar "Dina" Fayek who was murdered shortly before the interview. Haidar/Dina "worked in the prostitution industry as a transsexual madam, was a fixture in Baghdadi gay circles, [and was] always loud and fun and quick with a laugh. She never hid her orientation and indeed lived openly as a woman" (France 2007; see also Ireland 2006). But as al-Hilli's account of his own experience demonstrates, the regime's intelligence services exploited the vulnerability of gay men in Iraqi society by attempting to blackmail them into becoming spies, particularly if they were in contact with foreigners (France 2007). Nevertheless, the situation was not desperate in the 1990s for most men with non-normative gender and sexual embodiments and identities or who engaged in same-sex relations.

In 1994, a few years after the conversation between Hussein and tribal leaders in Saddam City, the daily newspaper *Babil*, which was owned by Hussein's eldest son 'Uday, ran an article on the "scandal" of an ensemble of "Egyptian" *mukhanathiyyin* (male-to-female transvestites) performing in a Baghdad restaurant. Numerous published photos depicted the performers in drag. According to the published account, which included the restaurant's name and address,

Figure 10.1 Baghdad Restaurant, *Babil*, January 13, 1994

Babil's secret camera managed to collect these gleanings of a roaming band of Egyptian queers [*al-nafar al-dal min al-mukhanathiyyin al-misriyyin*] who can be seen in these pictures like morally corrupt women ... Is this tolerable in the country of struggle and brave people?

(*Babil*, January 13, 1994, translated by the author)

This article was published when the regime was clamping down on Baghdadi nightlife. Saddam Hussein had banned the public sale of alcohol and ordered all nightclubs closed as part of an Islamization campaign (Bengio 1998, 176–191; Rohde 2013, 714–717), the "National Faith Campaign." These efforts were widely understood as symbolic gestures aimed at appeasing religious forces and suppressing shows of conspicuous consumption given the severe UN sanctions; most Iraqis could hardly afford to buy food. As a result, such performances were no longer publicized (see Figure 10.1).

Despite Saddam Hussein's declared aversion, the regime did not conduct organized assaults on gay men, and queer life continued. An Iraqi gay man ("Kemal") portrayed in an account by Afdhere Jama (2008, 49–53) reports moving from his native Najaf to Baghdad in the 1990s, where he eventually lived in a romantic relationship with a wealthy older man in the upscale Mansour district. Both participated openly in social life in the permissive enclaves of well-to-do Baghdadis. Later in the 1990s, after they had split up, Kemal worked for international NGOs and charities and lived "a good, stable life" in the Zaytouna neighborhood. He continues: "It was work, have fun, and [I] lived my life without any stress. I met various guys as lovers and although none of them worked out, I was still happy with my life" (Jama 2008, 52). Of course Kemal's account does not reflect the experiences of most Iraqis, who suffered greatly under UN sanctions, and it might be coloured by a degree of nostalgia given the deterioration that occurred after 2003. Still, by all available accounts, popular nightclubs known to be frequented by gays remained in 1990s Baghdad, including in upscale hotels, "gay cafés and cruising points on Abu Nuwas Street ..., among other gathering spots" (Luongo 2010, 99–100; Buckley 2007).

Although there was relative openness to male non-normative gender and sexual practices, by 2000 there was a full-fledged campaign against women deemed prostitutes by "Saddam's Feda'iyyin," a paramilitary group founded in 1994 and run by Hussein's eldest son 'Uday. This militia formed part of what is called the "shadow state" in late Ba`thist Iraq since it existed outside the Ministry of Interior and reported directly to 'Uday Hussein (Sassoon 2012, 149–150). In 2001, a team of French researchers who collected human rights testimonies from Iraqi refugees in Damascus and Amman, composed biographical accounts of 56 women who were publicly beheaded in daylight by the Feda'iyyin. According to their findings, these "were often single women (widows, spinsters) who may have been prostitutes but who most often have been or are mixed up in some form of opposition to the regime" (International Alliance for Human Rights/Human Rights Alliance France 2002, 21–22). Reportedly, party and security service personnel often accompanied the executioners, shouting slogans like "Hurrah for the glory of Iraq! Down with those who shame us" (ibid., 22). The victims' families and neighbors were forced to witness the events. Heads and bodies were exhibited in front of their homes for up to 24 hours after an execution. Estimates of the number of women killed in the course of this campaign vary widely, but number between 60 and 2000 (ibid., 23).

In times of conflict, the killing of women is regularly connected to the concept of "national honor." The fusion of women's bodies with a discourse of honor and shame is amply demonstrated by 'Uday Hussein's henchmen in this violent campaign against women (Al-Ali & Pratt 2009, 10, 80). This violence occurred outside formal state frameworks. The Iraqi Penal Code of July 1969 sanctions prostitution with a 3–6 months' prison sentence and a fine.[3] The code does not penalize consensual same-sex activities between adults unless committed in public or by married men, which makes them a valid reason for a woman to be granted a divorce. In 1981, Revolutionary Command Council (RCC) Decree No. 125 amended the Personal Status Law, declaring acts of "sodomy" by a married man to be adultery.[4] The often-cited RCC Decree No. 234 that turned prostitution into a capital crime was issued on October 30, 2001, after the end of the violent campaign against women "prostitutes." With regard to homosexual practices, the decree added "sodomy" committed without consent to the list of capital offences but it did not outlaw homosexual activities, as was often reported.[5] In 2003, the decree and all amendments to Iraqi law issued after 1984 were declared null and void by Paul Bremer, who was appointed as Presidential Envoy to Iraq by George Bush, leading the Coalitional Provisional Authority during the occupation (Global Justice Project: Iraq 2009). This effectively turned back the clock, applying the Iraqi penal code and all amendments issued up to the beginning of 1985. The 1981 RCC amendment to the Personal Status Law was not declared invalid after 2003.

Militia masculinities and non-normative masculinities in Iraq after 2003

Conservative forces in the region argue that LGBTQI communities and lifestyles are expressions of Satanism, contradict Islamic precepts and human nature, and are the result of corrupting foreign influences (Tolino 2014, 78–82). Ryan Richard Thoreson (2014) reminds us, however, that just as in contemporary Africa, the trope of a rising tide of homophobia elides political-economic differences in incidents of anti-queer animus. According to available evidence, targeted killings of supposed or known gay men and male to female transgender persons started as early as 2004 but went largely unnoticed in the generalized violence of the US war in Iraq, insurgency, and militia infighting. Reports of these killings surfaced in international media in 2006 and 2007. Based on testimonies from Baghdad and Basra, these reports attributed the 2004 killings to the Iran backed Badr Corps, which form part of the Islamic Supreme Council of Iraq (ISCI).[6] A fatwa published in 2005 on Grand Ayatollah Ali al-Sistani's website legitimized the killing of men engaging in acts of "sodomy." The fatwa was removed from the website as a result of protests by advocacy groups, according to media reports (Ireland 2006; Howden 2006; Buckley 2007, France 2007).

After 2008, the decreasing violence in daily life led to a surge in nightlife in Baghdad, Basra, Najaf, and other cities, including gay nightlife (Williams and Maher 2009; LGBT Asylum News 2010).[7] Sadrist militiamen, part of "Jaysh al-Mahdi" (Mahdi Army, established in 2003) and its offspring "'Asa'ib Ahl al-Haq" (League of the Righteous, formed in 2006), responded by "repositioning themselves as agents of moral enforcement" (McAllester 2009, 2).[8] In 2009, these young men, who were from the same Baghdad neighborhood that was a site of the 1991 uprising against Hussein's government, embarked on a campaign that targeted and killed men and boys who were identified as homosexuals (Human Rights Watch 2009, 12). The masculine political agency of this younger generation was based on a brand of Islamism that took root in the late 1990s under the influence of Mohammad Sadiq as-Sadr, the father of Muqtada as-Sadr (Baram 2014, 271–278). According to a *New York Times* story in April 2009, Shi'i clerics in Baghdad "devoted a portion of Friday Prayer services to inveighing against homosexuality." The journalists report that in a sermon the previous week, Sheikh Jassem al-Mutairi instructed the congregation that the "community should be purified from such delinquent behavior like stealing, lying and the effeminacy phenomenon among men." Homosexuality, he reportedly said, is "far from manhood and honesty" (Williams & Maher 2009).

In a September 2012, BBC "assignment" documentary by Natalia Antelava titled "Hunted to Death – Gay Life in Iraq," the filmmaker's interlocutors discuss their experiences of violence and report frequent arrests and being raped at police checkpoints (Antelava 2012, 3:00ff, 8:10ff).[9] A spokesperson for the prime minister who was interviewed, contends that the state cannot protect homosexuals, emphasizes that homosexuality is alien to Iraqi culture, and states that gay people should respect local customs (ibid., 17:32ff). There is only anecdotal evidence of targeted killings of lesbian or bisexual women as part of this campaign. The lack of available data may reflect the focus of Western NGOs and researchers "on 'public', political patterns of attacks on men," or the general invisibility of lesbian or bisexual women in Iraqi society (Human Rights Watch 2009, 42–43; see also International Gay & Lesbian Human Rights Commission 2014a, 5).

The 2009 Islamist campaign against Iraqi boys and men targeted as gay was largely ignored by the government and Iraqi media.[10] When addressed by mainstream Iraqi media sources, the narrative was hesitant and all but explicitly condoned the killings. A 2009 article by Sabah Mohsen Kazem, published in the daily newspaper *al-Sabah*, criticized what he called the "feminization of young men" due to Western cultural influences and warned against their corrupting effects on Iraqi society as a whole (Whitaker 2010, 5). Al-Saray (2009, 37), in a published background report on the ongoing campaign, argued:

> They are homosexuals [*al-mithliyyun jinsiyyan*] or puppies [*jarawi*], as these effeminates are being called here, who suffer from the kidnappers [*al-shiyala*]. These are groups that hunt and mostly kill them. The police are observing, because there is nothing in the text of the Iraqi law that forbids this phenomenon.

According to reports in international media, the police indeed turned a blind eye to these organized killings and at times even participated in the persecution of supposed gays (Williams & Maher 2009). Killings of men and boys targeted as gay also occurred in 2012 and 2014, though on a more limited scale, and were again attributed to Sadrist Shi`i militias (International Gay & Lesbian Human Rights Commission 2014b, 6–8).[11]

The US invasion and the fall of Saddam Hussein's regime altered the parameters of non-normative sexual and gendered living in Iraq. The increased availability of the Internet in Iraq after 2003 "increase[d] gay networking within Baghdad and outside of Iraq," and made gay sites like www.manjam.com or www.gaydar.co.uk known to a local audience (Luongo 2010, 106). In the chaos and economic crisis that followed the invasion, sex work increasingly became a source of income for younger men and even children, which heightened the visibility of homosexual practices and attracted the attention of Islamist militias (Jama 2008, 52). There was a parallel increase of women and girl sex workers after 2003, particularly forced prostitution (Organization of Women's Freedom in Iraq 2010, 6). The feminization and queering of colonized men has long been known as an imperial strategy of projecting power, and US forces in Iraq, including in the Abu Ghraib prison, followed this trodden path (Trexler 1995, 1–37; Razack 2005, 341–363; Tétreault 2006, 159–163; Hasso 2007, 34–37). There is not sufficient evidence, however, that interaction with global gay culture or invasion and war have significantly changed the meanings and experiences of homosexuality in Iraqi society.

Killing and defending Emos

For several weeks in early 2012, a wave of murders against teenagers and young adults who were identified as "Emos" (this label was used loosely to capture a range of non-conforming behavior) was reported in Baghdad and southern Iraqi cities. The murders were attributed to the Sadrist Mahdi Army and League of the Righteous. The victims, estimated to range between "well under two dozen to 100," were largely male (LeVine 2012; see also Al-Sharaa & Mohammed 2012; Al-Bayati 2012). Emos were accused of being devil worshippers, effeminate and homosexual. The Emo subculture originates in the United States punk scene of the 1980s and refers to "emotional hardcore" music (Levine 2012). Emo music has a "more 'pop' sound" and lyrically focuses "on emotional, expressive or confessional lyrics" (LeVine 2012). According to Mark LeVine, critics "consider the music effete, or feminine, as it lacks the hard and supposedly masculine edge of more traditional punk, hardcore or heavy metal" (LeVine 2012). More recent adaptations became popular in various Middle East countries in the 2000s (Büsser, Engelmann, and Rüdiger 2009; Le Renard 2013, 68). According to Al-Bayati (2012), "Emo kids first started to appear in Iraq in 2008; most of them are aged between 12 and 18, the vast majority are male and one imagines the same elements of rebellion that attract Western teens, also attract the Iraqi youth." A 15-year-old Emo girl from Najaf portrayed by Ned Parker in a *Los Angeles Times* story (2010), describes her love of US goth music, her attraction to the "Twilight Saga" film series, and fashion accessories attached to the Emo subculture. In 2012, this subculture was ubiquitous in upscale urban districts, particularly in bars, schools, music shops, salons, and certain clothing shops (Al-Arabiyya TV 2012; LeVine 2012; Jawad 2012).

In contrast to the relative silence in the Iraqi media regarding the targeted killing of assumed homosexual men in 2009, the spring 2012 violence against Emo youths triggered a much broader Iraqi reaction among leading clerics, government officials and media pundits. Reactions were largely critical of the killing campaign and argued for focusing on addressing the sources of youth alienation. The Emo subculture was considered to be a protest against prevailing conservative social traditions and the bleak situation in Iraq after years of civil war. One article compared the phenomenon of Emo youths with the emergence of breakdance subculture in 1980s Iraq. Whereas state authorities had suppressed breakdancers by arresting young men and shaving their hair, according to one account (Da'ud 2012) in the weekly *Al-Esbu`iyya*, today's Emo are being killed straight away. The article implies that under the former regime social non-conformity had not been as brutally repressed; it also highlights the impact of social media, especially Facebook, for the spread of the Emo subculture in Iraq. A female student identifying as Emo is quoted as saying that being Emo is solely about fashion and music and is not a sign of Satanism.

A media account by Al-Babi (2012) declares Emos "a scandal for Iraqi cultural and national identity" and calls for a concerted effort to imbue adolescents with values and a solid cultural identity in order to prevent such developments. Nevertheless, he holds the difficult social, political, and economic situation in Iraq under the former regime and the American occupation responsible for the estrangement of Iraqi youth. The author of the *Al-Esbu`iyya* account (Da'ud 2012) argues that violence is the wrong way to deal with the Emo phenomenon and calls on state authorities to protect Emos. Trying to counter the image of Emos as alien to Iraqi culture, the author relates their black clothes to the `abaya worn by war widows and argues that Emo culture is an attempt to break out of the cycle of violence. An unsigned op-ed in the same issue of *Al-Esbu`iyya* (Anonymous 2012a) declares that Emo subculture is a harmless reaction by youths to the difficult circumstances of life in Iraq. The author criticizes condemnation of Emos as contradicting individual freedom and democratic values. Similarly, a report on the proceedings of a conference at a teacher training college regarding Emos suggests that most participants thought they were harmless kids and saw the phenomenon as a response to the violence and insecurity of life in Iraq (Mawzan 2012).

Most accounts strongly criticized violence against Emos. Al-'Ubaidi (2012) likens the killing of Emo youths to the brutality of the former regime and calls upon today's authorities to act differently and according to democratic values, to protect young people and offer them chances for employment. Kazem (2012b) differentiates between those for whom being Emo is a temporary phase during their adolescence and those who are homosexuals (*mithliyyun*) or third sex (*al-jins al-thalith*). He cites social scientists who declare that, in either case, Emos cause no harm to society. Al-Jaburi (2012) identifies the "American occupation" as the main reason for the spread of Western cultural imports in Iraq such as Emos, but his criticism is directed against the government, which he attacks for failing to support youths and provide opportunities for them. He also identifies frustration as a main cause for the rise of sectarian extremists who turn against minorities. According to him, the killing of Emos is condoned by high religious authorities (*shakhsiyyat diniyya kabira*) and aims to spread fear in society as a whole.

An elaborate portrait of Emo culture published in the daily *Al-Zaman* by an unsigned author (Anonymous 2012b) explicitly counters erroneous views about Emos in Iraqi society. According to this article, being Emo is mainly about expressing emotions and a way for young people to come to terms with difficult transitory phases in their lives. The author notes that it is difficult to distinguish between male and female Emos because of their similar clothing choices. He stresses the difference between Emos and heavy metal fans in

Iraq. He contends that heavy metal fans are the real devil worshippers who had to be approached and reintegrated into society.[12]

In a marked contrast with 2009, Iraqi parliament members publicly condemned the killing of Emos and vowed to act against the perpetrators, and leading Shi'i clerics, including Muqtada Al-Sadr and Ali Sistani, denounced the killings and called for "ending the phenomenon in the framework of the law" (Anonymous 2012c; Human Rights Watch 2012). The chairperson of the Human Rights committee of the Iraqi parliament called for educational efforts to push back the influence of Emo culture, but added that violence is no solution (Kazem 2012a). While denouncing the killings, these figures believed that Emo subculture should have no place in Iraqi society. It is impossible to determine if the parliamentarians issued these condemnations out of personal convictions, or if they merely paid lip service to human rights and rule of law discourse. The broad public condemnation of the killings might have influenced their behavior at this point.

In the executive branch of the Iraqi government, discourse regarding Emo subculture was similarly disapproving but more repressive. In August 2011, the Ministry of Education "circulated a memo that recommended schools to curb the spread of Emo culture, which it called 'an infiltrated phenomenon in our society'" (Human Rights Watch 2012). The Ministry of Education issued a statement in 2012 that Emo youths would be prevented from entering schools, arguing that pupils had to be shielded from their corrupting influence (Zahrawi 2012). Statements from the Ministry of Interior, which oversees the police, instructed violent containment of Emos. On February 13, 2012 the ministry issued a statement on its website which stated that officials had been

> following up on the phenomenon of "Emo" or Satanists, and that they [the police] have official approval to eliminate them as soon as possible, because the dimensions of this community have begun to move in another direction, and are now threatening danger.[13]

Only a month later the ministry was compelled to issue a statement warning "radical and extremist groups attempting to stand as protectors for morals and religious traditions from any conduct against people based on a fashion, dress or haircut" (Human Rights Watch 2012). At the same time, the Ministry of Interior initiated a campaign to curb the further spread of Emo culture by sending police to close shops that sold Emo fashion and accessories, starting in Kadimiyya. Local functionaries in that neighborhood claimed that Emos contradicted the cultural values of Iraqi society and negatively impacted young people, whom they accused of blindly imitating Western influences (Al-Rawi and Kazem 2012; Human Rights Watch 2012). The repressive stance regarding social non-conformity reflected in these statements and the evidence of police involvement in repression suggest that a significant degree of overlap exists between parts of the Iraqi government and the informal militias behind most of the killings.

Conclusion

Non-normative gendered and sexual practices and identities are longstanding in Iraq and other parts of the region, and co-exist with hostility to same-sex relations and gender and sexual non-conformity (Rowson 1991, 671–693; Murray 1997a, 244–255; 1997b, 204–221; Westphal-Hellbusch 1997, 233–243). Despite Saddam Hussein's homophobic outbursts, there is no evidence of organized violence against supposed gays or cross-dressers by the Ba'thist government or allied non-state actors before 2003. Recent waves of violence against gender and sexual queerness in Iraq target the country's cultural heritage and are part of continuous attacks on Iraqi civil society, whose gender and sexual diversity is often unaccounted for in conventional narratives. Some observers have interpreted such attacks in Iraq and elsewhere as expressions of a struggle between tradition and modernity, constructing an Arab-Islamic civilizational block that refuses to respect human rights, with progress sometimes identified with the proliferation of visible gayness (Whitaker 2006, 2010). This position is indefensible and has been criticized (Haritaworn et al. 2008).

Violence against non-normative gender and sexual behaviors, enactments and identities has convincingly been attributed to the general erosion of the Iraqi state and the normalization of violence after decades of war, embargo and societal conflict (Al-Rachid & Méténier 2008, 114–117, 127–132; Green & Ward 2009, 612–616). A "culture of war" that centers the male soldier-hero as the acting subject is ubiquitous (Rohde 2010, 124–143; 2011, 100–104, 109–110; Dodge 2013, 256; Abdulameer 2014). This ideal of masculinity marginalizes and delegitimizes Iraqis who do not conform. The radical and traumatic changes experienced by Iraqis since 2003 have increased organized gender and sexual violence and outbreaks of moral panic that scapegoat non-conformists (Whitaker 2010, 5).

It is clear that several sectarian entrepreneurial formations have emerged in post-Saddam Iraq. Politicians and other figures preside over "informal" militia forces that act outside formal state structures. Some of these militias are widely understood to be associated with leading Shi`i actors in the central government and some are aligned with the Sunni insurgency. While these militias are not formally attached to the state, their acts are condoned by executive state officials who fail to prosecute the crimes and often issue inciting or endorsing statements. Moreover, police are often involved in violence against gender and sexual non-conforming people. All the dominant players pursue authoritarian political visions (Dodge 2013, 246, 249). In their fight for political control, they turn against Iraq's social and cultural diversity, notably in the realms of gender and sexuality. The organized anti-queer campaigns in post-2003 Iraq are reminiscent of the killing of women deemed prostitutes in 2000, when Saddam Hussein's son 'Uday initiated the campaign and the government legitimized the murders post-facto by issuing a decree that made sex work a capital offence. Before and after 2003, the victims' alleged deviant gendered and sexual practices were understood to embody ideological opposition.

Despite armed and well-financed attempts to repress diversity, Iraqi society remains multiple and vital in its gendered and sexual practices. Many communities, social spaces, and subcultures with different value systems exist and yet are not completely isolated from one another. Darle (2003, 145–160) has termed this state of affairs a "polysémie." While there is not necessarily widespread endorsement of such diversity, the vivid public debate and broad condemnation of the killings of Emo youth in 2012 is an encouraging sign that sexual and gender diversity will continue to be embraced in Iraqi society.

Notes

1 "Gays, Cross-Dressers, and Emos: Nonnormative Masculinities in Militarized Iraq" was originally published in the *Journal of Middle East Women's Studies* 12, 3: 433–449. Copyright 2016, Association for Middle East Women's Studies. All rights reserved. Republished by permission of the copyright holder, and the present publisher, Duke University Press. www.dukeupress.edu [Accessed April 8, 2016]:
2 Brown and Romano (2006, 56, 60–62); Al-Jawaheri (2008, 108–117); al-Ali (2005, 742–743, 754–755; 2007, 198, 207, 226–229; 2008, 413–416); Smiles (2008, 272–276); al-Ali and Pratt (2009, 78–80, 157–161); Campbell and Kelly (2009, 24–25); Fischer-Tahir (2010, 1391–1392); Ranharter and Stansfield (2015).
3 See Article 402 of the Iraqi penal code, which is available at www.iraq-lg-law.org/en/content/penal-code-no-111-1969-amended [Accessed April 8, 2016].
4 See *Al-Waqai al-Iraqiyya* No. 2863, December 21, 1981 and Articles 400 and 401 of the Iraqi Penal Code.
5 The decree is available at http://gjpi.org/wp-content/uploads/rcc-resolution-234-of-2001.pdf [Accessed April 8, 2016].
6 See https://web.stanford.edu/group/mappingmilitants/cgi-bin/groups/view/435 [Accessed April 8, 2016].
7 See also, a video apparently showing footage of a gay party at New Year's Eve 2009 in a Baghdad hotel: www.youtube.com/watch?v=OzGwq84FTjo [Accessed April 10, 2016].
8 For detailed and regularly updated portraits of these militias, see https://web.stanford.edu/group/mappingmilitants/cgi-bin/groups/view/143, https://web.stanford.edu/group/mappingmilitants/cgi-bin/groups/view/57 [Accessed April 8, 2016].
9 www.bbc.co.uk/programmes/p00xs1qb [Accessed April 18, 2016].
10 This claim is based on a systematic screening of the 2009 editions of four Iraqi daily papers and one weekly newspaper (*Al-Mada, Al-Manara, Al-Zaman, Al-Sabah*, and *Al-Esbu`iyya*), as well as of Internet statements by government officials or journalists that explicitly addressed the targeted killings of supposed gays. Only one article by Al-Saray, published in Al-Esbu`iyya, discussed this campaign. The newspapers are available in the press archive of Tel Aviv University's Moshe Dayan Center and on the internet.
11 Complementing the terror of Shi`i militias, the Islamic State since 2014 has reportedly killed men accused of having had sex with men in Deir Ezzor, Raqqa and Homs in Syria, and in Fallujah and Mosul (Cowburn 2016; Brydum 2015).
12 Despite the country's isolation, Heavy Metal was known and had its fans in Iraq during the 1990s as indicated by a writing "on an enclosure in the fine arts college in Baghdad" that celebrated the band Black Sabbath and its lead singer Ozzy

Osbourne (Faust 2015, 167–8). The documentary film "Heavy Metal in Baghdad" (2007) portraits the Iraqi metal band Acrassicauda, which was formed in Baghdad after the invasion of 2003. See www.youtube.com/watch?v=WuieVRO1DWg&no html5=False [Accessed April 11, 2016].
13 The quote was gleaned from a screenshot of the Iraqi Ministry of Interior website, which was shown in an al-Jazeera "Stream" on March 22, 2012 (www.youtube.com/watch?v=vPxrvCTXY0Q, screenshot at 15:40ff) that featured an extensive background interview with Yanar Muhammad and Ali al-Hilli on the massacre of Emo youths [Accessed June 12, 2015].

References

Abdulameer, Ali. 2014. "Nationalist Themes Coopt Iraqi Music, Again." *Al-Monitor*. January 12. Available at: www.al-monitor.com/pulse/originals/2014/01/iraq-songs-state-propaganda.html [Accessed April 10, 2016].
Al-Ali, Nadje. 2005. "Reconstructing Gender: Iraqi Women between Dictatorship, War, Sanctions and Occupation." *Third World Quarterly* 26, 4/5: 739–758.
———. 2007. *Iraqi Women. Untold Stories from 1948 to the Present*. London and New York: Zed Books.
———. 2008. "Iraqi Women and Gender Relations: Redefining Difference." *British Journal of Middle Eastern Studies* 35, 3: 405–418.
Al-Ali, Nadje and Nicola Pratt. 2009. *What Kind of Liberation? Women and the Occupation of Iraq*. Berkeley, CA: University of California Press.
Al-Arabiyya TV. 2012. "Iraqi Gay Community and 'Emos' Fear Abuse, Violence." March 14. Available at: www.youtube.com/watch?v=CwOi3L-DATE [Accessed April 10, 2016].
Al-Babi, 'Abd al-Hādi. 2012. "The Emo Phenomenon – A Scandal for Our Cultural and National Identity." *Al-Zaman*. March 24 (Arabic).
Al-Bayati, Shawkat. 2012. "Iraq's Threatened Emo Kids: 'We are Peaceful, we do not Worship the Devil.'" *Niqash*. March 14. Available at: www.niqash.org/articles/?id=3009 [Accessed April 10, 2016].
Al-Jaburi, Adel. 2012. "They are Killing the Emos." *Al-Zaman*. March 20 (Arabic).
Al-Jawaheri, Yasmin Hussein. 2008. *The Gender Impact of International Sanctions: Women in Iraq*. London: I.B. Tauris.
Al-Rachid, Loulouwa and Èduard Méténier. 2008. "Apropos de la Violence 'Irakienne'. Quelques Éléments de Réflexion sur un Lieu Commun." *A Contrario* 5, 1: 114–133.
Al-Rawi, Saray and 'Adel Kazem. 2012. "The Emo – Strange Accessories and Characteristic Clothes." *Al-Zaman*. March 4 (Arabic).
Al-Saray, Dhia. 2009. "The War Between the 'Puppies' and the Kidnappers." *Al-Esbu`iyya*. May 10–16 (Arabic).
Al-Sharaa, Hazim and Abeer Mohammed. 2012. "Iraq's Emo Youth Fear Threats." *Institute for War & Peace Reporting*. March 26. Available at: http://iwpr.net/report-news/iraqs-emo-youth-fear-threats [Accessed June 15, 2015].
Al-'Ubaidi, Sa`d. 2012. "The Emo – Wrong Treatment and Misunderstanding." *Al-Zaman*. March 24 (Arabic).
Anonymous. 2012a. "Why?" *Al-Esbu`iyya* 212. March 18–24 (Arabic).
———. 2012b. "Youth Culture in America Aims at Expressing Emotions." *Al-Zaman*. March 8 (Arabic).
———. 2012c. "The Government Denies any Persecution of Emo Youths and Calls for Respect of Personal Freedoms." *Al-Sabah*. March 11 (Arabic).

Antelava, Natalia. 2012. "Gay Witch Hunt in Iraq." *BBC World Service.* September 12. Available at: www.youtube.com/watch?v=1vvMCXI1Z14 [Accessed April 10, 2016].
Baram, Amatzia. 2014. *Saddam Husayn and Islam, 1968–2003: Ba`thi Iraq from Secularism to Faith.* Washington, DC and Baltimore, MD: Woodrow Wilson Center Press, Johns Hopkins University Press.
Bengio, Ofra. 1998. *Saddam's Word: Political Discourse in Ba`thist Iraq.* New York: Oxford University Press.
Brown, Lucy and David Romano. 2006. "Women in Post-Saddam Iraq: One Step Forward or Two Steps Back?" *NWSA Journal* 18, 3: 51–70.
Brydum, Sunnivie. 2015. "REPORT: ISIS Executes Nine More 'Gay' Men." *The Advocate.* August 28. Available at: www.advocate.com/world/2015/08/28/reports-isis-executes-nine-more-gay-men [Accessed April 10, 2016].
Buckley, Carla. 2007. "Gays Living in Shadows of New Iraq." *New York Times.* December 18. Available at: www.nytimes.com/2007/12/18/world/middleeast/18baghdad.html?_r=0 [Accessed June 14, 2015].
Büsser, Martin, Jonas Engelmann and Ingo Rüdiger eds. 2009. *Emo: Portrait einer Szene.* Mainz: Ventil Verlag.
Campbell, Perri and Peter Kelly. 2009. "'Explosions and Examinations': Growing up Female in post-Saddam Iraq." *Journal of Youth Studies* 12, 1: 21–38.
Cowburn, Ashley. 2016. "Isis has killed at least 25 men in Syria suspected of being gay, group claims." *The Independent.* January 5. Available at: www.independent.co.uk/news/world/middle-east/isis-has-killed-at-least-25-men-in-syria-suspected-of-being-gay-group-claims-a6797636.html [Accessed April 10, 2016].
Darle, Pierre. 2003. *Saddam Hussein Maître des Mots. Du Langage de la Tyrannie à la Tyrannie du Langage.* Paris: L'Harmattan.
Da'ud, Hassan. 2012. "Senseless Killing in Baghdad. Death Squads Hunt Emo Youths." *Al-Esbu`iyya* 212. March 18–24 (Arabic).
Dodge, Toby. 2013. "State and Society in Iraq 10 Years after Regime Change: the Rise of a New Authoritarianism." *International Affairs* 89, 2: 241–257.
Efrati, Noga. 1999. "Productive or Reproductive? The Roles of Iraqi Women during the Iraq-Iran War." *Middle Eastern Studies* 35, 2: 27–44.
Faust, Aaron M. 2015. *The Ba`thification of Iraq. Saddam Hussein's Totalitarianism.* Austin, TX: University of Texas Press.
Fischer-Tahir, Andrea. 2010. "Competition, Cooperation and Resistance: Women in the Political Field in Iraq." *International Affairs* 86, 6: 1381–1394.
———. 2012. "Gendered Memories and Masculinities: Kurdish Peshmerga on the Anfal Campaign in Iraq." *Journal of Middle East Women's Studies* 8, 1: 92–114.
France, David. 2007. "Dying to Come Out: The War Against Gays in Iraq." *GQ.* January. Available at: www.gq.com/news-politics/big-issues/200701/ali-Hilli-gay-iraqi-spy [Accessed April 10, 2016].
Global Justice Project: Iraq. 2009. "Homosexuality and the Criminal Law in Iraq: Updated." May 21. Available at: http://gjpi.org/2009/05/21/homosexuality-and-the-criminal-law-in-iraq/ [Accessed June 12, 2015].
Green, Penny and Tony Ward. 2009. "The Transformation of Violence in Iraq." *British Journal of Criminology* 49, 5: 609–627.
Haritaworn, Jin with Tamsila Tawqir and Esra Erdem. 2008. "Gay Imperialism: Gender and Sexuality Discourse in the 'War on Terror.'" In *Out of Place: Interrogating Silences in Queerness/Raciality*, edited by Adi Kuntsman and Esperanza Miyake, 9–33. York: Raw Nerve Books.

Hasso, Frances. 2007. "Culture Knowledge' and the Violence of Imperialism: Revisiting The Arab Mind." *MIT Electronic Journal of Middle East Studies* 7: 24–40. https://franceshasso.files.wordpress.com/2013/02/culture-knowledge-hasso.pdf.

Howden, Daniel. 2006. "Sistani Renounces Fatwa on Gays." *The Independent*. May 6. Available at: www.independent.co.uk/news/world/middle-east/sistani-renounces-fatwa-on-gays-478396.html [Accessed June 10, 2015].

Human Rights Watch. 2009. "They Want Us Exterminated." Murder, Torture, Sexual Orientation and Gender in Iraq." August 18. Available at: www.hrw.org/sites/default/files/reports/iraq0809webwcover.pdf [Accessed April 8, 2016].

———. 2012. "Iraq: Investigate 'Emo' Attacks." March 16. Available at: www.hrw.org/news/2012/03/16/iraq-investigate-emo-attacks [Accessed April 10, 2016].

International Alliance for Human Rights / Human Rights Alliance France. 2002. "Iraq: An Intolerable, Forgotten, and Unpunished Repression." Paris, March 13. Available at: www.refworld.org/docid/46f1465f0.html [Accessed April 10, 2016].

International Gay & Lesbian Human Rights Commission. 2014a. "We're Here. Iraqi LGBT People's Accounts of Violence and Rights Abuse." Available at: www.outrightinternational.org/sites/default/files/WereHere_IraqLR.pdf [Accessed April 10, 2016].

———. 2014b. "When Coming Out is a Death Sentence. Persecution of LGBT Iraqis." November. Available at: www.outrightinternational.org/sites/default/files/ComingOutDeathSentence_Iraq_0.pdf [Accessed April 10, 2016].

Ireland, Doug. 2006. "Shia Death Squads Target Iraqi Gays." *Gay City News* 5, 12: March 23–29. Available at: http://gaycitynews.com/gcn_511/iraq.html [Accessed April 10, 2016].

Jama, Afdhere. 2008. *Illegal Citizens. Queer Lives in the Muslim World*. N.p.: Salaam Press.

Jawad, Laith. 2012. "Ministry of Interior: Emos Give up on Clothing and Accessories." *Al-Zaman*. March 5 (Arabic).

Kazem, 'Adel. 2012a. "The Marja'iya Denounces Emo Killings and Parliament Calls for Educational Efforts." *Al-Zaman*. March 8 (Arabic).

———. 2012b. "The Authorities Stop the Killing of Teenagers." *Al-Zaman*. April 2 (Arabic).

Kazem, Sabah Mohsen. 2009. "The Feminization of Young Men: Diagnosis and Treatment." *Al-Sabah*. May 7 (Arabic).

Le Renard, Amélie. 2013. "Les Buya. Subversion des Normes de Genre en Arabie Saoudite." In *Jeunesses Arabes. Du Maroc au Yémen: Loisirs, Cultures et Politiques*, edited by Laurent Bonnefoy and Myriam Catusse, 68–77. Paris: Découverte.

LeVine, Mark. 2012. "Killing Emos, and the Future, in Iraq." *Al-Jazeera*. March 20. Available at: www.aljazeera.com/indepth/opinion/2012/03/201231911938716976.html [Accessed April 10, 2016].

LGBT Asylum News. 2010. Gay Life in Iraq. Interview with Michael Luongo (part one). October 25. Available at: www.youtube.com/watch?v=4mqyBjXyO2g [Accessed April 10, 2016].

Luongo, Michael T. 2010. "Gays under Occupation: Interviews with Gay Iraqis." In *Islam and Homosexuality*, Vol. 1, edited by Samar Habib, 99–110. Santa Barbara, CA: Praeger.

Mawzan, Qasem Hussein. 2012. "Conference on the Emo Phenomenon." *Al-Sabah*. March 20 (Arabic).

McAllester, Matt. 2009. "The Hunted." *New York Magazine*. October 4. Available at: http://nymag.com/news/features/59695 [Accessed April 10, 2016].

Murray, Stephen O. 1997a. "The Sohari Khanith." In *Islamic Homosexualities. Culture, History, and Literature*, edited by Stephen O. Murray and Will Roscoe, 244–255. New York: New York University Press.

———. 1997b. "Some Nineteenth-Century Reports of Islamic Homosexualities." In *Islamic Homosexualities. Culture, History, and Literature*, edited by Stephen O. Murray and Will Roscoe, 204–221. New York: New York University Press.

Organization of Women's Freedom in Iraq. 2010. "Prostitution and Trafficking of Women and Girls in Iraq." March 5. Available at: www.peacewomen.org/assets/file/Resources/NGO/dispvaw_prostitutiontraffickingiraqwomen_owfi_march2010.pdf [Accessed April 10, 2016].

Parker, Ned. 2010. "An Iraqi Girl's Thinly Veiled Teenage Rebellion." *Los Angeles Times*. December 14. Available at: http://articles.latimes.com/2010/dec/14/world/la-fg-iraq-goth-girl-20101214 [Accessed April 10, 2016].

Ranharter, Katherine and Gareth Stansfield. 2015. "Acknowledging the Suffering Caused by State-Mandated Sexual Violence and Crimes: An Assessment of the Iraqi High Tribunal." *Middle Eastern Studies* 52, 1: 27–45.

Razack, Sherene H. 2005. "How is White Supremacy Embodied? Sexualized Racial Violence at Abu Ghraib." *Canadian Journal of Women and the Law* 17, 2: 341–363.

Rohde, Achim. 2010. *State-Society Relations in Ba'thist Iraq. Facing Dictatorship*. London: Routledge.

———. 2011. "War and Gender in Ba'thist Iraq." In *Gender and Violence in the Middle East*, edited by Moha Ennaji and Fatima Sadiqi, 97–114. London: Routledge.

———. 2013. "Change and Continuity in Arab Iraqi Education: Sunni and Shi'i Discourses in Iraqi Textbooks Before and After 2003." *Comparative Education Review* 57, 4: 711–734.

Rowson, Everett K. 1991. "The Effeminates of Early Medina." *Journal of the American Oriental Society* 111, 4: 671–693.

Saghieh, Hazim. 2006. "'That's how I am, World!' Saddam, Manhood, and the Monolithic Image." In *Imagined Masculinities. Male Identity and Culture in the Modern Middle East*, edited by May Ghoussoub and Emma Sinclair-Web, 236–248. London: Saqi.

Sassoon, Joseph. 2012. *Saddam Hussein's Ba'th Party. Inside an Authoritarian Regime*. Cambridge, MA: Cambridge University Press.

Smiles, Sarah. 2008. "On the Margins: Women, National Boundaries, and Conflict in Saddam's Iraq." *Identities: Global Studies in Culture and Power* 15, 3: 271–296.

Tétreault, Mary Ann. 2006. "The Sexual Politics of Abu Ghraib. Hegemony, Spectacle, and the Global War on Terror." *National Women's Studies Association Journal* 18, 3: 33–50.

Thoreson, Ryan Richard. 2014. "Troubling the Waters of a 'Wave of Homophobia': Political Economies of anti-Queer Animus in sub-Saharan Africa." *Sexualities* 17, 1–2: 23–42.

Tolino, Serena. 2014. "Homosexuality in the Middle East: An Analysis of Dominant and Competitive Discourses." *DEP (Deportate, Esule, Profughe)* 25: 72–91.

Trexler, Richard C. 1995. *Sex and Conquest: Gendered Violence, Political Order, and the European Conquest of the Americas*. Ithaca, NY: Cornell University Press.

Westphal-Hellbusch, Sigrid. 1997. "Institutionalized Gender-Crossing in Southern Iraq." In *Islamic Homosexualities. Culture, History, and Literature*, edited by Stephen O. Murray and Will Roscoe, 233–243. New York: New York University Press.

Whitaker, Brian. 2006. *Unspeakable Love. Gay and Lesbian Life in the Middle East*. London: Saqi.

———. 2010. "Pride and Prejudice: The Targeting of Gay Men in Iraq." *Near East Quarterly*. November 28.

Williams, Timothy and Tareq Maher. 2009. "Iraq's Newly Open Gays Face Scorn and Murder." *The New York Times*. April 7. Available at: www.nytimes.com/2009/04/08/world/middleeast/08gay.html?_r=0 [Accessed April 10, 2016].

Woods, Kevin M., David D. Palkki, and Mark E. Scott eds. 2011. *The Saddam Tapes: The Inner Workings of a Tyrant's Regime, 1978–2001*. Cambridge, MA: Cambridge University Press.

Zahrawi, Fajr Muhammad. 2012. "Ministry of Education: No Place for Emos in Schools." *Al-Sabah*. March 12 (Arabic).

Zollner, Barbara. 2010. "Mithliyyun or Lutiyyun? Neo-Orthodoxy and the Debate on the Unlawfulness of Same-Sex Relations in Islam." In *Islam and Homosexuality*, Vol 1, edited by Samar Habib, 193–221. Santa Barbara, CA: Praeger.

Index

Abdel-Jaouad, Hédi 139
Abelove, Henry 100n8
abject art 80, 85n3
Abject Art: Repulsion and Desire in American Art (exhibition) 85n3
abortion 56, 61, 70
Aboutaleb, Ahmed 26, 27
AFŽ (Women's Antifascist Front), Yugoslavia 55, 56, 57
Ahimeir, Abba 113
Ahmed, Sara 50
al-Ali, N. S. 134n5
Aldrich, Robert, *Colonialism and Homosexuality* 112
All-Polish Youth 70
Alperen Hearths (youth organization) 157
American Psychiatric Association 57; Diagnostic and Statistical Manual of Mental Disorders 164
Amsterdam 25, 29
Anatolia Muslim Youth 157
Anderson, Benedict 2, 43
Antelava, Natalia 177, 178
anti-Semitism 2, 95, 96, 109, 116
Antifascist Council of the People's Liberation of Yugoslavia (AVNOJ) 55, 56
Arabic literature 121–134; androgyny in 128, 129–133; female homosexuality 123–125, 126; male homosexuality 126–128; patriarchal society 121, 123, 124, 125
Ars Homo Erotica (exhibition) 72, 73–74, 81
art, Eastern European 71–85; art history and homophobia 81–82; disruptive power of negativity 80–81; subversion 80–81

Art Guys, The (Michael Galbreth and Jack Massing), *The Art Guys Marry a Plant* (performance) 83, 84
"'Asa'ib Ahl al-Haq" (League of the Righteous) 177, 179
Ashkenazi, Dr. Tuvia 112
asylum and sexual orientation 6, 39–52; case study 46–49; Norwegian asylum regulations 44–45, 46
Austria 57
autodiegetic narrators 144, 152, 153
AVNOJ (Antifascist Council of the People's Liberation of Yugoslavia) 55, 56

al-Babi, 'Abd al-Hādi 180
Babil (newspaper) 174, 175
Balboa, Vasco de 82
Barakāt, Hodà, *Ḥāǧaraḍ-ḍaḥk (The Stone of Laughter)* 121, 128, 129–133
Basta, Mus'ad, *The Ostrich Egg* 121
Bawer, Bruce 39
al-Bayati, Sahwkat 179
Belgrade, University of 58
Bensmaïa, Réda 140
Bhabha, Homi 2
Bild (newspaper) 88
binarism 10, 96, 121, 123, 125–126, 129, 140–146
bisexuality 91, 140, 143, 151, 178
Black Pink Triangle 159, 166
Blažević, Dunja 57
Blüher, Hans 92, 93; on forms of homosexuality 94–95, 96
Bolkestein, Frits 34n2
Böll, Heinrich 61
Bosnia 55, 56

Index

Boudjedra, Rachid 143; *The Repudiation* 146
Bourdieu, Pierre 33
Boyarin, Daniel 109
Bracke, Sarah 20, 24
Brand, Adolf 91
Bremer, Paul 176
Brnabic, Anna 62
Brown, W. 24
Buckley, Carla 174
Buden, Boris 59, 63, 64
Buijs, Laurens et al. 2012 29, 35n4
Buruma, Ian 34n2
Bush, George W. 176
Butler, Judith 19, 63, 98, 99, 133, 134

Campaign for the Reform of the Turkish Penal Code 168
Castells, Manuel 26
Catholicism 58, 60, 61, 70, 72, 82
censorship 69, 71, 73, 80, 82, 83, 128, 133
Chávez, Karma R. 50
Chevallier, Denis 78
Chraïbi, Driss, *The Simple Past* 143
Çicek, Cemil 168
"civil Islam" 20, 26, 27–28, 29
colonialism: art as propaganda 82; 'degeneration' 112, 113; and effeminacy 96; feminization 178, 179; and language 99, 138, 140; Zionist 109
Comrade Woman: The Women's Question: A New Approach? (Drugcažena. Žensko pitanje. Novi pristup?) (conference) 57, 58
Croatia 57–65, 74, 75; *In the Name of Family* (*U ime obitelji*) initiative 62
CSD Berlin (pride association) 98, 99
cultural assimilationism 23
cultural essentialism 22
cultural protectionism 20
culturalism 3, 5, 20–22, 24–28, 30, 32–34

Dačić, Ivica 60
Darle, Pierre 183
Davar (newspaper) 107, 108, 110, 111, 112, 116
de Bry, Theodore, *America* 82
degeneration 4, 89–97, 112–116, 117; "psychic degeneration" 112
Deleuze, G. and Guattari, F. 122, 123
Devarrieux, Claire 142
di Bartolo, Taddeo, *The Last Judgment* 82

Dietz, Gabriele 161
diffusionism 8
Đinđić, Zoran 60
Dirt and Domesticity: Constructions of the Feminine (exhibition) 85n3
"discretion reasoning" on asylum 44–45
Djaziri, Eyet-Chékib: *A Fish on a Swing* (*Un poisson sur la balançoire*) 139, 140, 145–146, 153; *A Promise of Pain and Blood* (*Une promesse de douleur et de sang*) 139, 153
Dota, Franko 65n5
Doubrovsky, Serge 152
Dresselhuys, Ciska 24
Drucker, Peter 23
Dugandžić, Danijela 56
Duggan, Lisa 42, 134, 152

East Side Story (video installation) (Grubic) 74, 75–76
ECHR (European Convention on Human Rights) 158, 164, 165, 166
Eelmaa, Liisi and Hint, Minna, *Heard Story* (video installation) 76, 77–78
effeminacy: in art 82; Germany 90, 94–98; Iraq 173, 177, 178, 179; Jewish 7, 109, 112, 116; North African literature 140, 144, 145, 149
Egypt: Egyptians in Iraq 174, 175; literature 128, 144, 145; Matmon on homosexuality in 115; mythology 125
Eisenstein, Zillah 76
Ekremoğlu, Selahattin 164
El-Moumni, Khalil 28
Emos 179–181
Eng, David 43, 51
Enloe, Cynthia 2
Erdogan, Recep Tayyip 160, 168
Erol, A. 160
Al-Esbu'iyya (weekly newspaper) 179, 180
Estonia 76, 77
"ethical moments" 28, 34
EU (European Union): and Poland 69, 70, 71; pressure on Turkey 164, 168; protection of LGBTQ citizens 69; and Serbia 60, 61, 62
European Convention on Human Rights *see* ECHR
exclusionism 2
"exilic degeneration" 116

Fassin, D. 41
Fassin, É. 42

Index

Fassin, É. and Salcedo, M. 19
Faust, Aaron M. 173
females: Freud and 94; gender equality 56; Germany 92; homosexuality 3, 4, 9, 97, 123–125, 126; and Yugoslavia 59
feminism: and citizenship 161; Polish art 83; rejection of 91, 92–93; and secularism 21
Fordism 23
Fortuyn, Pim 24, 39
Foucault, Michel 34, 141; *The History of Sexuality* 80
Frankenstein, Carl, *Youth Neglect* 112, 113
Fraser, N. 160
Freud, Sigmund 93–95; "Leonardo da Vinci and a Memory of His Childhood" 94; *Three Essays on the Theory of Sexuality* 94; *Totem and Taboo* 95
Friedlaender, Benedict, *The Renaissance of Eros Uranios* 91, 92

Gabriel, Timothy, *Love Does Not Harm* (conceptual public sculpture) 79
Galbreth, Michael, *The Art Guys Marry a Plant* (performance with Massing) 83, 84
Gender Bazaar, The: Feminine/Masculine in the Mediterranean (exhibition) 78–79
German Empire 89, 90
Germany 88–99; Community of the Special Individuals (*Gemeinschaft der Eigenen*) 91; gender/race division 93, 94–95, 96; homosexuality and Jewishness 93, 95–96; homosexuality and Nazism 96–97; masculinity 89–96; *Wandervogel* youth movement 92, 93; *Wissenschaftlich-humanitäres Kommitee* (Scientific-Humanitarian Committee) (WhK) 91
Geschiere, Peter 25
Gilman, Sander 109
Gleichen, Heinrich von 100n7
Gordon, N. 125
Great Britain: change in attitude 118; criminalization of male homosexuality 57; Wolfenden Committee *Report of the Committee on Homosexual Offenses and Prostitution* 159
Grubic, Igor: *East Side Story* (video installation) 74, 75–76; *Monument and Flowers* (photographic series) 74

Härm, Anders 76, 77–78
Hasso, Frances S. 152
Hathaway, James and Popjoy, Jason 45
Hayes, Jarrod 140, 144, 148
Heidegger, Martin 122
Heimsoth, Karl-Günther 96
Herzer, Manfred 100n8
Hester, Hester 153n2
heteronormativity: in Arabic literature 121, 123; and art 71, 72, 73, 80; Fordism 23; Germany 3, 96; Mosse on 2; in North African literature 138, 152; Norway 40, 49; Yugoslavia 57; Zionism 7
Hide/Seek: Difference and Desire in American Portraiture (exhibition) 82
hijab 24
al-Hilli, Ali 174
Hirschfeld, Magnus 91, 93, 94, 95, 96, 115, 116
Hitler, Adolf 97
homonationalism: Mepschen on 5; and the Netherlands 34; and North Africa 152; and Norway 40, 42–44, 49, 51; Puar on 19, 20; Western values and 6
homonormativity: Netherlands 33; "new" 42–43, 152; Norway 6, 41, 42–44, 49, 50, 51
humanism 30, 31, 59
Hungary 5, 6
"Hunted to Death – Gay Life in Iraq" (documentary) 177, 178
Hurriyet (newspaper) 157

Ibrāhīm, Sonallah, *The Committee* 128
IDF (Israeli Defense Forces) 117
"imagined communities" 43, 45
Institut für Sexualwissenschaft, Berlin 115
Institute for Hygiene and Sexual Sciences, The, Tel Aviv 115
Iran–Iraq war 8, 172, 174, 177
Iraq 172–184; "'Asa'ib Ahl al-Haq" (League of the Righteous) 177, 179; Coalitional Provisional Authority 176; Emos 179–181; female prostitution 176, 178; Human Rights committee 181; internet 178; Iraqi Penal Code 176; "Jaysh al-Mahdi" (Mahdi Army) 177; masculinities 172–183; "National Faith Campaign" 175; Personal Status Law 176, 177; "Saddam's Feda'iyyin" (paramilitary group) 176; Sadrist Mahdi Army 179

ISCI (Islamic Supreme Council of Iraq) 177
Islam: female homosexuality 125; and globalization 9; Iraq 173–175, 177–178, 182; on male homosexuality 8, 27–32; Netherlands 19–34; Norway 39; on pederasty 146, 153; as pre-progressive 33; Turkey 157; *see also* North African literature
Israel: identification 7; LGBT historiography 108; representations of sodomy 107–118
Israel, Society for the Protection of Personal Rights 108
Israeli Gay, Lesbian, Bisexual and Transgender Association 108
Istanbul 156–159, 164, 166, 168
Italy 57
Iton Meyuchad (weekly) 108, 109, 110, 111, 114–115, 116

al-Jaburi, Adel 180
Jama, Afdhere 175
Jansen, Wilhelm 91
"Jaysh al-Mahdi" (Mahdi Army) 177
Jensen, Uffa and Schüler-Springorum, Stefanie 2
Jivraj, S. and De Jong, A. 33
Johnson-Davies, Denys 125
"Judeo-Christian" tradition 22, 27

Kaczyński, Jarosław 70
Kaczyński, Lech 70
KAOS (Gay and Lesbian Cultural Research and Solidarity Association), Turkey 164–165
Kayral, Kürşat 164–166, 167
Kazem, 'Adel 180
Kazem, Sabah Mohsen 178
Khouri, Mustafa 109, 110, 111
Kingdom of the Serbs, Croats, and Slovenes 55
kinning 40, 49, 51
Klauda, Georg 149
Korkuc, Wojciech 83, 84
Kosofsky Sedgwick, E. *Epistemology of the Closet* 121, 122
Krakow Feminist and Gay Parade of Equality 70
Kristeva, Julie 85n3
Kuwait, invasion of 174

Lambda Istanbul 157, 158, 159, 164, 166, 167
League of Polish Families 70

"lean citizenship" 23
Le Madame (club) 72
Lentin, A. and Titley, G. 24
LeVine, Mark 179
Li, L. 125
Listhaug, Sylvi 41
Ljubljana 57
Long, Scott 39
Love and Democracy (exhibition) 71, 72, 81
Love is Love. Art as LBGTQ Activism: from Britain to Belarus (exhibition) 81

McAllester, Matt 177
Macanović, Slobodanka 66n15
McClintock, Anne 2, 3
Maclure, J. 161
McDonald, K. 75
Maghribi literature 138–153; ethnographic 141; first-person narratives 139; gay culture 148, 149–150, 151; gender binarism 143–145, 146; pederasty theme 146–151
Mai, Nicola and King, Russell 48
Majewska, Ewa 72
Männerbund 93, 94, 95, 97
Marcouch, Ahmed 20, 26, 27, 28–32
Marcuse, Max 116
market rationality 23
masculinity: as active 140; construction of 148; Egypt 128; Germany 88–97; and identity 3, 4; Iraq 172–183; Islamic 48; and nationalism 2, 76, 151; in North African literature 129–132, 145; and Zionism 7, 114
Massad, Joseph 122, 123, 151, 152
Massing, Jack, *The Art Guys Marry a Plant* (performance with Galbreth) 83, 84
Matmon, Dr. Avraham 115, 116
Mayer, Eduard 91
Meyer, B. 21
Meyer, Richard 80
Mirutziu, Alex, *Tears are Precious* (video performance) 74
Montenegro 57
Morgenbladet (newspaper) 41
Morocco 149–150
Mosse, George 2, 151
MUCEM (Musée des Civilisations de l'Europe et de la Méditerranée) 78–79
multiculturalism 11n2, 19, 31, 39, 42
Murray, Stephen O. and Roscoe, Will 152

Mus'ad, Ra'ūf, *Baiḍat an-na' āma* (*The Ostrich Egg*) 126–128
al-Mutairi, Jassem 177
Myong, Lene and Bissenbakker, Mons 43, 50

Nablus 112
Nasseri, Karim: *Chronicles of a Hammam Child* (*Chroniques d'un enfant du hammam*) 139, 146, 147; *The Sailor from Magador* (*Le Marin de Magador*) 139; *Soulaimane's Secret* (*Le Secret de* Soulaimane) 139; *Wedding and Funeral* (*Noces et funérailles*) 139, 147
national identity 2, 25, 42, 73, 144, 180
National Museum, Warsaw 72, 73–74
nationalism 2–3; and anti-Semitism 7; Croatia 75; Eastern Europe 76; Egypt 128; Germany 95, 96; and globalization 9, 10; Netherlands 22–23, 32; Norway 39; Poland 70–71; Yugoslavia 55, 58–61, 64, 65, 66n13; *see also* neo-nationalism; sexual nationalism; ultranationalism
neo-nationalism 5, 22–24
"neoliberal communitarianism" 23
neoliberalism 1, 5, 22, 23, 41, 48, 63
Netherlands: "civil Islam" 27–28, 29; homophobia 19–34; human rights 30–31; immigrants as "preprogressive" 23, 24, 26; immigration and integration 21, 22, 25–29, 30; Labor Party (PvdA) 20, 26, 31; Moroccan immigration 29–30; "El-Moumni affair" 28; Muslim communities 27; neo-nationalism 22, 23, 24; New Right culturalism 27; populism 30; as post-progressive 20, 21, 22–24; postfeminism 24; pragmatic approach 22, 25; same sex marriage 138; secularization of 20; sexual democracy 19–21; sexual nationalism 19–34; sexuality and liberal Muslims 26, 27–28, 29; social democracy 24, 25–26; "third wave" feminism 24
Night of Long Knives 97
Nordau, Max, *Muskeljudentum* 116
North African literature 138–153; ethnographic 141; first-person narratives 139; gay culture 148, 149–150, 151; gender binarism 143–145, 146; pederasty theme 146–151

Norway 39–52; application for family reunification 40, 41; asylum regulations 44–45, 46; case study 46–50; Conservative Party (Høyre) 39; Directorate of Immigration (UDI) 40, 44; Equal Marriage Act 43, 44; homonormativity 41, 42–44; Immigration Appeals Board (UNE) 40; marriage immigration 40–41; tolerance of sexual minorities 43
Nussbaum, Martha C., *From Disgust to Humanity: Sexual Orientation and Constitutional Law* 81
Nwachukwu-Abgada, J. O. J. 124

O'Donnell, G. 161
Olive, B. A. 124
Opzij (feminist monthly) 24
Orientalism 19, 48, 49, 51, 141
Otherness 3, 21–22, 32–33, 58, 59, 99, 141
Oudenampsen, M. 22

Palestine 3, 7, 107–110, 115–116
Papić, Žarana 57
Parker, Ned 179
Parris, David 142
passivity 109, 130, 140, 143–145
patriarchy: and Arabic literature 121, 123, 124, 125; Egypt 128; Germany 92, 99; Iran 46; Maghribi 138; and non-conformity 8; Poland 71; Turkey 167; Yugoslavia 57, 58, 59
Perreau, Bruno 148, 153
Perrone, Roberto 158, 159
persecution, as grounds for asylum 44–45
Pink Life (association) 165
pinkwashing 7, 63, 118, 142
Piotrowski, Piotr 73
Poland: All-Polish Youth 70; anti-refugee stance 70, 71; art and homophobia 70–74, 83, 84; collapse of Communist system 70; criminalization of abortion 70; decriminalization male homosexuality 70; entry to EU 70, 71; feminism 70, 83, 84; films 72; influence of Catholicism 70; Law and Justice Party 70, 71; League of Polish Families 70; move to right 70, 71; *Movement for Moral Hygiene* 83
Põldsam, Rebeka 76, 77–78
Polisiewicz, Aleksandra, *The Reanimation of Democracy – the March for Equality Moves On* (film) 72

populism, right-wing, rise of 5, 6, 8, 24, 30, 71, 72
post-progressivism 20, 21, 22–24, 26, 33
Postcolonial Studies 142
postcolonialism 8, 22, 143, 144, 153
postfeminism 24
Poznań 70, 72
pragmatism 21, 22, 25, 32, 34
Pride Parades 48, 51, 60, 62–64, 70, 75, 156–157
Prins, B. 34n2
psychoanalytic approach 79, 80, 93, 125
Puar, Jasbir 19, 20, 42, 99, 151
Pupovac, Ozren 55
Putin, Vladimir 97

"queer liberalism" 43

Rainbow Association, The 166
Rachid O. 138, 140, 141; *The Dazzled Child* (*L'Enfant ébloui*) 139, 144, 147–148, 150; *Illiterates* 142; pederasty as theme 146, 147–149; *Several Lives* 148–150, 150, 151; *What Remains* 148
racial hygiene 90, 91–92
Rajkowska, Joanna, *Le Ma!* (film) 72
Reanimation of Democracy, The – the March for Equality Moves On (film) (Polisiewicz) 72
Rebucini, Gianfranco 148
recognizable sexual identity 45, 48, 49, 50
"relational subjectivity" 50
Ressouni-Demigneux, Karim 81
"reverse discourse" 80–81
Rif'at, Alīfa: "Badriyya's Husband" 125, 126; female homosexuality 123–125, 126; "My World of the Unknown" 121
Röhm, Ernst 96, 97
Romania 6, 74
Rüdin, Ernst 90, 91
Russia 5, 44, 61, 79, 98

al-Sabah (newspaper) 178
Saddam Hussein 172, 173–174, 175
"Saddam's Feda'iyyin" (paramilitary group) 176
as-Sadr, Mohammad Sadiq 177
al-Sadr, Muqtada 177, 181
Said, Edward 122, 141, 142
al-Saray, Dhia 174, 178
Saslow, James M., *Closets in the Museum: Homophobia and Art History* 82
Scheffer, Paul 25–26

Schilling, Diebold, *Die Grosse Burgunder-Chronik* 82
Schinkel, Willem and van Houdt, Friso 23
Schwartz, Mordechai 109, 110, 111
Scott, Joan 21
Sears, Alan 23
secularism, Western, as superior 19–21, 24, 32, 61
Seidman, *The Enemies of Youth* 112
Serbia: and abortion 61; Civil Code 56; criminalization of homosexuality 57; and EU 60; feminism 61; Gay Pride Parade 75; LGBTQI groups 58, 61–63, 65; nationalism 58, 60, 64; views of West 5; *Women in Black* 61
sex workers 150, 160, 161, 174, 176, 178, 182
sexual democracy 4, 19–21, 31, 42
sexual nationalism 20–27, 32
"sexularism" 21
SFRY (Socialist Federal Republic of Yugoslavia) 58, 59; Penal Code 57
Sharmacharja, Shamita 76
Shower of Homophobic Insults, The (sound installation) 78–79
al-Sistani, Ali 177, 181
Slovenia 57, 62
Smithsonian Institution 82
snake, as symbol 123–125
sodomy: in art 82; Iraq 176, 177; and Zionism 4, 107–118
Sofer, Yehudah 108
Solberg, Erna 43, 44
Somerville, Sibhan B. 97
Southern, Ell 72
Spijkerboer, Thomas 45
Split, Dalmatia 63
stereotypes 10, 80, 83
Stretenovic, Dejan 75
substantialism 24, 25
Süddeutsche Zeitung (newspaper) 88

Taïa, Abdellah 139, 140; *An Arab Melancholia* 150; *The Red of the Fez* 144–145; *Salvation Army* 150, 151; Zekri on 141
Tallin 76, 77–78
Taylor, Charles 160
Tel Aviv 113–115, 117
Thoreson, Ryan Richard 177
Tinin, Louis-Georges ed., *The Dictionary of Homophobia* 81
Titanic (satirical magazine) 97, *98*
Tito, Josip Broz 56
Tokheim, Vegard Rødseth 39

Index

transgenderism 3, 160, 163, 174, 177
transnationalism 73, 151–152
transvestism 160, 161, 163, 174
Triisberg, Airi 76, 77–78
Tully, J. 161
Tunisia 8, 145
Turkey 156–168; AKP government 163; Alperen Hearths (youth organization) 157; Anatolia Muslim Youth 157; Black Pink Triangle 159, 166; Campaign for the Reform of the Turkish Penal Code 162; Civil Code 156, 158, 165, 166; Confederation of Progressive Trade Unions (DISK) 160; Constitution 156, 158, 166; Criminal Code 163; democratization 160–162; EU accession process 162, 163; Great Union Party 157; hate-crime legislation 162, 163; human rights 162–163; Justice and Development Party 157, 160; KAOS (Gay and Lesbian Cultural Research and Solidarity Association) 164–165; landmark cases 164–167; Law on Associations 164; Law on the Powers and Duties of the Police 163; LGBT organizations 159–160; Misdemeanor Law 163; People's Democratic Party 160; Pink Life association 165; Public Employees Trade Union (KESK) 160; The Rainbow Association 166; Republican People's Party 160; struggle by LGBT for legal recognition 159–160; trade unions 160; Women's Platform for the Reform of the Turkish Penal Code from a Gender Perspective 164; see also Lambda Istanbul
TV Sirens (feminist collective) 72

al-'Ubaidi, Sa'd 180
'Uday Hussein 176, 182
Uitermark, Justus 20, 27
ultranationalism 83, 85, 157
UN Refugee Convention 42
Untold Stories (exhibition) 76
US (United States): art 79, 80, 82, 83, 84; deportations 44; overseas military interventions 42

Van Gogh, Theo 29
Verkaaik, Oskar 22
Verkaaik, Oskar and Spronk, Rachel 21
Vojvodina 57
Vucic, Aleksandar 62

Wandervogel (youth movement) 92, 93
Warsaw 70, 72; National Museum 72, 73–74
Waschitz, Yossef 112
Weedon, C. 122
West Germany 57
Westerwelle, Guido 88, 97
Wilders, Geert 22, 30, 32
Williams, Timothy and Maher, Tareq 177
Wolfenden Committee, Report of the Committee on Homosexual Offenses and Prostitution 159
Women in Black (network) 61
Women's Antifascist Front, Yugoslavia (AFŽ) 55, 56, 57
Women's Platform for the Reform of the Turkish Penal Code from a Gender Perspective 164
Woods, Kevin M., Palkki, David D. and Scott, Mark E., eds. 173, 174

Yediot Ahronoth (newspaper) 117
Yeni Akit (newspaper) 157
Yishuv (newspaper) 4, 7, 108–110, 113, 114, 115, 117
Yugoslavia 55–65; AFŽ (Women's Antifascist Front) 55, 56, 57; AVNOJ (Antifascist Council of the People's Liberation of Yugoslavia) 55, 56; break-up of 58–59, 60; Criminal Code 57; decriminalization of male homosexuality 57; feminism 56, 57, 58–59, 61; gay culture 57; gender equality 55, 56; heteronormativity 56, 57; legalization of abortion 56; LGBTQI 58, 59, 60, 61; liberalization 57; moral authority of Church 59, 60–61; new Yugoslav Constitution 56; normalization of violence 58; party membership barred to gays 57; regional authority 57; return to patriarchal norms 58–59
Yuval-Davis, Nira and Anthias, Flora 2

Zagreb 57, 62, 63
Zagreb, University of 58
Zaharijević, Adriana 59
Al-Zaman (newspaper) 180
Zekri, Khalid 140, 141, 142
Zigon, J. 27, 28
Zionism: heteronormativity 7; homosexuality as threat 117; Levantinization and degeneration 113–116, 117; national identity 3; representations of sodomy 4, 107–118

 Taylor & Francis eBooks

Helping you to choose the right eBooks for your Library

Add Routledge titles to your library's digital collection today. Taylor and Francis ebooks contains over 50,000 titles in the Humanities, Social Sciences, Behavioural Sciences, Built Environment and Law.

Choose from a range of subject packages or create your own!

Benefits for you
- Free MARC records
- COUNTER-compliant usage statistics
- Flexible purchase and pricing options
- All titles DRM-free.

Benefits for your user
- Off-site, anytime access via Athens or referring URL
- Print or copy pages or chapters
- Full content search
- Bookmark, highlight and annotate text
- Access to thousands of pages of quality research at the click of a button.

REQUEST YOUR FREE INSTITUTIONAL TRIAL TODAY — **Free Trials Available** We offer free trials to qualifying academic, corporate and government customers.

eCollections – Choose from over 30 subject eCollections, including:

Archaeology	Language Learning
Architecture	Law
Asian Studies	Literature
Business & Management	Media & Communication
Classical Studies	Middle East Studies
Construction	Music
Creative & Media Arts	Philosophy
Criminology & Criminal Justice	Planning
Economics	Politics
Education	Psychology & Mental Health
Energy	Religion
Engineering	Security
English Language & Linguistics	Social Work
Environment & Sustainability	Sociology
Geography	Sport
Health Studies	Theatre & Performance
History	Tourism, Hospitality & Events

For more information, pricing enquiries or to order a free trial, please contact your local sales team:
www.tandfebooks.com/page/sales

 Routledge Taylor & Francis Group | The home of Routledge books

www.tandfebooks.com